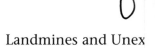

Landmines and Unex

'McGrath is now among the few who can stir the sluggish conscience of the world on the curse of landmines and unexploded ordnance. Because of his example, I truly believe that some of the world will suffer less if this book is a success.' Lord Deedes

'There is a global landmine epidemic which is out of our control. Once you accept this fact there are only two options; ignore it, or do something. This book is an essential resource for those who take up the challenge.' Dr Hans Husum, War Surgeon and author of *War Surgery Field Manual* and *Save Lives, Save Limbs*

'McGrath's expert contribution to the "understanding" of the tragedy posed by landmines forcefully matches the courage of his analysis in unfolding the political and humanitarian challenges, and shortcomings, that still need addressing.' Nicoletta Dentico, Executive Director, Médecins Sans Frontières Italy, and the Italian Campaign to Ban Landmines

'Offers invaluable insights for all those working in conflict areas, making it required reading. We will turn to it again and again.' Dr Sultan Barakat, Post War Reconstruction and Development Unit, University of York

'McGrath is the most knowledgeable person I know on the topic of landmines, and one of the most passionate advocates of their ban. He is pragmatic and deeply compassionate, as this book shows.' Dr Chris Giannou, Surgeon & Co-ordinator of Health Activities, International Committee of the Red Cross

'An invaluable resource for anyone wanting to understand the impact of these persistent killers, and how best to respond to them.' UK Working Group on Landmines.

Landmines and Unexploded Ordnance

A Resource Book

Rae McGrath

Pluto Press
LONDON • STERLING, VIRGINIA

First published 2000 by Pluto Press
345 Archway Road, London N6 5AA
and 22883 Quicksilver Drive,
Sterling, VA 20166–2012, USA

British Library Cataloguing in Publication Data
A catalogue record for this book is available from
the British Library

ISBN 0 7453 1264 0 hbk

Library of Congress Cataloging in Publication Data
McGrath, Rae.
    Landmines : a resource book/Rae McGrath.
        p. cm.
    ISBN 0–7453–1264–0 (hbk.)
        1. Land mines—Safety measures. 2. Land mines—Economic aspects.
    3. Land mines—Social aspects. 4. Ammunition. 5. Bombs. I. Title.

UG490.M34 2000
327.1'743—dc21
                                                            99–052952

Designed and produced for Pluto Press by
Chase Production Services, Chadlington OX7 3LN
Typeset from disk by Stanford DTP Services, Northampton
Printed in the EU by T.J. International, Padstow

Dedication

To the late Abdul Baseer, Sayed Aqa, Din Mohammed, John Hicks and Omar who started this journey with me

to Chris Howes and Houn Hourth, humanitarian deminers, who were murdered by the Khmer Rouge

to all the field engineers who go to work in minefields

and to Debbie.

Contents

List of Illustrations

Acknowledgements

A book of this nature can never be the work of one person since it brings together the shared experiences and skills of many people, all of whom deserve to be recognised. I acknowledge this fact unreservedly here without embarking on the risky business of naming some while overlooking others.

Some however have been directly involved in providing invaluable assistance, support and advice and I would be remiss if I failed to properly acknowledge that input.

Medico International and Thomas Gebauer have been a constant source of practical assistance and encouragement, not least for their financial support during the most intense period of research and writing. Their commitment to eradicating landmines and improving the future prospects for mine-affected communities is total and unreserved. I hope that their enthusiasm for this book is repaid by seeing it finally in print.

Special thanks are due to Sayed Aqa and to the Mine Clearance Planning Agency for sharing so much information and to John Rodsted and Sean Sutton for permission to use their excellent photographs. Mines Advisory Group, Norwegian Peoples Aid and Handicap International have all been extremely helpful and given me access to project and technical information. Special thanks also to Howard Thompson of HMT Insurance Brokers for his support and advice.

Finally, my thanks are due to Roger van Zwanenberg and Pluto Press for their patient encouragement and continuing enthusiasm as I shifted around the world during the writing process, at times out of contact in Africa or elsewhere for months on end.

Abbreviations

AMREF	African Medical and Research Foundation
ASA/SCA	Agricultural Survey of Afghanistan (a section of) the Swedish Committee for Afghanistan
BAC	battle area clearance
BM	bench mark
CBU	cluster bombs
CIA	Central Intelligence Agency, US
CMAC	Cambodian Mine Action Centre
CPR	cardio pulmonary resuscitation
DDA	Department for Disarmament Affairs
DGPS	differential global positioning system
ECHO	European Community Humanitarian Office
FAO	Food and Agriculture Organisation
GPS	global positioning system
ICBL	International Campaign to Ban Landmines
ICRC	International Committee of the Red Cross
IDPs	internally displaced people
INAROE	Institucao Nacional Angolana de Removacao dos Obstaculos Explosivos (Angolan national demining organisation)
IRC	International Rescue Committee
IP	intermediate point
KLA	Kosovo Liberation Army
Lao PDR	Lao People's Democratic Republic
LSN	Landmine Survivors Network
MAG	Mines Advisory Group
MCC	Mennonite Central Committee
MCPA	Mine Clearance Planning Agency
MDC	Mine Dog Centre
MDG	Mone Dog Group
MGRS	Military Grid Reference System
MLRS	Multiple launched rocket system
MPLA	Movimento Popular de Libertacao de Angola (governing party, Angola)
MTM	mouth-to-mouth

NATO	North Atlantic Treaty Organisation
NGO	non-governmental organisation
RP	reference point
SIPRI	Stockholm International Peace Research Institute
SP	start point
TP	turning point
UN	United Nations
UNDHA	United Nations Department of Humanitarian Affairs
UNDP	United Nations Development Programme
UNHCR	United Nations High Commissioner for Refugees
UNICEF	United Nations Children's Fund
UNITA	Uniao Nacional para a Independencia Total de Angola (opposition guerilla army, Angola)
UNMAS	United Nations Mine Action Service
UNOCA	United Nations Office of the Coordinator for Afghanistan
UNOCHA	United Nations Office of the Coordinator of Humanitarian Assistance to Afghanistan (this superceded UNOCA)
UNOPS	United Nations Office for Project Services
UTM	Universal Transverse Mercator
UXO	unexploded ordnance
WFP	World Food Programme
WHO	World Health Organisation

There is a sort of sail which may be called the original of all sails. It is the sail with which antiquity is familiar. It brought the ships to Tenedos and the Argo carried it. The Norwegians had it when they were pirates a thousand years ago. They have it still. It is nearer a lug sail than anything else, and indeed our Deal luggers carry something very near it. It is almost a square sail, but the yard has a slight rake and there is a bit of a peak to it. It is the kind of sail which seems to come first into the mind of any man when he sets out to use the wind. It is to be seen continually to-day hoisted above small boats in the north of Europe.

But this sail is too simple. It will not go close to the wind, and in those light and variable airs which somehow have no force along the deck, it hangs empty and makes no way because it has no height.

Now when ... the Arabs left their deserts and took to the sea ... They took this sail which they had found in all the ports they had conquered ... they lightened and lengthened the yard, they lifted the peak up high, they clewed down the foot, and very soon they had that triangular lateen sail which will, perhaps, remain when every other evidence of their early conquering energy has disappeared. With such a sail they drove those first fleets of theirs which gave them at once the islands and the commerce of the Mediterranean.

Hilaire Belloc
'Esto Perpetua'

You can just muddle along and do things as best you can or you can do things properly. For the professional there should be no choice.

'Doc' Tom Spencer
Master Ropeworker and Instructor
School of Electrical and Mechanical Engineering, REME 1970

Preface

It was four o'clock in the morning and the harsh Australian twang on the other end of the telephone was giving me a headache: 'What is it like ... clearing landmines in Afghanistan? Is it dangerous? How many of your team have been killed?' The mistake I had made was to stay late in the American Club bar. It had been a rough trip back over the border from Afghanistan and then through the Kurram Tribal Agency by ramshackle bus, arriving dusty and thirsty in Peshawar after more than twelve hours on the road. The news that an Australian journalist wanted to do a telephone interview in the middle of the night was not welcome and the decision to have a few drinks after dinner had been lacking in good judgement in the circumstances. I kept my cool and answered with applaudable sobriety, suppressing the yawn that threatened to engulf my answer. Twenty minutes later the journalist had his interview and I dropped into a dead sleep.

It was 1988 and landmines were just beginning to make the feature columns, if not the headlines. I had no idea that night but I was to spend many hours over the coming years giving that same interview, the media only slowly learning the subject and, even now, nearly a decade later, many interviews start with those same questions: 'What is it like? Is it dangerous? How many of your colleagues have been killed?' I probably took too long to realise that my job had expanded to include education. I was to become a teacher, whether I liked the idea or not. My pupils would be the media, donors, aid agencies, politicians, soldiers and the public-at-large.

In 1990 I wrote a short handbook for aid workers, funded by the Norwegian Afghanistan Committee, entitled *Mines in Afghanistan*.[1] Although everyone knew that the country was overrun with landmines very few of the relief workers who travelled across the border from Pakistan into Afghanistan had more than a cursory understanding of the risks involved. That short manual probably raised more questions than it answered – the problems were ones that still plague agencies who produce landmine-awareness resources today. What is the sense of advising someone not to do something which may be an essential part of their work if you cannot offer an alternative? Seemingly obvious cautionary advice may, on closer examination, be useless in reality. A classic warning would be, *never go into minefields*! That seems like a sound groundrule for anyone working in a mine-affected region but, in practice, is almost irrelevant in terms of the risks facing the community and travellers in such an area. If a minefield was surrounded by barbed-wire fencing with clearly visible warning signs only a fool would climb over the wire and walk across the field, and such a fool would, in any event, be unlikely to heed advice to the contrary. In fact, very few minefields have such markings, so an understandable response would be, 'how do I recognise a minefield?' The answer is straight-forward, because there is no certain way, no general rule, which can protect the layman from straying into a mined area. It is, 'in most cases you *cannot* recognise a minefield'. There are cautionary guidelines which will reduce the risks faced by anyone who must travel by foot, animal or vehicle in an area suspected of being mined. But since the majority of people in such circumstances will have a prime reason for being there – farming, water or firewood collection, agricultural survey, animal vaccination, any number of essential tasks – many of these cautionary rules will present a severe obstacle to their work. In fact, if observed religiously, most tasks would be impossible to implement. It is worth clarifying this point by examining two common pieces of advice offered to aid and development workers: first, 'when in a vehicle look for and avoid driving over irregularities in the road surface, particularly small depressions which may indicate a buried mine', and second, 'always stick to well-used tracks'.

Certainly no one can argue that, if observed, these precautions would diminish the risks of falling victim to a landmine. But, given that irregularities and depressions are the rule rather than the exception on the highways and tracks of most mine-affected countries, one would have to travel at walking pace to observe the first example. It is a good idea but, faced with the need to actually get from one location to another within a reasonable time, totally impractical. The second example presents a more complex problem; it is certainly excellent advice but as a firm and fast rule it presents problems for anyone working in a post-conflict environment. How, for instance, could a United Nations High Commissioner for Refugees (UNHCR) field officer conduct surveys of potential repatriation routes for returning refugees under such a restriction? Many day-to-day activities of rural aid and development workers would be impossible, or at least severely limited, if they confined their travel to well-used tracks and roads. The weakness of such well-meant advice is that it offers no accompanying solution which would enable people to observe it in practice. Solutions do exist, but they are mostly linked to the survey, marking and clearance of minefields and offer no rapid resolution which would remove the risks to anyone who lives or travels in a mined area. Some projects, such as the survey of repatriation routes, could be preceded by specialist mine survey teams, but no such facility could be made available to every shepherd who set out to graze his livestock or to every aid worker.

In 1994 I published a more comprehensive manual,[2] aimed again at development workers operating in mined countries, which I prefaced with a stark warning which is worth repeating here:

> There is a frightening and illogical tendency among expatriate aid representatives working with communities in a mined environment to assume their own indestructibility, often, at the same time, voicing concern for the threat to the indigenous population. It should be superfluous to point out that no-one is immune from the sudden and shocking horror of a mine explosion: the only protection lies in understanding the threat and adjusting your life accordingly. But there are no guarantees of safety, except, of course, that the foreign worker may select the final option and leave the country. For the indigenous community the choice is starker: live with the mines or abandon your land; and often not even that level of choice exists.

That will always be the case until the world is rid of landmines. I certainly had no idea when I gave that nocturnal interview in 1988 that, ten years later, landmines would have captured so much international attention But *attention* should not be misinterpreted as necessarily indicating *understanding*. Most involved agencies and individuals understand that the solution in general terms lies in the implementation of four parallel initiatives:

- the eradication of landmines already disseminated
- stopping the continued use of landmines
- organising interim initiatives to limit the impact of landmines
- providing treatment and support services for victims and their families.

It follows that the direct response to landmines requires action by the engineering, international advocacy, education, health and social welfare sectors at least. Of course, this scale of response requires substantial funding and therefore international donors must be a partner in the solution. Ten years ago this overall sector of post-conflict activity did not exist except, inasmuch as that a person who stepped on a landmine would be given medical treatment and possibly prosthetic support. The development of what might be termed an 'integrated landmine response', has only been generally accepted as a viable approach during the past seven years. International advocacy has, through the work of the International Campaign to Ban Landmines (ICBL), achieved dramatic results culminating in the signing of the Ottawa Treaty in December 1997 by 122 countries. Unfortunately the campaign weakened at the last moment and unforgivably supported a treaty with a weakened definition – which defines landmines by their design rather than effect. The remaining three areas of response have failed to achieve the same dynamic progress. Which brings me to the reason for writing this book and, by a circuitous route, back to my middle-of-the-night interview in Peshawar.

Non-governmental organisations (NGOs) have, as in the case of the landmines campaign, been the pioneers of humanitarian mine eradication. The world had no effective answer at all to the problem of landmines prior to the inauguration of the two UK-based NGOs, the Halo Trust and the Mines Advisory Group (MAG), and the Afghan NGOs, the Mine Clearance Planning Agency[3] and Afghan Technical Consultants. Despite differing philosophies, especially regarding advocacy, these organisations laid the operational groundwork for all subsequent mine-clearance initiatives. This, paradoxically, is one of the reasons that widescale landmine eradication has been slow to progress. To understand this argument there is a need to identify the key agencies involved in the process of clearing landmines and summarise their roles.

KEY AGENCIES AND THEIR ROLES

Governments of Mine-affected Countries

It goes without saying that the government of a country should have the ultimate responsibility for the eradication of a problem which threatens its citizens, its development and its economy, but with few exceptions the governments of the worst-affected nations have followed the process rather than led it. To some extent this can be justified, or at least understood, in a post-conflict scenario where an emerging administration is struggling with an overwhelming mass of equally urgent demands. But somewhat ironically those countries with the weakest government structures have seen the most impressive progress in mine clearance because external agencies have effectively imposed eradication programmes with little or no government consultation or involvement. However, this is a short-term benefit likely to have long-term negative repercussions.

The United Nations

The UN is probably the only viable umbrella for an international response to landmines and, having accepted that role, has, with few exceptions, shown itself to be institutionally incapable of adequately or effectively meeting the challenge. The reasons for this failure would provide material for several volumes, but all have their roots in the improbability of implementing complex field-engineering programmes from within a monolithic structure dominated by a core staff unconnected with, and ignorant of, the engineering processes involved, but with ultimate control and influence over them, and who support the bureaucratic *status quo* above all other considerations. Despite what may seem like a damning dismissal of the UN's capacity to achieve success in this field I believe that its continued involvement is essential. It may be that the recent handover of operational responsibilities for landmine response from the UN Department of Humanitarian Affairs (UNDHA) to the UN Mine Action Service (UNMAS) and the UN Development Programme (UNDP) is a positive reorganisation. I will, however, and in this I am not alone, require convincing. The NATO intervention in the Balkans and the willingness of NATO governments to circumvent the UN Security Council in order to bomb Serbia and Kosovo has damaged the UN in the eyes of much of the world, a fact which has escaped the attention of President Clinton and Prime Minister Blair in their euphoric conflict afterglow. This is not an indication that there was much international support for Serbian actions against the Kosovar Albanians – many of the countries who strongly oppose the way NATO bestowed on itself the authority to act in place of the

United Nations would have supported military action by a UN-sponsored force. The fact is that rich industrial nations can afford not to take the UN seriously, while for the debt-ridden nations of the South it is often the only international forum where they have a voice. Countries blighted by the explosive remnants of war may be as critical of the UN attempts at establishing national mine-clearance programmes as I have been – perhaps more so – but their complaints will never overshadow their belief in the concept and philosophy of the UN and its value to them.

Non-governmental Organisations

NGOs have been the driving force in the demining[4] process but, perhaps unfortunately, they do not have the capacity to make any substantial impact on the global problem. In addition, NGO involvement must now be separated into two categories: those with in-house specialist capacity and an organisational philosophy to underpin their mine-related action; and those which subcontract technical specialists to run demining programmes. The latter can be considered for practical purposes as commercial operations.

Commercial Demining Companies

Commercial operations vary greatly in capacity, from those which accept contracts and simply hire landmine specialists from the open market to conduct operations, to companies who retain an in-house specialist capacity. They are, to some extent, irrelevant in themselves since the ultimate responsibility for their success in completing their tasks must lie with the contracting agency.

The Donors

Donors pay the piper but, in the field of landmine eradication, have rarely been clear about what tune they are paying him to play. This is critical because, regardless of moral or other imperatives, all the implementing agencies must keep their donors happy – that may not be the ideal to which humanitarian agencies aspire, but it is fact.

The Media

It may seem unusual to include the media as an involved agency but their role has been substantial, both as a positive medium, pressing for action to eradicate landmines, and as a damaging influence through their demand for, and dissemination of, statistics which have little relevance to the engineering process and which have often been misleading in the extreme and been instrumental in diverting attention from real issues in favour of media-friendly 'factlets'.

So we are faced, it would seem, by an unimpressive overall international response, interspersed with dramatically successful but limited field initiatives. Yet there is a vast resource of experience at every level of operation which should make a very different result possible. The deficiency lies in the fact that there is no easily available and usable source of information to which involved agencies and individuals can refer when establishing, implementing and evaluating a demining initiative. Similarly, there is no guiding reference covering the overlap of mine-related activities in the health, education and other sectors to form truly integrated programmes.

This book aims to remedy that deficiency, perhaps a bold and, some would undoubtedly say, presumptuous ambition, but none the less one that is overdue. When I first discussed the possibility of writing a definitive manual – a how-to-do-it reference book – with colleagues, their response was discouraging – 'you must be mad', they said. I knew what they meant – the field of humanitarian mine clearance may be comparatively new but it has never been lacking in controversy. Despite their doubts I have been hugely assisted in the task of researching this book by the enthusiasm and support of those same colleagues and many others. Where it applies, I apologise in advance for teaching many highly professional grandmothers to suck eggs – they need no instruction but they will recognise the need for other readers to understand the basic principles. Aimed primarily as a practical reference for everyone involved directly or indirectly in mine-action programmes it should also, as a resource for the media, remove the need for me to answer too many press calls in the middle of the night.

Where it does not detract from the instructional or technical content I have not avoided the opportunity to express my personal opinion on the pages that follow, especially in relation to the manufacture, export and military use of landmines and ordnance. Those who know me and those who have worked with me would be surprised if I did otherwise. Some may feel that the book is too damning of what may seem at least well-meaning attempts to address the plight of mine-affected communities and the victims of landmine explosions. I would agree that I have, quite deliberately, sometimes been blunt when I could have been diplomatic – I make no apology for that, this is not a celebration of international benevolence, it is an attempt to offer a resource based on engineering and practical management experience which may help to improve the lot of the families who live in the world's minefields. If the cost of achieving that is a few sour faces in London, Washington, New York or Geneva it's a price worth paying. Readers may have differing opinions, but it is worth remembering that mine are expressed not from any political soapbox but from hard-won personal experience. I do not believe in general disarmament, although I would wish for a world where such an aspiration would be realistic. But I do believe in simple justice – something which is ill-served by the arms industry – and the entitlement of people who have suffered the horrors of war to enjoy the opportunities and the freedom from fear which should come with peace. During 18 years in the British military I never heard an experienced soldier express any opinion which contradicts those beliefs.

Rae McGrath
Langrigg, Cumbria
August 1999

1

An Introduction to Landmines and Unexploded Ordnance

Their hindsight was better than their foresight.
Robert S. McNamara

THE DEVELOPMENT OF LANDMINES

Rudimentary landmines were first used in the American Civil War, but they came into their own and into the sphere of military strategy in the First World War with the deployment of the first battle tanks. The tanks were virtually immune to small-arms fire and could traverse contested land between entrenched armies while providing cover for advancing infantry troops. It was a frightening, exciting and challenging development for strategists and generals, many of whom were already suspicious of any technology which impinged on their 'war of position', as the military terminology of the day defined the strategy of deadlock. The landmine offered a solution which could be developed, manufactured and deployed quickly. It consisted simply of a container of high explosive with a pressure switch which would initiate an explosion when a tank drove over the patch of ground under which the mine was buried. And so, with the tank, came the anti-tank mine. These early anti-tank mines could, however, be discovered easily by sappers and, once lifted and reburied in a new location, used against enemy tanks, so some form of protection was required to prevent opposition forces stealing landmines. The solution was another type of landmine designed to explode when contacted by a soldier – the anti-personnel mine. Development of these new weapons was sporadic and they varied in design from comparatively clumsy pressure devices to fairly sophisticated mines which, when initiated, sprang into the air before exploding, spraying shrapnel over a wide area – these became known as bounding mines.

Weapon designers and military strategists were quick to recognise the wider potential for such weapons and, in the years between the world wars, both the anti-tank and anti-personnel mines were integrated into the fighting strategies of the major military powers. But not all armies saw the landmine as a mass-produced weapon; certainly the British army still viewed the landmine as an extension of a different mine warfare – a feature of the First World War practised by enlisted coal miners who would attempt literally to *undermine* enemy trench systems and destroy them by detonating massive underground explosive charges. It is perhaps interesting to compare these mines, a development of virtually static trench warfare, with anti-tank and anti-personnel mines, a product of mobile fighting. On the 7 June 1917 British sappers blew up the Messines Ridge with 19 simultaneous explosions using a total of 424,182 kilograms of high explosive over a front exceeding ten miles. The miners had tunnelled a total of 7,625 metres – over five miles – in order to place the charges at depths ranging from 14 to nearly 17 metres; two of the tunnels had taken more than a year to complete. German and British mining units also fought underground wars, attempting to intercept enemy workings and either break through and attack or set a charge and destroy the enemy miners and their tunnels. By 1934 the British army, or at least the Royal Engineers, had recognised that future wars were unlikely to demand such tactics and, in any event, belatedly recognised their limited impact (and, given that the following quote came from an official manual and can be assumed to be conservative in its judgement, perhaps the military had also recognised the total madness of such subterranean warfare). Indeed, the manual of military engineering printed that year stated:

> Those who directed the active period of mine warfare during the Great War generally concede, however, that the results achieved were seldom commensurate with the expenditure of personnel, material and time involved, and it is improbable that military mining will ever again be employed so indiscriminately. The later stages of position warfare in this campaign clearly demonstrated that, given large resources of artillery and tanks, mining ceased to play a useful part in assisting the assault.[1]

It is worth noting, however, that despite these comments the manual dedicated more than a hundred pages to the subject of military mining and its complexities, even emphasising the fact that personnel should be billeted close to the underground workings because 'In general, the miner does not march well; work will suffer if the men have to walk much more than a mile before going on shift.'

But there is one important and relevant similarity in strategic thinking relating to underground mining and the later arguments developed to justify the widescale use of landmines; that of damaging enemy morale.

> Against field defences the moral effect of a successful mine explosion will frequently be out of all proportion to the material damage done, and the main object of a mining offensive should, therefore, be so to demoralize the enemy as to render a surface attack overwhelming.[2]

In other words, the process of secret tunnelling and exploding underground charges was judged to have achieved no great strategic advantage and so the tactic was, thereafter, primarily justified by reference to its peripheral impact on the enemy, despite the fact that the actual instances where enemy morale was so damaged as to allow their positions to be overwhelmed were rare. This phenomenon, however, is not rare, the vested interests in maintaining any given military strategy involve far wider considerations than just the seemingly obvious assessment of whether it actually achieves its stated military aims.

In contrast the manual afforded only one nine-page chapter to landmines and traps. The chapter is interesting, however, and it is worth observing that the basic objectives of landmine warfare have changed little in the intervening 64 years, although the complexity of the terminology is now far more advanced, rendering it more impressive and mystifying to the layperson.

> Land mines are explosive charges laid in the ground with the object of delaying the advance of the enemy by impairing his morale, destroying his personnel and transport, or interrupting his communication after the evacuated terrain has fallen into his hands.[3]

The manual referred to three classifications of landmine, defined according to their method of operation. A contact mine was buried just below the surface and designed to be detonated by the pressure on the ground surface caused by the passage of troops or vehicles (therefore including both anti-tank and anti-personnel mines). Clearly in 1934 the British army was not relying on mass-produced landmines since the manual referred to the contact mine simply as a 'charge of explosive' contained in a 'specially designed box (or a shell)' with 'some form of contact firing arrangement'. These mines were to be sown 'as a rule' in fields or belts which could be of 'considerable extent' in order to 'render it practically impossible for a body of troops or vehicles to pass through the field without exploding at least one of their number'. This was to be done by burying rows of mines approximately 6 feet apart or 'connecting the mines together by planks of wood'. Second was the somewhat confusingly designated observation mine, simply a mine which was remotely detonated employing an electric detonator and concealed cable when the enemy were observed to be passing over it. The manual recommended that this type of mine should contain more explosive than a contact mine and suggested including stones as tamping for the charge to increase its destructive effect. The third type of mine described was a delay action mine, although since the delay techniques described range from lighted candles with trails of gunpowder to alarm clocks and water dripping on to electrical contacts it can be assumed that this was not, at the time, a fully developed technology.

The manual also examined in detail the anti-tank mine:

> The most suitable design of mine for employment as a tank obstacle is still a matter of experiment; but it will probably be a contact mine, disc-shaped, say 7½ inches diameter by 2½ inches deep, will contain about 4lb of explosive and weigh about 7½lb filled ... It will be rendered sensitive in a manner similar to a Mills grenade, by inserting a capped detonator and will then be fired by any heavy load pressing anywhere on the upper surface.[4]

It is interesting that, despite the acceptance of a new kind of mobile battle involving armoured fighting vehicles, the specific design of anti-tank mines was not further advanced 16 years after the end of the First World War. However, strategies for the use of mines against enemy tanks had been adopted and consideration also given to the employment of dummy minefields to confuse, among others, enemy air reconnaissance. Anti-tank mines were to be deployed across roads, defiles or between the edges of craters in roads and the verge, at intervals of 12 inches. They were also to be deployed to strengthen a non-explosive tank obstacle and, finally, in a minefield which due to the policy of laying mines at close intervals would normally only consist of a single row, but which, at key points, could be strengthened by a second row of mines laid opposite the gaps in the first row and also 12 inches apart. In addition, larger, less concentrated minefields, were recommended to disorganise enemy tank assaults and deter reinforcements or second attacks on the same front. Such minefields, 200 yards deep, were to contain 3,500 mines to each mile of front. A trained mine-laying party consisting of one non-commissioned officer and ten soldiers was estimated to be capable of laying 40 mines in 'ordinary loam soil' in 5 minutes and in metalled roads in 25 minutes. In general, anti-personnel devices were still viewed as protection for anti-tank mines to deter their removal.

Both Nationalist and Republican forces made wide use of anti-tank mines during the Spanish Civil War, with soldiers on both sides developing detection and clearance techniques in order to remove and redeploy enemy mines. The ease with which this exploitation of enemy resources was achieved was noted by observers from Germany and other countries which led to the development of anti-lift devices being incorporated into anti-tank mine design and an increased emphasis on the use of anti-personnel mines to protect anti-tank mines.[5]

Probably the first widescale use of anti-personnel mines in their own right, deployed separately from anti-tank mines, was in the war between Finland and Russia. The Finnish forces made extensive and effective use of cast-iron fragmentation mines, mounted on wooden stakes just above the ground, which were initiated when the enemy disturbed a hidden tripwire. Mines of this type, virtually unchanged in design and method of operation, have remained in use ever since. But inevitably it was the Second World War proper which gave the development of landmine design and tactics for their deployment an urgency which had previously been lacking. Contrary to popular belief, minefields consisting entirely of anti-personnel mines were soon enshrined in military strategic thinking and commonly laid for their nuisance value, and were, in fact, referred to as 'nuisance minefields'. Defensive and barrier minefields consisting of both anti-tank and anti-personnel mines were often massive in scale: at the Battle of Gazala in 1942 British forces laid more than half a million mines over a 40-mile front and later that year, at El Alamein, both sides laid so many minefields that many German fields were incorporated into British defences and vice versa. It was in North Africa that strategists developed the concept of the landmine as a force multiplier – meaning, in simple terms, that mines might be used to reinforce the fighting capacity of an outnumbered force or, conversely, to improve the superiority of a stronger force. (This concept, in recent years, has taken on a more pragmatic economy-based rationale; determining the role of landmines as force multipliers thus enabling cash-strapped armies to reduce expenditure on manpower and more expensive weapon systems.) The development of new landmines was an ongoing process. The Germans introduced the S-Mine, a bounding fragmentation device packed with a mixed fragmentation load of ball bearings and steel fragments which exploded at a height of approximately 2 metres and had an effective range of up to 30 metres. The Italians, to emerge in the 1970s as the world's most prolific landmine producers, foreshadowed the technology of the future by making use of air-delivered scatterable mines against British troops. As the opposing forces improved their detection and clearance technology so they each introduced landmines which were increasingly difficult to detect – the use of Bakelite and other plastic compounds became a common feature of landmine construction.

In Okinawa, Japanese minefields accounted for more than 30 per cent of allied tank casualties. But it was the Soviet army which made widest use of landmines. At Kursk in 1943 a massive German tank assault was routed by Soviet mixed minefields with a density of more than 4,000 mines per square mile.[6] The Soviet Union laid more than 220 million landmines during the Second World War, mostly on their own territory and, although over 50 million were reported to have been cleared by the end of the war, clearance operations are still mounted annually by Russian troops. Field Marshal Rommel, convinced of the utility of landmines by his experiences in the Desert War, incorporated over 5 million landmines into the Atlantic Wall defences which faced the invading allied forces in 1944. Rommel is reported by some sources to have wanted to build a minefield stretching the length of the vulnerable French coast consisting of over 50 million mines.

With the end of fighting and the dawning of the Cold War, barrier minefields became a common feature of national border defences – sometimes, as in the case of East Germany, designed to keep the population in rather than the more traditional role of keeping the enemy out. The war in Korea acted as a further development ground for landmine technology but also led to the common use of improvised and simply-constructed mines by the Chinese and North Korean forces, including mine cases made of wood, glass bottles, oil drums, clay pots and bamboo.[7] The North Korean use of mines became more effective as the war progressed, eventually accounting for a large percentage of UN tank losses and over 300 fatalities and 2,400 wounded among US troops.

Although the concept of the landmine as a weapon which could be used to close off wide areas of land from use by an enemy force (and incidentally, by definition, any person or animal) had been used to a limited extent during the Second World War, it was the advent of the US intervention in Southeast Asia and the introduction of a whole new 'family' (a somewhat obscene generic term used by the US military and the arms industry to refer to weaponry of related role or design) of air-delivered weapons which irrevocably enshrined the area-denial philosophy into military thinking. Even in retrospect and with the experience of the recent techno-war in the Gulf it is difficult to conceptualise the scale of the US deployment of air-delivered mines, and perhaps the only way is to examine US procurement figures. Air-dropped anti-personnel mines were normally delivered to their target in dispensers – commonly a bomb casing which opens in mid-air to dispense its load over a wide area – which contained up to 4,800 mines. Other mines were fired from tubes mounted on fighter aircraft. US Department of Defense figures quoted by the Stockholm International Peace Research Institute (SIPRI) in 1978[8] gave procurement figures for just three types of area-denial anti-personnel mine during the three years 1966 to 1968.

XM-48 Button Bomblet
A small anti-personnel mine normally dispersed from a 10-tube tactical fighter dispenser.
Procurement:
1967   13,625,000
1968   31,700,000
Total   45,325,000

BLU-43 and BLU-44 Dragontooth anti-personnel mines
These mines were forerunners of the infamous Soviet-manufactured Butterfly mine. They were deployed from SUU-13 dispensers each containing 4,800 of the mines.
Procurement:
1966   2,222,400
1967   17,664,000
1968   11,587,000
Total   31,473,400

XM-41E1 Gravel anti-personnel mines
A small canvas-covered chemical-fused mine designed to be hand laid by troops, scattered from helicopters or dispensed from a 10-tube tactical fighter dispenser.
Procurement:

1967	11,250,000
1968	26,150,000
Total	37,400,000

The fact that the United States procured over 114 million anti-personnel mines of just three types in a period of three years gives a clear indication of the enshrinement of the area-denial concept within the military psyche of the time. In addition to the BLU-45 anti-vehicle mine, the US had in use at least a further ten types of air-delivered anti-personnel mines during the Southeast Asian conflict for which no procurement figures are available. The war with Vietnam also led to a confusion of definitions between air-delivered landmines and submunitions. The latter were often, either by design or malfunction, *de facto* landmines by their effect and, especially in Laos where the US air force conducted an unprecedented area-denial campaign, have similar long-term implications for post-conflict communities. Reports that US ground forces suffered heavy casualties from their own air-disseminated mines are credible given the scale of deployment and the highly mobile nature of the ground war. A declassified US intelligence document[9] states that landmines and boobytraps accounted for 65–70 per cent of US marine corps casualties in Vietnam during 1965.

The area-denial concept, despite its complete failure to gain any perceivable long-term tactical victory or even advantage for the US forces and their allies in Southeast Asia, was adopted by virtually every major military force during the 1970s and dominated design thinking among manufacturers. But these mines and their accompanying delivery systems, while highly profitable, gave producers who were used to regular contracts from their domestic forces a problem. Such expensive systems were required to have a long service life and, therefore, manufacturers were faced with dramatically increased periods between orders and much higher research and development costs. The strategy adopted by many companies, most notably in Italy, was to increase their export market (and, usually, dispense with any associated moral considerations involved in such trade) for standard hand-laid anti-tank and anti-personnel mines, while competing for lucrative high-technology mine systems. Arms-export restrictions were rarely a problem and most governments turned a blind eye to infringements, while some actually helped exporters overcome inconvenient laws. A number of producers negotiated subcontracted manufacture or assembly of mines with companies in states where legal restrictions on exports were less strict than their own or more easily overcome. A few countries made a business of providing end-user facilities for arms shipments – most notably Singapore and Nigeria, which also assisted in the covert sale of landmines to armies and guerilla forces subject to embargoes – while a handful of companies, one of the largest operating out of Europe, specialised in the logistics of illegal arms shipments. The lucrative nature, enormous scale and widespread acceptance of this underground trade can best be illustrated by examining the source of landmines used in three of the major conflict areas of the past 25 years:

Horn of Africa – Somalia conflicts and Ethiopian-Eritrean War
Belgium, Bulgaria, China, Czechoslovakia, Egypt, former East Germany, former West Germany, Italy, Pakistan, United Kingdom, United States, former Yugoslavia.

North Iraq – Iran/Iraq War, internal Iraqi actions, Gulf War
Belgium, China, Czechoslovakia, Egypt, former East Germany, Iran, Iraq, Israel, Russia, Singapore, United Kingdom, United States, former Yugoslavia.

Mozambique – War of Independence, Civil War, South African insurgency
Belgium, Bulgaria, China, Czechoslovakia, France, Italy, Portugal, former Rhodesia, Russia, South Africa, United Kingdom, United States, former Yugoslavia, Zimbabwe.

Iraq/Kuwait – mines emplaced by Iraqi forces during the 1990 invasion of Kuwait and the 1991 Gulf War
Anti-personnel:

VS-50/Valmara 59/Valmara 69/P-25/VAR-40/SB-33 Italy	
PMN	Russia and Iraq
Type 72a	China
M409	Belgium
MON-50/MON-100	Russia

Anti-tank:

VS-1.6/VS-2.2	Italy

L9A1 Barmine	United Kingdom
TM-46/TM-57/TM-62M	Russia
Type 72 AT	China
M3	Belgium
PT-Mi-Ba 3	Czechoslovakia
MAT 76	Romania

In addition the following anti-tank mines were found in Iraqi bunkers in Kuwait:

SB-81	Italy
HPD-F2	France
ATM-6	Austria

These lists are sourced from agencies involved in the clearance of landmines, declassified intelligence reports and from known shipments – they may not be comprehensive nor may the mines have necessarily been exported directly from the source country. It is common for weaponry to be sold on after the initial purchase, often several times – there is a thriving and lucrative second-hand arms industry. The fact that a government may have superficially strong limitations on arms exports is not any real indication of the actual situation – the United Kingdom is a classic example of this fact (even disregarding recent, highly publicised, infringements of national and international embargoes). The Royal Ordnance-manufactured Mark-7 anti-tank mine was, for many years, standard British army equipment. Since it went out of service with the British army to be replaced by the L9A1 Barmine, it has become the archetypal low-cost weapon for government and guerilla forces throughout the world, purchased legally as government surplus stores and sold on by the second-hand arms trade. It would be a mistake to believe that the used-arms trade is necessarily conducted secretly – in fact, one company, Interarms (UK), had maintained one of the world's most comprehensive second-hand weapons emporia in a warehouse in Manchester from which it supplied customers throughout the world with every type of military equipment and lethal weaponry. (Happily, in December 1997, it was demolished as part of a road-widening project. A local resident who had long been concerned by the presence of the Interarms warehouse described it as 'One of the few concrete arms reduction measures ever taken in the UK.') However, it is believed that Interarms has another similar facility somewhere on the M4 corridor. Interarms is a high-profile business and its owner, the late Samuel Cummins, who started his career working for the CIA procuring weapons for the Guatemalan coup and was once said to maintain sufficient stock in his warehouses to equip 40 divisions, claims that none of his sales are illegal, and adds that the morality of such sales is a matter for the government: 'if they didn't want me to sell them they wouldn't issue the licences'.[10]

It is certain that the activities of landmine manufacturers have placed governments in embarrassing situations in recent years and left their military forces at risk of having to face mines manufactured in their own country. A US Defense Intelligence Agency list of Iraqi landmine holdings[11] immediately prior to the Gulf War is notable less for what it reveals than for what it fails to reveal. The partly declassified document has censor's black strike-outs through selected mines supplied in recent years, often indicating the suppliers to be the United States or its allies. One conventional anti-personnel and three conventional anti-tank mines are censored under the category of 'classified'. However, in a list of twelve scatterable mine types in the Iraqi arsenals, six are censored, three as 'secret' and three as 'classified'.

Developments such as self-destruct and self-neutralising landmines, usually a feature of remotely delivered devices, often used as an example to illustrate the humanitarian concern of producers and the military, are actually a by-product of the strategic weakness of scatterable mine systems. As recognised by the US Defense Intelligence Agency in its 1992 review of trends and projections in landmine warfare, 'due to problems which may be encountered in remote delivery of mines (e.g. command and control procedures for determining where and when the landmines are to be placed, the notification of units which may need to enter those areas, and the accuracy of the emplacement systems), friendly forces may be called upon to breach their own scatterable landmines'.[12]

There are considerable differences in reliability estimates of self-destruct devices incorporated in landmines. Most manufacturers and military accept (although often only off the record) that 10 per cent failure rates are the probable reality when mines are deployed correctly. However, this is only part of the story because mines are not always deployed in the correct way. This is particularly true of air-delivered landmines which must usually be deployed within certain critical parameters – most commonly related to the speed, height and trajectory of the delivery aircraft. If the pilot is flying at the wrong speed or height when the mines are deployed this would lead to arming failures. While a mine which has not been armed will not perform its military role it will still remain a serious threat to anyone who disturbs the device; it will often then arm and explode. Mines in this condition are unlikely to self-destruct or self-neutralise since these mechanisms are a function of the arming cycle.

One of the most disturbing developments in landmine design occurred because of military concerns that the enemy might be able to develop effective clearance techniques. It is ironic that a defensive minefield, once breached by the enemy, becomes a greater potential threat to the defending than the attacking force. In those circumstances the minefield becomes an unknown quantity to the troops who laid it because the enemy may have added mines of their own, widened the perimeters or closed known safe lanes – in effect the minefield changes sides. The first, perhaps most obvious, response by designers was to manufacture landmines which contained no metal, thus defeating the most common and effective detection method which locates the metallic content of the mine. However, such mines have obvious disadvantages if the deploying force has, subsequently, to clear its own minefields. Additionally, with the globalisation of the arms market, the possibility that one country could have exclusive access to non-metallic mines became unlikely and, therefore, the encouragement of such developments were counter-productive. None the less, such landmines have been manufactured and deployed – former Yugoslavia being the most prolific producer. The TMA series of anti-tank mines are constructed of plastic and polystyrene and employ non-metallic friction-sensitive fuses; they therefore cannot be detected using metal-detection equipment. It is, of course, ironic that these devices are now threatening the people and the postwar recovery of the former Yugoslavian states. However, most military forces preferred a midway solution and encouraged the development of mines with small amounts of metal which made their detection difficult but not impossible. The Italian companies, Valsella, Tecnovar and BPD Difesa, specialised in both anti-tank and anti-personnel mines which met these requirements and for many years cornered the commercial market, ensuring that devices like the TC series of anti-tank mine and minimum-metal-content anti-personnel mines could be found on virtually every battlefield of the past 25 years. China, Pakistan and France have also produced many low-metallic-content mines.

A more direct and, in the context of post-conflict mine-clearance operations, insidious development to deter the removal of mines by the enemy was the anti-lift or anti-disturbance device. This could be a design feature of the mine or an improvised boobytrap. The most common examples of the latter are achieved by linking the mine to a concealed explosive device, such as a grenade, by a hidden wire. Any attempt to move the mine will (normally) pull the pin from the grenade or firing device and cause an explosion which will kill or injure the deminer. Such improvised traps are only limited by the expertise and imagination of the operative and the availability of materials. One Russian-manufactured anti-personnel mine, the MS-3 pressure-release mine, was designed specifically for such deployment. When used as an anti-lift device it is placed under the primary mine and will detonate as soon as the weight of the mine is removed.

However, many anti-tank mines have one or more in-built fuse-wells to accommodate anti-lift devices. These may be simple pressure-release or pull-initiated switches which detonate the mine when it is lifted, but more dangerous are devices which cause the mine to explode when it is exposed to light, through a photo-electric cell similar to that used in cameras or a tilt switch which detonates the mine when the switch is moved through a predetermined angle. Probably the most effective and immoral type of anti-lift device are magnetic sensors, such as the South African M8943A1, which respond to the signal of a metal detector, causing the mine to explode. While most other devices can be defeated by pulling the mine from a safe distance, magnetic-influence-type mechanisms are likely to claim at least one victim before clearance teams become aware of their presence and revert to non-magnetic detection methods. Of course, from a military viewpoint, if the breaching party were working in a forward area the demining operations would probably cease following the explosion since they would come under fire. Humanitarian deminers working in peacetime do not have the luxury of abandoning the task.

Possibly the most prolific distributor of anti-disturbance devices for landmines is the Belgrade-based Federal Directorate of Supply and Procurement who market the Superquick US series of electronic fuses which are available in six versions: USA-T Acoustic Fuse; USI-T Inertia Fuse; USS-T Light-Sensitive Fuse; UST-T Thermal Fuse; USE-T Time Fuse; UST-T Vibration Fuse. Although anti-lift and similar devices are normally a feature of anti-tank mines they have also been incorporated into some anti-personnel mines such as the Chinese Type 72b, which has an electronic tilt mechanism which detonates the mine when it is tilted through an angle greater than ten degrees. Once armed the mine is identical to the Type 72a minimum-metal-content pressure-blast mine, the only visible difference being the shape of the safety-pin clip which is removed on arming (round in the 72a, triangular in the 72b), although due to the high metal content in the Type 72b it can easily be differentiated when located by a metal detector.

LANDMINES – THE PROBLEM RECOGNISED

Despite their long history and the high value placed on landmines by the military, their general recognition as a pariah among the para-phernalia of modern weaponry did not occur until the mid-1980s. It should, perhaps, have been Vietnam, Cambodia and Laos which first alerted the world to the scale of landmine use being employed by the military and the peripheral impact on non-combatants, especially in the aftermath of the conflict. But Vietnam and Laos were subject to enforced isolation from many of the Western indus-trialised countries by the United States' laws on trade or contact with enemies, a restriction which it encouraged its allies and trading partners to observe. This was an especially ironic fate for Laos, with whom the US had never formally been at war and, indeed, whose national integrity President Kennedy had committed his country to protect. The US, had, however, effectively destroyed the greater part of its infrastructure and, either by design or casual curiosity, used it as a live testing ground for new weapon systems. It is also true, and understandable, that for many years neither Vietnam nor Laos, particularly the latter nation, sought assistance from the Western world and so their internal problems remained largely unrecognised. Cambodia, like Laos, had suffered the consequences of providing a convenient military haven and staging post for the North Vietnamese forces; it subsequently became another target for the US military. But the Vietnam War proved only a preface to the well-documented horrors which would overtake Cambodia: the Khmer Rouge, invasion and liberation by Vietnam, civil war, the shameful UN intervention followed by more civil war. It is not surprising, in the midst of such misery, that the toll being taken by landmines was hidden for many years.

So it was Afghanistan that first drew the attention of the world to the problem of landmines. The Soviet military and Afghan government forces employed anti-personnel mines of every kind on a massive scale. There was no pretence that the widescale use of mines was directed purely at the military opposition – the policy was area-denial and any area which could not be controlled by the Soviets was to be denied to the *mujahideen*. But this time there were witnesses, not just the international media, but medical-aid agencies who found themselves facing hitherto unparalleled casualties among non-combatants, large percentages of whom were landmine victims requiring, most commonly, limb amputations.[13] There were additional factors involved; this was a classic good-versus-bad story for the Western media – invasion by hugely superior (and communist) external force being resisted by brave but poorly armed local fighters with colourful history. The facts were, as ever, somewhat more complex, but why spoil a good story with detail? For once the press had almost got the story right, but would hardly have been so well-served by well-informed sources had it not been for the fact that virtually the whole intelligence community of the Western world had gathered on Afghanistan's borders to assess the Soviet army in action, to try to get hold of samples of its latest weaponry and, of course, to ensure that, come what may, the Soviet machine suffered defeat. Although the impact of landmines and references to their indiscriminate nature became an increasingly common feature of news reports from the Afghanistan warfront it was to be more than eight years after the Soviet invasion before the international community began to react in any meaningful way.

It would, of course, be misleading to ignore the many other wars during this period where landmines played a key and subsequently hugely damaging role. Mozambique, Angola, Somalia, Ethiopia, Iran, Iraq, Nicaragua and other countries were all suffering the impact of landmines on their civilian populations, but the fact went virtually unrecorded.

It is interesting to examine why it took so long for the world to respond and, even then, why it was non-governmental organisations who led the way in the face, initially, of concerted opposition from virtually all the major military powers in the world. The argument of the major powers has always been that it is the irresponsible use of landmines by indisciplined forces of less-developed nations and guerilla armies which account for civilian casualties and large-scale land-denial – the inference being that the landmine as an indiscriminate weapon is really a Third World strategy. This argument simply does not stand up against even cursory examination. No single landmine type has been developed initially by a lesser military power; in every case they have been first used in combat by the major powers – they have served the interests of the military and the arms industries of those powers. They have continued to do so when they have been donated or sold as military aid to favoured governments or opposition forces – the foreign policy of the donor nation being served and the arms industry continuing to profit, the United States, China and Russia being the major culprits. Later, when new technologies were introduced into the armouries of the superpowers' own forces, old landmines were sold off as surplus, often with no control over their eventual destination. The casual nature of this foreign military aid and the sale of landmines by major powers with no apparent concern regarding what they now, almost without exception, refer to as 'irresponsible use' is easily explained – the landmines were being used a long way from home. None of the major development and manufacturing countries had experienced the national trauma of having landmines laid in their own fields in the years since the beginning of the Cold War. But most of those nations had controlled or dabbled in other wars – combat by proxy is the luxury of great nations – and when they had been forced to send troops to foreign fields, landmines were only a small part of a big picture; returning soldiers who had been disabled by mine blasts were war heroes not mine victims. And after the boys came home the curtains were drawn on the foreign battlefields – that was yesterday, and who wanted to hear about foreign farmers and their families being blown apart in fields anyway? The war was over, that was someone else's problem. The Cold War was the time of the superpowers and the would-be superpowers, countries who fought their wars on other nations' land – Africa, Asia and Central America provided battlefields for those few great states to play global Monopoly. It was no great wonder that the world at large took so long to wake up to the landmine crises.They were simply not aware it existed, and it was not in the interests of those best placed to know of its existence – the military and those who designed mines to be a persistent and indiscriminate weapon – to advertise their knowledge.

It was humanitarian organisations directly involved in work with mine-affected communities who defined the reason why landmines had become such a problem.

1. They are indiscriminate once deployed.
2. They are victim-triggered.
3. They are persistent in that their effects continue indefinitely after a war ends.

These are the properties of all landmines, not just anti-personnel mines. The reason that the subsequent campaign focused on the latter was that their use could not be justified on the grounds of military utility and their impact on non-combatants was disproportionate, making their use illegal under existing international conventions. That is not to say that the anti-tank mine is necessarily an acceptable weapon, but it is certainly possible to justify its military utility and difficult to argue that its impact on non-combatants is disproportionate. However, recent moves by manufacturers and military to blur the definitions as to what can be defined as an anti-tank mine by using such vague terminologies as 'anti-material mine' and 'area-denial munition', negotiating for the legal addition of anti-handling devices, and thus introducing the possibility that anti-tank mines of the future could incorporate the properties of anti-personnel mines, will undoubtedly lead to calls for a ban on anti-tank mines. Despite the international concern caused by the humanitarian, economic and environmental impact of landmines, especially anti-personnel mines, there still persists a stubborn belief in the weapon's military utility in some circles. This was well illustrated in Jane's Special Report, *Trends in Landmine Warfare*, published in August 1995:

> *Anti-Lift Devices* – We believe that at least 20% to 30% of mines laid should contain an anti-lift device to assist in delaying breaching/neutralisation. However it may be possible to include an anti-lift device in 100% of mines at very little extra cost and in the interests of commonality.

This view conveniently ignores the fact that the number of mines actually cleared by soldiers is insignificant compared with the great majority cleared by civilian humanitarian teams. The definition of 'little extra cost' clearly refers only to the cash-balance sheet and not to the cost in human life, which would apparently be sacrificed in the interests of 'commonality'.

CHARACTERISTICS OF MODERN LANDMINES

Landmines may best be characterised by their mode of operation and activation, the method of deployment, or a combination of those characteristics.

Mode of Operation

Blast: A blast is a wave of air driven at ballistic speed from the site of the explosion. A blast mine is one from which the blast effect of the explosive content of the mine is the primary cause of injuries or damage sustained by the victim or target.

Fragmentation: A fragmentation mine contains an internal packing of fragments, usually metallic, or a segmented outer casing designed to break into fragments. When dispersed at ballistic speeds by the force of the explosion the main cause of injury to the victim, or damage to the target, is a result of being struck by those fragments.

Bounding: A bounding mine, usually of the anti-personnel fragmentation type, employs a primary charge designed to lift the mine to a predetermined height (normally 1–2 metres) before the main charge is initiated. Most bounding mines are activated by tripwire.

Type of Activation Mechanism

Pressure: A mine which is activated by direct pressure from above. Most anti-tank and many anti-personnel mines employ this method of activation.

Tripwire: A tripwire-activated mine has a wire or filament attached to a pull switch on the mine which causes the mine to detonate when a predetermined load is placed on the tripwire. The other end of the tripwire extends to a fixed object, often a metal stake driven into the ground or, in some cases, another mine. Some mines may have more than one tripwire.

Pressure release: A comparatively rare type of activation where the mine is detonated when a preapplied source of pressure is removed from the mine. Most commonly used as an anti-lift device when placed under an anti-tank mine or as a boobytrap.

Proximity: Some mines can be equipped with a fuse which detonates the mine when a victim or target passes within a predetermined distance of the mine.

Remote firing: Some mines, notably those designed to disperse fragmentation over a set field of effect – known as directional or ambush mines, can be activated by a pull wire or a similar device or may employ radio signal or other remote firing methods. The mine is fired from an observation point. Most such mines can also be activated by means of a tripwire as above.

Deployment Method

Hand emplacement: Most mines can be hand emplaced. Pressure mines are normally buried just below the surface or camouflaged.

Mechanical emplacement: Some anti-tank and anti-personnel mines, usually pressure mines, can be buried or surface laid by purpose-designed mine-laying machinery.

Remote deployment: Most modern anti-personnel mines and many anti-tank mines are designed to be disseminated by remote means. They may be free-fall air-delivered, either directly from pods or carriers on fixed-wing aircraft or helicopters. They may be part of a cluster bomb system or be carried to the vicinity of their target area in artillery carrier rounds, or by rocket or mortar fire. Some mines may be sown from ground-based systems mounted on tracked or wheeled vehicles. All mines deployed by these methods will lie on the surface of the ground but may be difficult to see due to camouflage and colouring of the mine and, in some cases, by the irregular shape of the outer casing.

Scatterable: Scatterable mines are remotely delivered, normally from aircraft, and are designed to disperse over a wide area after release, normally due to the incorporation of wings or fins into the casing design.

UNEXPLODED ORDNANCE – GARBAGE OF WAR

Landmines are a post-conflict problem because of their wide impact and the specific nature of their design which causes people to fall victim to them so easily. They also deny the use of valuable land once the population become aware of their presence. However, modern war leaves behind other explosive debris in addition to landmines, and this is referred to by the military and those agencies who must deal with its safe disposal under the generic term 'unexploded ordnance' – normally shortened to UXO. UXO can be defined simply as 'any object containing explosive of any kind which has been deployed and failed to detonate, or has only partly detonated, or such objects which have been abandoned in any condition'. The list is as long as the catalogues of weapon manufacturers: submunitions, tank shells, artillery ammunition, bombs, rockets and missiles of every kind, mortars, hand grenades, rifle grenades, bulk explosive, light-weapon ammunition, detonators, illumination flares.

In general, UXO does not constitute the same level of threat to civilians as do landmines. First, because it is usually visible and clearly recognisable for what it is, in most circumstances it requires considerable manhandling or disturbance in order to make it explode. But that is not always the case (some submunitions are an exception and are dealt with below). However, any explosive item is intrinsically dangerous and even a detonator, although normally containing only a small charge of explosive material, may explode in response to the heat of a hand closed around it – the result will be the loss of several fingers at least. Bombs may contain hundreds or even thousands of pounds of high explosive with the capability to devastate a large area and cause deaths and injuries on a large scale. All UXO was originally designed to explode, cause material damage and kill people; usually it has failed to function as a result of some fault in the arming process or it has been deployed incorrectly – all it takes to cause an explosion is for someone to take some action which will overcome that initial malfunction. One reason that this happens quite commonly is related to postwar economic difficulties facing the community. Everyone is looking for a way to improve their circumstances and nothing of value is abandoned or ignored, collection of scrap is a common and often lucrative way to make money. All armies leave behind two things – destruction and junk.

But the junk often helps to pay, albeit indirectly and unintentionally, for reconstruction – UXO is part of that junk. Scrap metal of all kinds has value, particularly aluminium, a common component of fuses, and copper, which is often used in ordnance manufacture. It is not unusual to find scrapyards containing sufficient explosive to destroy the town in which they are located. Soon after their teams began work in Xieng Khouang Province in Laos, MAG ordnance disposal experts checked the contents of a scrapyard in Phonsavan, the provincial capital. They found a 3,000-pound bomb among many items of live ordnance. On my first visit to North Iraq I was taken to a shallow bunker only yards away from the edge of a refugee camp where local men had brought thousands of items of ordnance. Among their nightmare collection I discovered a fused hand grenade with a very thin piece of electric fuse wire acting as a pin – the only restraint on the arming lever and the only thing saving the nearby refugees from disaster. Stories like these are not unusual, but are the norm in post-conflict communities struggling to recover in an environment where risk is not an uncommon feature of daily life and where a few kilograms of aluminium or copper may provide enough money to feed a family for one or maybe two days. Fuses smashed off projectiles with heavy hammers, and copper driving bands driven off shells with hammers and chisels after heating them over an open fire are merely additional hazards in a perilous existence. Mortar rounds are especially dangerous because they have direct impact fuses which can be initiated by a heavy blow or from being dropped on the ground. One rather surprising, but common, phenomenon is to find that communities who have lived through long periods, often years, of war and have been literally inundated with ordnance, are almost totally unaware of the potential destructive force of the items of UXO for which they scavenge or, quite commonly, allow their children to collect. A common response when asked about the risks involved in disturbing UXO is, 'it's been lying there for a long time and not exploded – it must be safe after all this time' or 'if it didn't detonate after falling thousands of feet from an aeroplane then it's not going to explode just because I hit it with a small hammer'.

Although the immediate risks to human life caused by the presence of items of unexploded ordnance are less than those presented by landmines, their disposal is nevertheless an essential and major component of any clearance programme. The number of explosive ordnance items deployed in modern war is immense – during the 1991 Gulf War allied forces alone deployed 250,000 individual weapons from the air totalling 88,500 tons, and an additional 20,000 to 30,000 tons of artillery and multiple-launched rockets were fired.[14]

LANDMINES BY ANOTHER NAME – SUBMUNITIONS

A submunition is any air-delivered munition, normally a bomblet or mine, carried within and released from a projectile, warhead or dispenser. This category of ordnance encompasses a wide range of weaponry which becomes more complex and prolific with every passing year – as with so many other modern weapons they saw their first really comprehensive use during the Vietnam War. The carriers for many submunitions are referred to as cluster bombs or, in the terminology of the US forces, CBUs – each such carrier will often contain many hundreds of submunitions. Many submunitions explode on, or shortly following, impact, but many fail to arm properly or simply do not explode as designed. These are UXOs but, because of the density in which they are disseminated and the fact that they are commonly small in size they present a much greater problem than normal unexploded ordnance, more akin to the post-conflict impact of landmines. They also present a complex clearance situation, especially since many submunitions have similar external characteristics but may have a variety of design capabilities. Failure rates are high and, once the bomblet fails to function in the designed manner, it may act as a *de facto* anti-personnel mine because it is likely to explode due to the contact or proximity of a person. Undoubtedly the most dramatic and horrifying example of this failure of submunitions to operate as designed can be found in Southeast Asia. In his belated *mea culpa* for his complicity in the Southeast Asian debacle, Robert McNamara records his assessment of the ever-escalating US bombing raids:

> I did not believe that strategic bombing would work unless it targeted production sources, denied access to basic products, and prevented the use of substitute products and means ... I believed that bombing to interdict the flow of men and supplies would work only in specific instances. It was unlikely to be effective in North Vietnam and Laos because of the terrain, the low volumes of supplies required, and the ability to substitute alternative routes and means of distribution ... led me to conclude that no amount of bombing ... short of genocide, which no one contemplated – could end the war.[15]

This is an illuminating view, given that the United States is estimated, in my view conservatively, to have dropped more than 300 million bomblets on Indochina (in addition to over 60 million anti-personnel mines).[16] It was clearly the duty of the US administration to have preassessed the reliability of a weapon type they intended to use on such a scale and to consider the potential impact on non-combatants and post-conflict communities. Even a 1 per cent failure rate, given the deployment figures used by Prokosch, would leave 3 million unexploded and potentially dangerous bomblets scattered across the rural areas of three countries in which a fragile system of subsistence agriculture is vital to the survival of the population. McNamara, as US secretary of defense, certainly had such data available, although the research had been conducted to confirm the lethality of the bomblets rather than from any humanitarian concern. One such test conducted on 3 March 1966 at Nellis Air Force Base to test and evaluate the impact pattern of the BLU-26 bomblets dropped from a CBU-24/B 'Sadeye' cluster bomb resulted in one alarming and enlightening item of peripheral data. In a controlled situation an F-4c released the bomb in a 45-degree dive at an altitude of 5,500 feet with a 5-second fuse set to function the release of the bomblets at an altitude of 1,908 feet; 663 bomblets were spread over an impact area measuring 900 x 400 feet – 173 of them failed to explode. A failure rate of more than 26 per cent.

The key factor is that this was a test in a controlled situation. The pilot, whose name was Larson, was not flying in enemy airspace over ground controlled by a hostile force, there was no ground fire, no harrying enemy fighters. He was flying over Nevada, USA – all Larson had to do was undertake a delivery of a cluster bomb unit on to a set target at a prespecified speed, trajectory and altitude. One must assume that this test mission was considered to be a textbook example since the results were included as an annex to an official report[17] and therefore a dud rate of 26 per cent appears not to have been uncommon. There can have been very few pilots, if any, who experienced such an uneventful bombing raid over Indochina and precision was certainly not always the order of the day:

> Sullivan's biggest headache was controlling the secret U.S. air strikes. In the early months of 1965, navy jets had hit the wrong target three days in a row. In another incident a jet missed its target by twenty miles and bombed a village where Sullivan had been just the day before on a goodwill visit. He found it embarrassing to have to send some young USAID field guy in there to apologize and hand out money for the loss of innocent lives.[18]

This combination of unreliable submunitions and criminally careless, ill-trained or badly tasked aircrews explains the situation which faces communities and ordnance eradication teams in Southeast Asia today. MAG roving disposal teams operating in six districts in Xieng Khouang Province of Laos destroyed 20,044 items of unexploded ordnance in a twelve-month period during 1996/97, 10,407 of which were bomblets.[19] A survey conducted by Handicap International in Laos during 1996 found that 25 per cent of the villages in the country still suffer contamination from UXO with 865 villages reporting UXO in the centre of their villages and 713 having heavy UXO contamination in surrounding areas. The bombing of Laos ceased in 1973, a quarter of a century ago.

Laos is exceptional because of the scale of submunition deployment and the total failure by the US administration and armed forces to give any consideration to the long-term post-conflict implications of weapons which they knew, or should have known, would outlast any military purpose. (It may be too late to indict those responsible for war crimes but it is certain that the United States has a duty to assist those communities it so criminally damaged. Any US funding to Laos should be seen as reparations, not aid.)

In a sane world the lessons of the Vietnam War would have been learned, but the opposite is the case. Arms manufacturers have difficulty keeping up with orders for new submunitions and the military are willing customers. During the 1991 Gulf War 2,500 multiple-launched rockets (MLRs) were fired by British forces alone – a total of 1,610,000 submunitions.[20] Such enormous numbers would be of less concern if one could be certain that the MLRs 'improved conventional submunitions' that the British soldiers were firing were less prone to failure than the Vietnam War-era munitions. The fact in practice is that the greater percentage of submunitions which fail to explode become *de facto* landmines and no battlefield evidence exists to support the claims of manufacturers, often bolstered by politicians and the military, that failure rates have been reduced to less than 1 per 1,000. The claim is not merely ludicrous, given the available evidence in the form of devastated humanity and destroyed environment, it is criminally irresponsible.

Perhaps the most insanely stupid deployment of cluster munitions is happening as I write, in Kosovo. NATO, with a stated mandate of providing a safe environment into which Kosovons can return, are using cluster bombs against Serb ground units. Searching perhaps for some logic behind this strategy, *The Times* headlined a report on 7 April 1999: 'Cluster-bombing ends frustration of Harrier pilots.' On the same day the *Independent* could also find no better reasoning behind the strategy than the improvement of the morale of Royal Air Force pilots and ground crew:

> It has considerably raised morale at the base. Wing Commander Graham Wright, in overall command of the RAF detachment in southern Italy, said 'People were over the moon, because we had done something productive'.

The ground attacks used BL-755 cluster bombs, a well-established weapon with a high 'kill' probability against a range of armoured or 'soft' targets such as trucks.

It will be some time before Wing Commander Wright's definition of productivity can be tested in full. The lessons of Laos, Vietnam, Cambodia and Iraq would indicate that these British-made submunitions will be at least as productive in killing and maiming Kosovons and denying them their land as they were at achieving a combat advantage for NATO.

WHAT IS A MINEFIELD?

It is probably inevitable that, when the word 'minefield' is mentioned, the unenlightened mind conjures an image of a rectangular stretch of land, perhaps undulating and bearing the scars of battle, but separated from the surrounding landscape by barbed wire and signs with skull and crossbones proclaiming 'BEWARE – LANDMINES!' 'ACHTUNG MINEN!', or whatever language is appropriate. Unfortunately this tempting illusion says more for the influence of Hollywood on our lives than it does about reality. Certainly no one who has lived or worked in a heavily mined environment would visualise such a minefield. A minefield is any area of land which contains landmines – it may stretch for many miles and contain 10,000 mines or, equally likely, it may be the patch of land at the rear of a small town house and contain maybe two or three mines. A mountain may be a minefield, so may a river bed, a short wooded path from a village to the tubewell or an irrigation ditch. A minefield may be marked or, more likely, sporadically marked; it may even be fenced, but these are the exceptions rather than the rule.

The reason for this denial of safe land in peacetime is the result of the perceptions which soldiers must adopt in order to fight a war. In combat every feature of landscape must be perceived by the soldier as threatening, advantageous or of no relevance to his position. However, this is not a static judgement, as the battle ensues the scenery is in a state of constant flux. Of course, this purely military judgement of the threat or value offered by a physical feature is complicated by the fact that the opposing force may assess the same feature in the opposite manner. Thus a defending force will look for 'dead ground', the military term for any area of landscape within range of a defended position which cannot be overviewed or covered by effective fire from that position and which, therefore, can conceal movement by enemy soldiers or vehicles. The attacking force will be looking for 'cover', areas which will hide an advancing force or a firing point. In other words, both commanders will be looking at the same piece of ground, the same feature, but what they see will be different, and their subsequent actions will be based on that purely combat-orientated assessment. So the defending commander will, perhaps, send his sappers to lay mines along the likely approach to, and the line of, a trench which dissects the view to his front and, because soldiers of all nations differ little in their training, the attacking commander will assume that the trench is mined and decide either to accept some casualties in return for the advantage of cover or to adopt a strategy which does not involve using the cover offered by the trench. These will be just two of many such tactical decisions made by those two commanders during that day and, as with the trench, many of those decisions will gain neither great advantage nor great loss. At the end of the day, or after an hour, and perhaps without any great battle, both forces may move to a different location, new positions, and begin to review the new battlefield landscape once again; each looking for dead ground and cover. Many such areas will be battlefields more than once during the ebb and flow of war, those same assessments being remade, from different angles by different soldiers, and mines being laid as required at that moment in time. With peace the land can once again be viewed in a non-military way, and the farmer will, in time, return to clear and repair his neglected irrigation ditch. His perceptions are not those of the soldier; trench, dead ground and cover have no place in an agricultural vocabulary. But his ditch is still mined.

Of course, with the proliferation of remotely delivered landmines, a commander may simply call for air support to lay his mines, in which case the trench will be merely one feature within a strip of land to 'be denied' to the enemy. It is at that point in time that wider calculations may come into play. For instance, pilots will not wish to be recalled to mine the same area more than once, since the element of surprise may be lost and they are more likely to encounter response from enemy ground forces. The obvious strategy in the circumstances is to *be sure*, and so instead of deploying the minimum number of mines to achieve the objective required by the defending ground commander, the maximum number are deployed. No one complains, the defending forces feel more secure, the pilots will reload and fly other missions elsewhere, the attack may happen anyway or maybe not, the presence of the mines may influence the outcome of any action that follows, or they may not. This is not to infer that minefields laid in conventional war situations are always a matter of careless military delinquency; given time and a belief in the necessity for a doctrinaire minefield covered from well-prepared positions with overlapping fields of fire most commanders would use the option. All too often, however, soldiers simply do not have time to do things by the book, they do the best they can in the circumstances and their priorities are survival, achieving a tactical edge and inflicting casualties on the enemy. But it is not just between the soldier and the civilian that perceptions of minefields differ, there is a considerable gap between the strategic planner's reasons for deploying mines and those of the fighting soldier. The standard strategist's jargon is that remotely delivered mines are laid to 'canalise' enemy forces, or, as British military strategists define their projected use:

> to disrupt the enemy's use of critical areas and routes; attack and disrupt key points and logistical installations; to canalise and delay the enemy and thereby create suitable targets for other weapons systems to engage ... In this overall context, landmines are deemed to contribute to the maintenance of high tempo, by causing delay to and lack of cohesion for the enemy.[21]

It is probably inevitable that all strategists present the enemy as a flock of sheep blindly moving into each trap and disregard the possibility that the enemy may, inconveniently, have plans of their own. Strategy documents rarely refer to soldiers or people, as though admitting that each unit was made up of individual human beings would somehow weaken the tactical integrity of the plan. I will always remember a sergeant major I served under pronouncing through gritted teeth following a lecture on tactics to our unit by a very young officer, 'Thank you, Sir, I have always been impressed by the steely toughness of tacticians, so valuable when planning the battle from a distance.' Landmines are remarkable in the gap which seems to separate the confidence of the manufacturers and tacticians from the soldiers who must fight with and against them.

Compare, for instance, the assured tone of the UK strategy quoted above with the misgivings of one of the world's most experienced fighting soldiers:

> We kill more Americans with our mines than we do anybody else. We never killed many enemy with mines ... What the hell is the use of sowing all this [air-delivered scatterable mines] if you're going to move through it next week or next month? ... I know of no situation in the Korean War, nor in the five years I served in Southeast Asia, nor in Panama, nor in Desert Shield/Desert Storm where our use of mine warfare truly channelised the enemy and brought them into a destructive pattern ... In the broader sense, I'm not aware of any operational advantage from the broader deployment of mines.[22]

General Gray sees people and soldiers, rather than statistics massaged and exaggerated to meet the expectations of higher echelons. It may be said that this is the key factor in relation to minefields – they are not *military* places, they are simply places – places which are temporarily put to military use, usage which will impact the peacetime population, their activities and environment to the same or greater extent than the military. Anywhere a battle has been fought or over which a military plane has flown or which is within the range of mortar, artillery or rockets may be a minefield – the only definition is that *landmines are present*.

2

Landmines and Unexploded Ordnance – Post-conflict Impact

Their war kills
Whatever their peace
Has left over
      Bertolt Brecht

DIRECT IMPACT

The Human Body

There is a certain delicacy in the terminology employed by arms manufacturers to advertise the effects of their weapons. A common phrase in use is 'soft targets', which means people. The fact is that the buyers and the sellers wear smart suits, not camouflaged battledress, and have wives and children at home who would flinch at the realities of their profession if it were to be explained with honesty: 'the ball bearings from this mine will blow damn great pieces of flesh and bone out of any person within 30 metres' or 'an incidental benefit of this bounding mine is that the high fragmentation pattern will ensure massive facial injuries and blinding among all age groups from 10–12 years upwards'. Everyone has their sensitivities, and although such descriptions are perfectly accurate they are unduly unpleasant and may adversely affect a company's reputation. In fact, so careful are manufacturers in this regard that their advertising material for the most horrendous weaponry rarely makes mention of human targets at all. Understandably, neither do the arms companies mention the long-term post-conflict capabilities of their weapons, despite the fact that most landmines and many other items of ordnance are far more effective in action against peacetime communities than in their wartime role against military targets.

The Vulnerable Aid Worker

Ken Rutherford travelled to the Horn of Africa in 1993 as a monetisation training officer with the US aid agency, the International Rescue Committee (IRC), to establish credit unions in the Gedo region of Somalia close to the border with Kenya. Four months into his assignment, on 16 December, he went to inspect a lime-producing plant near the town of Luuq, accompanied by several local IRC staff and credit union members in a Toyota Landcruiser. The driver drove on to the verge of the road to avoid a donkey cart; there was a violent explosion and the vehicle filled with dust. Ken remembers seeing somebody's severed foot through the clearing dust – it was several minutes before he realised that it was his own. His radio had been blown from his belt by the blast and was lying several yards away from the vehicle. He crawled out of the vehicle, dragged himself to it and called the IRC base. His local colleagues helped to prop him up against the vehicle and elevated what remained of his lower limbs, comforting him until he was taken, in a pick-up truck some 20 minutes later, to the African Medical and Research Foundation (AMREF) hospital in Luuq. The doctor at the hospital could do little and determined that Ken must be urgently evacuated to a fully equipped hospital, the nearest being more than 800 kilometres away in Nairobi – a long and difficult drive in the best of circumstances on a very basic road system. The doctor was fearful that Ken would not survive the journey, but equally certain that he would die if he could not be transferred to a suitable hospital. Luckily an AMREF aeroplane was in the area and was able to land. During the flight Ken was losing so much blood that the doctor and nurse who accompanied the plane gave him direct transfusions from their own bodies. What remained of his lower leg was surgically amputated soon after his arrival at the hospital and he was transferred by air to Geneva where three operations were conducted over five days in an attempt to save his left foot. Three days before Christmas Ken was flown to Colorado to a hospital near to his parents' home where he underwent a further three operations on his left foot. Just over three years later he made the decision to have his left foot surgically amputated. Ken Rutherford is not just lucky to be alive, he is lucky to have been a foreign aid worker. If he had been Somali he would undoubtedly have died from his injuries.

The Deminer as Mine Victim

In early 1990 Din Mohammed, known to everyone as 'Dinnie', was returning from a day clearing mines near to Chamkani in the Paktia Province of Afghanistan. He had been working for more than two years on a humanitarian demining initiative in support of a World Vision-funded rural rehabilitation programme and, as a member of the *mujahideen*, had been my guide to the local Soviet-laid minefields when I first went to Afghanistan in 1987. Exactly what happened that day is not too clear, but Dinnie stepped on a buried landmine, probably a PMN blast mine, close to some trees at the edge of the narrow dirt track. One of his legs was ripped apart, the other severely damaged by fragmentation, and the flesh and muscle was torn from his right arm by the metal armrest of the Schiebel metal detector he was carrying. Luckily the explosion was heard and Dinnie was found and carried on a makeshift stretcher to the clinic in Chamkani, but with few facilities and drugs there was little the doctor could do. A pick-up truck was found and, with Dinnie made as comfortable as possible in the back, it set out for the Pakistan border town of Parachinar. I have made that trip myself many times, and the several hours of corrugated earth road that jars the nerves can only be described as misery; that however was sat in the driving seat of a Landcruiser with good suspension and shock absorbers, and it is impossible to imagine the pain which Dinnie underwent in the back of a battered pick-up. They reached the International Red Cross emergency station near the Afghanistan–Pakistan border late at night, the paramedic examined Dinnie, did his best to stabilise his condition, and told the driver to get him to Peshawar, a further five hours' driving, as fast as possible. The International Committee of the Red Cross (ICRC) Hospital for Afghan War Wounded in Peshawar was always crowded and a large percentage of its patients were victims of landmines. Dinnie had not long come down from surgery when I arrived at his bedside. One leg had been amputated just below the knee and the other was a mess, and the doctors were not sure if they could save his right arm. They said he was literally grey from loss of blood when he arrived in Peshawar. Din Mohammed is lucky to be alive. If he had stepped on a mine in a more remote area, or at a time when no one was close enough to hear the blast, or if he had slid into a ditch out of sight of the track after being blown up, he would have bled to death at the site of the explosion.

Dying Alone – the Child at Risk

A small boy, about nine years old, was following his goats as they grazed in the mountains. His name is not known. He was probably playing a little, throwing stones maybe, or he would have noticed the small green mine that blew his foot off at the ankle. From what we know of how people react, from the memories of those who have survived, the little shepherd boy probably hopped or dragged himself to where his foot lay – it would have been quite close to him. He would have tried to put his foot back on to the bleeding stump of his ankle. He would have cried or maybe just sat lonely and quiet and helpless and slipped into unconsciousness. His goats must have stayed until after he died, probably until wild dogs arrived at the scene. We have no way of knowing exactly what happened; the dogs found him days before we did. He was certainly a 'soft target'.

The Facts as Figures

In March 1995 the ICRC released an analysis of landmine casualties including data collected on 23,767 survivors[1] – the statistics were blunt testimony to the landmine as a means of damaging the human frame:

Mine injured dying in hospital	3.7 per cent
Mine victims losing one or both legs	28 per cent
Survivors injured by stepping directly on a mine	29 per cent
Survivors sustaining fragmentation injuries	48 per cent
Mine victims requiring blood transfusions	37 per cent
Amputees requiring blood transfusion	75 per cent

Mine victims spend an average of 22 days in hospital on their first visit and a large percentage return because of wound and stump infections and for second and sometimes third amputations. But there is no comparison to be usefully made between the conditions prevailing in the hospitals who accept the great majority of incoming mine victims and the pristine conditions to be found in most Western European and United States surgical facilities – the latter have paid, trained staff, a well-stocked pharmacy, modern equipment, a reliable source of electricity and several ambulances with trained paramedic crews. Such conditions would have seemed of a fairy-tale nature to the surgeon I met in Penjwen, North Iraq, in 1993 who only undertook surgery, mostly amputations, after dark – by so doing so he could stretch the meagre ration of fuel available for the generator since the lights in the hospital had to be on at night anyway. The availability of drugs and trained theatre staff in most mine-affected countries is low to non-existent. In both Cambodia and Angola it is common practice for the patient's family to purchase whatever drugs the hospital recommend on the local market; if they are not available or the family cannot afford to buy them the patient must do without them. The administration of anaesthetics to a patient undergoing limb amputation is not a widespread practice in most rural hospitals, simply because the drugs are not available or are beyond the budget of the family or the hospital. Proprietary brands of painkillers may be the only pain relief administered prior to surgery in such cases.

But, horrific as it may seem, the lack of modern refinements in the operating theatre may be a minor part of the trauma which a mine or UXO victim undergoes. What exactly happens when a person activates a landmine or causes a piece of ordnance to explode? The following descriptions are common scenarios.

Victim Stands on Buried Blast Anti-personnel Mine

Hollywood is wrong – there is no 'click', just noise and confusion. Few mine casualties know exactly what has happened to them for some minutes, some do not even realise immediately that they are the victim. A surprising number recall a feeling of foreboding or of experiencing an unusual stillness in the moments before the explosion although, with due respect to those people, this may be more related to a need to come to terms with the horror of the moment in retrospect, rather than an actual premonition. Typically, the mine's pressure plate is 5 centimetres below the ground's surface. Only a few kilograms of downward pressure is required and, as the foot meets that mechanical requirement, a chain of reaction is initiated. A striker is released and drives down under spring pressure into the detonator which explodes and, in turn, initiates the main explosive charge, perhaps 200 grams or more of high explosive. This process, from pressure to detonation, takes less than a tenth of a second.[2] The explosion of the main charge causes a wave of pressure to move upwards at a velocity in excess of 1,000 metres per second, contacting the bottom of the foot and driving up through the limb. Moving within the pressure wave are items of debris from the mine casing and its components; earth, stones and vegetation from the ground immediately above the mine and pieces of footwear and parts of the foot, all accelerated by the blast to become high-velocity, irregularly shaped projectiles. Most of the injury sustained is caused by the blast pressure wave – a mine containing 150 grams of high explosive may amputate the leg at thigh level. In the above situation there is also a strong possibility that the pressure wave has caused abdominal injuries. Fragmentation is likely to have penetrated deeply into the rectum, small intestine and bladder and may have caused serious injury to the reproductive organs, especially in the case of a male casualty. Although the casualty's other leg was not directly above the mine, blast wounds may range from superficial secondary fragmentation injuries to serious damage resulting in amputation. One third of such cases sustain, in addition, upper-body injuries, typically penetrating fragment injuries to the head and eyes, often resulting in partial or complete blindness and damage to the upper limbs. The latter injuries are often caused when the casualty is carrying something which is caught in the blast pressure wave; it is common, for instance, for deminers who are carrying a detector with an arm-retaining cuff fitted to have flesh and muscle stripped from the arm as the cuff is driven up the limb.

The casualty may well be conscious and confused and will often try to stand up despite the visible injuries. Some survivors of mine explosions have told of making several attempts to stand and walk before they accept, or realise, the extreme nature of their physical injuries. This may be especially true of children, who may not immediately connect the explosion and their own condition. That this seeming alienation from reality is a common factor in many landmine incidents is supported by the number of survivors who remember attempting to reconnect a foot or part of a limb traumatically amputated by the explosion. If the casualty is alone when the incident takes place survival to reach expert medical aid depends on a combination of the following factors:

- the seriousness of injuries, the onset of shock
- the behaviour of the casualty
- the timely arrival of assistance
- the action taken by rescuers
- the evacuation process.

Loss of blood may not be extreme in the case of smaller mines even though amputation may result. However, in cases such as those described above both internal and external bleeding is likely to be considerable and circulatory shock will result. Individual casualties will react differently to their injuries, although there is evidence from the testimony of survivors that panic is not necessarily a reaction. There is considerable risk, however, if the casualty does panic and, in any case, when any attempt is made to crawl away from the incident site. Unless the incident was the result of an isolated landmine, which is the exception and certainly not the rule, the risk of initiating another explosion is considerable, especially as the victim may be disorientated and unable to remember or recognise the direction of travel up to the time of the incident and is likely to move further into the minefield. The state of mind of the casualty at this stage can be judged from the account given by Tun Channareth, the Khmer double-amputee who accepted the Nobel Peace Prize on behalf of the ICBL, of the minutes following the mine explosion. With both his legs massively injured and abandoned by his military unit except for a friend who was paralysed with fear, Channareth attempted to cut his legs off with an axe because he could not drag himself out of the minefield, he referred to them as 'a dead weight'. Happily, the horror of this scene seemed to bring his comrade to his senses; he took away the axe and managed to get Tun Channareth to hospital.

When rescue arrives the result depends on those present having some knowledge of landmines. If the rescuers are ignorant of the risks or, as often happens, are related to the casualty and react without thought, it is probable that they will fall victim themselves. The behaviour and age of the casualty can also be a factor – if he or she is in extreme pain or panic and calling or screaming loudly, or if the victim is a child, the rescuers are more likely to succumb to the pressure of the moment and approach carelessly or without thought, which will increase considerably the possibility of further explosions. Having safely reached and extracted the casualty, survival then depends, in cases where the injuries are extreme, on their ability to arrest bleeding and find the fastest means to get to a surgical facility. The benefit of delay in order to stabilise the casualty's condition depends entirely on the skill and training of the medic; if trained properly such first aid is vital, if not it can be fatal.

Vehicle Strikes Anti-tank Mine

There are several reasons why a wheeled civilian vehicle may initiate an anti-tank mine, the most obvious being that the mine's design is such that a lesser pressure than would be applied by a battle tank is sufficient to begin the explosive chain. Alternatively, the mine may have been adapted to respond to less than the original design pressure or may explode due to damage or deterioration of the internal mechanisms. However, the fact that such incidents have become increasingly common in recent years may indicate that many anti-tank mines are, in actual fact, anti-vehicle mines, designed to explode at a lower pressure than would be necessary if the intended target was solely battle tanks. There is also a specific class of landmine designed to destroy a wide range of vehicles of varying weights, the best example of this type of device is the M7A2 anti-vehicle mine, manufactured in the United States, which is often deployed with two or more mines interlinked to maximise effect. It is also common practice among soldiers to 'boost' the effect of a landmine by laying an anti-tank mine in tandem with an anti-personnel mine, thus the initiation pressure required is that of the anti-personnel mine which acts as a detonator for the larger mine.

It is not unusual for a vehicle to be blown up on a road which has been considered safe for some time, which may lead to the assumption that the mine was newly laid – this is not necessarily the case. Anti-tank mines, especially when laid by inexperienced or poorly trained troops, are often buried too deeply and only explode after a period of time when the surface of the road has become compacted or, in the case of unmetalled routes, when rain and weathering has removed the surface strata of the road. Anti-tank mines may also be laid off the main carriageway on the verge, often accompanied by anti-personnel mines, the latter frequently being part of a minefield which may extend for some distance in depth, parallel to the road.

> The truck was carrying a mixed load typical of the developing world, consumer goods, building materials, firewood and as many people who could afford the journey and find a space on top of the cargo. The driver and his mate had made the trip several times since the road reopened following a fragile ceasefire between the government and the rebel army. At first vehicles only travelled in escorted convoys, but confidence was returning and truck drivers

were making the best of the new trade by travelling together in informal unescorted convoys which, in any event, avoided the need to pay the inevitable 'fees' to escorting soldiers. There had been no security incidents and village talk along the way, normally more reliable than official proclamations, was that the rebels had withdrawn from the area some months ago. There were known to be minefields close to the highway and travellers were warned not to stray far into the bush. The road was potholed and little of the original metalled surface remained, destroyed bridges were negotiated over precarious but serviceable timber and steel trackways or through river bed diversions, deep craters in the road had been loosely filled with rubble.

The truck had stopped at a roadside stall and the passengers had stretched their legs and bought fruit and now they were moving again, the day's trip was half completed and a few of the passengers were singing as they slowed approaching the obstacle. It was an old tanker and its overloaded rear axle was jammed solidly between two rocks in a shell crater, a group of sweating men were struggling with long poles attempting to lever one rock from under the tanker, they paused to wave the truck past. The driver crunched into low gear and pulled around the edge of the crater. The driver's mate remembered the engine cover seeming to push his face into the corner of the cab and then a blast of heat before the scene changed to spinning green and he found himself lying under a tree looking at the smoking truck lying on its side. The driver died trapped in his mangled cab, both legs amputated by the blast – the engine block lay 20 metres away in the centre of the road. Two of the passengers who were sat on the top of the cab were also thrown into the road, both were uninjured apart from superficial cuts and bruises. The remaining passengers, seven men, two women and one six-year-old boy, were either thrown off the truck or jumped from it following the explosion. Two men and one woman sustained serious leg and upper-body injuries from the fall and items of cargo falling on them, the child was trapped under the truck and died from crush injuries soon after being rescued. All the remaining passengers were injured by anti-personnel mine explosions in the few minutes following the truck hitting the mine, one man subsequently died. The driver of the tanker which was partially blocking the highway causing the truck to drive on to the verge was killed while trying to help one of the passengers from the minefield.[3]

When vehicles hit mines it is not uncommon for deaths and injuries to occur from people being thrown or jumping from the back of the vehicle.

Anti-personnel Fragmentation Mine Explosion

The three men were returning from digging cassava beyond the river outside the town perimeter defences. There wasn't any choice really, they lived on the railway sidings with their families in rotting wooden railroad wagons, the relief planes had stopped more than two weeks before and there had been no food for the thousands of displaced families in the town for several days. It was many months since the last shellings and there had been an effective truce for some months, although the army still strictly kept the cordon around the town. The continuing fighting which had stopped the food aid flights was over a hundred miles away in another province, but all the roads into the town were mined and no convoys could get in and, equally, no vehicles could leave.

They joined other small groups of men and boy scavengers as they neared the river, calling to friends and comparing their luck. The man only saw the tripwire a second before the boy in front of him walked through it, all the time struggling with the slipping load on his scrawny shoulder. He said later that time seemed to stop – the boy's body appeared to dance for a moment as black and red seemed to smear blotches on his light T-shirt and trousers, then his head jerked and seemed to twist as his body flopped to the ground. They could smell the explosive and, well versed in the lore of minefields, they approached the bodies slowly and carefully. The boy was dead – the stake mine had been only feet from him, another man had died with the blade of his small shovel embedded in his throat. A third man was badly injured and bleeding heavily from several shrapnel wounds, one in his stomach looked serious. The men called to each other, one boy was missing but no one wanted to venture far to search for him, they thought two mines had been linked to the tripwire and there could be many more in the area. They shouted for the boy and eventually he emerged from some trees, frightened, all the men knew him, he was simple minded and lame in one leg. They all screamed at him when he began a hobbling run, crashing through the long grass towards them, then they crouched silently and watched, flinching, waiting for the inevitable. He seemed to somersault before they heard the explosion and, even at that distance, they were spotted with blood as the fragmentation tore into his body. It could only have been a claymore mine – they could see his lifeless body sprawled unnaturally in the flattened swathe of grass stretching out in a widening arc from where the mine had been hidden. They fashioned a litter from their blankets and hoisted the wounded man between them, heading carefully for the river.

The person who related the above story did not know if the man they carried back to town survived; they took him to the hospital and left. Someone knew the man's family and said they would inform them. Some men went back the following day with family members and some soldiers to retrieve the bodies. Fragmentation mines usually kill the person who initiates them and injure those nearby. The killing range can be up to 30 metres, and fragmenting submunitions have a similar impact on the human frame. Survivors often sustain substantial scarring and disfigurement, amputations are common as is total or partial blindness.

Vulnerability

Vulnerability by Lifestyle

Although landmines, by design, are random in their impact on post-conflict communities, the circumstances which dictate that a victim detonates a mine or UXO are often related to one or more of three factors: occupation, season and age.

Certain occupations among subsistence communities must be considered as extremely vulnerable; they have in common the fact that they are also essential to the survival of the community. The following list is not comprehensive, but does represent the most common tasks being carried out by victims at the time of their death or injury:

- fuel collection/woodcutting
- clearing vegetation from overgrown farmland/irrigation systems
- ploughing/planting

- grazing livestock
- collecting water
- playing
- collecting battle scrap/metal.

There are more generalised headings such as migration and repatriation – the fact that refugees and internally displaced people are vulnerable by definition of their situation is clearly evident – but the tasks listed above account for a large percentage of mine casualties from all population groupings residing permanently in or transiting mine-affected areas. The reason is comparatively clear – each occupation requires, or makes it likely, that the subject will be the first person to enter a given area since fighting ceased. Some, such as fuel collection and woodcutting, involve a constant process of breaking new ground which is apparent from the number of mine casualties who are carrying out those jobs when they are blown up.

Vulnerability may shift seasonally between groups and occupations, sometimes a result of obvious task rotation, as illustrated by the agricultural cycle, but also resultant of complex and less apparent influences. In most subsistence, especially remote, rural areas where snow is heavy during winter, fuel collection – often carried out by women – increases dramatically in the weeks leading up to the coldest time of the year. The increase in mine casualties during prewinter fuel stockpiling activities may, at first investigation, seem inexplicably high and this particular example is a good indicator of the complex nature of the link between occupation and vulnerability to landmines. The need to gather, transport and store large quantities of fuel wood within a limited timeframe requires an increase in the labour force, so children are commonly taken along either to help gather and carry kindling or simply because some mothers have no one with whom to leave them. Consequently three new areas of vulnerability must be considered: first, that children are less cautious and aware of the risks and therefore more likely to trigger an explosion. Second, the involvement of children leads to tighter groupings in the vicinity of any explosion – they are less strong than the women and tend to work in small teams. In addition, mothers with babies and very young children on their backs are also likely to be more numerous. Thus the number of victims affected by each detonated landmine is likely to be higher than at other times of the year. Third, the presence of young children changes the immediate response of bystanders following a mine explosion. A mother seeing her child blown up is likely to react instantly and without caution, the same is true in the case of a child whose mother triggers a mine – the chances of further detonations caused by desperate attempts to rescue, assist and comfort victims in minefields are considerably increased in such circumstances.

Vulnerability by Age

Vulnerability as a result of age relates primarily to the very young and the very old. The latter category of potential victim is, to some extent, self-explanatory; an old person is likely to be less aware of surroundings, may not respond to visual warnings and may be generally confused, especially during a period of conflict or in the immediate aftermath of war. But there may also be other contributory factors – elderly members of a community may not be included in mine-awareness classes, for example, or, if they do attend, may be unable to see or hear sufficiently to benefit. Culture can also play a part – it may, for instance, be considered disrespect-ful for a young instructor at a mine-awareness class to target confirmatory questions to community elders, in turn it may be considered indicative of lack of wisdom for elders to ask questions concerning parts of the instruction which they have not understood.

The vulnerability of the very young can be related directly to three factors: physical, behavioural and occupational. It may seem too simplistic to state that children often fall victim to landmines because they are small – it is, none the less, a fact. In countries such as Iraq, where large numbers of anti-personnel mines have been surface laid and are therefore visible, children often fall victim simply because they cannot see the mine they stand on as they approach it. Why cannot the child see what, to the adult, is clearly visible? Because the child is too small and has a lower viewpoint – the mine is hidden from its view behind vegetation.

Children, even those who have been warned about the dangers of landmines and who have attended risk-limitation lessons, are prone to increase their vulnerability through behaviour which, in the cir-cumstances, is high risk. Play, necessarily examined as an occupation, is an undisciplined activity which demands that children often run, climb and hide without paying close attention to their immediate environment, and are unlikely always to observe boundaries imposed by adults for reasons of safety. A child will chase a ball or follow a kite without thought of danger, the excitement of the game will nearly always outweigh other considerations or behavioural limitations.

Vulnerability – the ICRC Experience in Bosnia and Herzegovina

The ICRC has released data from its operations in Bosnia and Herzegovina[4] which illustrates how vulnerability can be affected by season, population movement, occupation, age and other considerations.

> During the war (1992–1995), there was an increase of the number of victims during May–September and a significant increase during the winter ... explained by a reduction of movement ... Since the end of the war (January 1996), the general trend shows an increase during February to April corresponding to farming activities. The number of victims [in the postwar period] has decreased in September to January ... activities such as cutting wood in rural areas have maintained a certain number of injuries during July to September ... The elderly (65+) represent 5% of the victims.

The ICRC report also notes:

> In 1996 544 persons were injured by mines and UXO ... 23% of the casualties were children ... between January and September 1997, 217 persons were injured ... 19% of the casualties were children ... the proportion of children injured during the war was lower (around 10%). 80 to 90% of all mine victims [in Bosnia and Herzegovina] are male, mostly engaged in manual labour activities at the time of the accident. Since January 1996, an increasing number of internally displaced people (IDP) and returnees are being injured (40%). During the war, on average, 20% of mine victims were IDP or returnees.

Landmines and Community Confidence

Landmines and Farmers

The fear of mined land is a major negative influence on post-conflict rehabilitation. It is easy to empathise with the affected communities, although perhaps difficult to understand the complex nature of their plight, but, for anyone involved in any capacity with the landmine crisis, comprehension is essential since this factor is central to the whole issue.

Subsistence farmers are a direct human interface with the physical environment, they must understand their land in order to survive, to say they *love* the land is a misnomer – they *need* it. I have watched a farmer sift soil lightly through his fingers, an intent gaze as the wind spreads the grains, gently rubbing earth between thumb and fingers – man with complete dependence on the land and, by necessity, intimate with its properties. The only fear of the land for such farmers is that it will fail them, starve them, starve their families. War may drive them from their homes and from their fields, sometimes for years, but war is a human flaw and when they return they treat their land as an old and faithful partner in survival. These are the people who suffer most from landmines, initially because ignorance of modern warfare means that many farmers and their families are killed and maimed before they learn that their land is unsafe.

Farmers are not, by their nature, given to an easy acceptance of defeat, thus the first response of many is to make attempts to clear mines from their land themselves in the same determined manner they would adopt in repairing a plough or a water pump. The result, although often after initial success, is virtually always devastating – the land erupts, killing or crippling the farmer. Fear sets into the community, even for those who have had no accidents and have seen no mines on their land; how can they tell if their land is safe? And when one or two people are blown up on land that has previously been ploughed and planted the fear is total and is not based on a dread of the technology of war but on a mistrust of the land itself.

The formulae is then simple and perverse; each family must get into the business of risk assessment. There are no guidelines, at first just a basic and largely inappropriate rural logic, and as the toll of victims grows experience takes on the role of teacher, but the dilemma itself becomes no simpler with time. The solution to each threat exposes the family to alternatives which are only marginally preferable – in some cases the options, although physically safer, offer an impossibly unrealistic course of action. Deprived of all or some of their land a farming family must decide how to survive and, supposing that they have decided that searching and clearing the land for mines themselves is an unacceptably high risk (they may have arrived at that assessment through the death or injury of one or more of their number) an option may be to hire someone to clear the land. Mine-clearance services are often offered by former soldiers or fighters and, invariably, are not a solution since clearance techniques tend to be haphazard and offer no guarantee of success. In the same manner of many ill-informed advisers to donors and governments these demining entreprenuers will often justify incomplete clearance of land by arguing that, having at least removed some mines, they have made the land safer for the community. If the family choose that option there comes a time when they must demonstrate their confidence in the work for which they have paid – it is not hard to imagine the trepidation which would attend that venture, nor the growing confidence with each day's work completed safely and the devastation if the land, sooner or later, proves to be unsafe after all. In some communities, usually the poorest, families simply accept the risk of death or maiming as a new factor in their lives – in the most heavily mined areas of Cambodia it is not unusual to encounter families who have lost several members to mine explosions but who still farm and graze the same land. When questioned regarding the inherent dangers in this lifestyle their answer is characteristically one of acceptance, a threat accepted because it is marginally the lesser risk when measured against total destitution. But the loss or maiming of a member of the family group reduces its survival capacity and, when the main breadwinner is killed or unable to work, the role must be taken on by another family member – nearly always younger, less experienced and more vulnerable.

Mined Land – the Rural Economy and Food Security

So far I have only related this fear of land to its impact on the immediate community, but quite clearly the potential implications are of a wider nature. In countries where landmines have been disseminated extensively over arable land the impact on a postwar economy may be enormous, although landmines may not always be identified as the cause by economists searching for a less specific and, for them, more conventional culprit within the confusion of post-conflict society. There is, however, a logical and clearly apparent link between mines on farmland and the national economy in any nation emerging from war where agricultural rehabilitation, the ability to meet domestic food demand, is a key factor in recovery. If many farmers are unable or unwilling to work their land to its full capacity this is obviously a food security issue – domestic food production will not achieve targets. It is comparatively rare to see more than a passing reference to landmines in agricultural assessment reports and even where references are included there is little attempt to properly assess their impact. A 1997 Food and Agriculture Organisation/World Food Programme (FAO/WFP) report on crop and food supply in Afghanistan[5] *did* recognise the existence of landmines in relation to agriculture but, remarkably, drew no conclusions as to the scale of their impact in relation to food supply although it did make some unspecified adjustments to (extrapolated) estimates to allow for their presence: 'the Mission based its 1997 estimate on the official 1967/68 data, updated by the 1992 satellite information, and modified downwards to take account of the direct effects of war, mines and displacement of rural people'. The report also noted: 'Although handicapped by war damage and locally by mines, agriculture is recovering quickly following the relative peace of the last two years in the south of the country.'

The unaddressed but essential question must be, how much more quickly would agriculture recover if there were no mines? 'The existence of mines remained a constraint on planting in some areas although de-mining has already released some of the better land.'

This observation seems unusually specific. Farmers constrained from planting seeds are constrained from *farming* – if the land is mined it cannot be prepared for planting or, subsequently, harvested. Any farmer relying on such land would be redundant. The report illustrates a common failing of many agencies involved in specialist sectors of aid and development: while recognising that landmines have an impact on their specialised area of operations and, often, are an obstacle to their work, no response is incorporated into their subsequent programme design and implementation. Very often this failure to respond is related to funding; agencies are aware that the eradication of landmines is a costly undertaking and avoid the obvious option to work in partnership with demining organisations based on the possibly justified belief that, having recognised the need for a mine-action sector within their field of operations, this may ultimately divert funds from their own budgets. The question will remain in every such case; if mines are an obstacle to credible operations, how can those programmes be implemented without incorporating a mine-eradication element?

In the case of food security any time wasted in responding directly to the landmine problem, regardless of how daunting in terms of scale and cost that may appear, are myopic and, in some instances, criminally so. The obstacle is normally a two-pronged obstruction:

- restricted access to arable and pastoral land negatively affects food production
- mined roads limit or make impossible the delivery of food aid.

The national and international response will inevitably focus on food deliveries, typically to displaced and returnee populations initially, by airlift to main urban centres. In areas where farming access is affecting, or is subsequently discovered to have an impact on, local food supply the airlift will need to be expanded. The costs of airlifts are enormous and the logistics make no sense other than in pure emergency and humanitarian terms, however what makes even less sense and eventually costs more is to delay the commencement of an engineering response to the landmines. What inevitably delays that response is a lack of funds or, to be more precise, a lack of a decision regarding the source of funding; meanwhile the situation in population centres dependent on the airlift deteriorate and place the overall logistical framework of the relief operation under greater strain. The irony of such situations is cruelly apparent: that landmines have never been so successful in disrupting the logistic chain in wartime as they are in peacetime, especially during the post-conflict transition phase. It should be added that airlifts tend to focus attention on locations accessible by air at the expense of those which are not, thus often forcing communities who are cut off from support and aid by mined roads and the lack of landing facilities to abandon their homes and move to displaced people's centres in areas accessed by the airlift.

Mined Land, Reconciliation and Peacekeeping

Countries in transition from war to peace may find that landmines laid by all combatant forces present a very real obstacle to reconciliation. Initially this may be through a straightforward lack of trust in the peace process by field commanders who will not mark, give information regarding, or remove their minefields. It is may, as discussed above, be due to the lack of access for peacekeeping personnel and the drain on budgets imposed by the use of aircraft to maintain operational integrity. But later the impact of landmines may become more complex and destructive. It is common for each force to be responsible for removing landmines to allow access to peacebuilding missions, normally made up of officers from formerly opposing armies, and for access to containment areas. It is unfortunately rare to find any military formation, government or guerilla, which is as expert at locating and removing its mines as it was previously in deploying them, it is not unusual for sappers to miss mines during clearance operations. A subsequent explosion, especially if it involves casualties to soldiers from either side or to members of the peacekeeping forces, leads to accusations that one side or the other has laid new mines on a previously cleared road. Even if the authorities responsible for clearing the road accepted blame it is unlikely that the damage to mutual trust would be fully repaired and such an admission would damage confidence in subsequent clearance operations and, inevitably, slow down the business of reconciliation. This innate ability of the landmine to disrupt both the logistics of, and the confidence in, a return to peace is ultimately costly in both humanitarian and economic terms.

The Cultural Cost

Culture may survive the longest and cruellest wars, often because communities grasp at and cherish the things which represent normality and stability. Even the young, who may have exchanged tradition for fashion before the fighting began, seek some common bond and meaning when their families and friends are threatened and separated by war. It is in the confusion and disappointment of peace that the strands of culture begin to unravel most easily. Like a shipwrecked man whose delight at reaching land is short-lived when faced with the trials of survival on a bare rocky island, so communities who have learned to deal with the challenges of conflict are often defeated by the ordeals of emerging peace. Anyone who has worked in such a situation will have heard expressed many times a sentiment that could be paraphrased thus: 'Peace seems to have few advantages over war.'

Peace brings expectations which, even in the best of post-conflict circumstances, are not realistic, especially for the poorest communities, displaced people and returning refugees. Because landmines outlive warfare and present different, and largely unexpected, problems in a peacetime environment, they are a major reason for the breakdown of social structures which would, in all likelihood, otherwise survive.

The Family Unit

The effect on the family unit and the traditional roles of each member are a classic example of the impact of widescale landmine use on rural society and the way in which lifestyle adjustments adopted in response to problems caused by landmines may prove irreversible in practice. The detail will differ from country to country, but the overall effect will be similar. The following is a sample family group from a subsistence farming community.

Grandfather is sick and contributes little. He may, on occasion, look after the youngest children.

Grandmother is a strong influence within the group. She teaches the children prayers and tells traditional stories, and teaches the girls traditional dances and ceremonies. She was also influential in holding the family together at height of war when they were forced to leave their village for some months. She suffers from failing eyesight but collects kindling from nearby woodland, looks after several domestic animals kept in the family compound, and helps with cooking. She makes important decisions about suitable timing and dates for auspicious occasions and key tasks – a quasi-religious role.

Father is a farmer. Carries out all major farming tasks and is the main group interface with the community. He is the group decision maker but, in some important matters, he consults with his wife, eldest son and mother. He conducts trade with local markets and travels to purchase commodities which are not available locally, such as fertiliser.

Mother is responsible for the household and budgeting income. She maintains a small garden plot producing vegetables and several fruit trees, and also a poultry smallholding. She makes all daily domestic decisions, brings up and allocates tasks to the children. She acts as the family doctor.

Eldest son understudies his father. He is largely involved in manual agricultural labour but with a special responsibility for irrigation and livestock. His role and responsibilities within the family group will increase with time.

Eldest daughter understudies her mother and is being prepared for marriage. She is responsible for the baby and younger children and ensures they go to school (although did not attend school herself) and complete allocated chores. She accompanies other village females for water and firewood collection and washing clothes.

Other children are two girls and two boys aged between six and fifteen years. They share household duties, with both boys taking turns grazing the family's goats, usually in a mixed flock with other village animals. All go to school for three hours each day. The eldest of the two boys will begin full-time education when he reaches twelve years old. There is also a baby boy, nearly 18 months old, who the daughters look after as directed by their eldest sister.

Interdependence Within the Family
This is a fairly representative rural family group which, with some variations as regards custom and practice, could exist in any developing country. They are reasonably successful and forward-looking but still totally reliant on their land and their traditional way of life for survival – they have no alternative living options and no state-provided assistance to cushion them in times of difficulty. The critical factor is the interdependence of the group; there is little room for adjustment of roles, and with the exception of the grandfather and the baby each group member has a full day. There are only two areas of latitude, both involving the children – playtime and education. The latter would be sacrificed begrudgingly by the parents since most subsistence communities value the opportunity to educate their children very highly; the decision to send the second-eldest son into full-time education is in itself an important and sacrificial decision and will increase the workload of other family members. If for any reason, such as sickness, a member of the family is unable to work, their tasks must be shared by the rest of the family – they are essential and cannot be left undone.

Dependence on the Land and the Elements

The war will have eaten into, and probably removed, any reserves the family possessed. Having to leave their land will have tested each member and may have already caused some breakdowns in the family structure – the young are often more adaptable and resourceful in such situations and, perhaps, the eldest son may have been better able to deal with the challenges presented by migration and displacement. This would possibly now strain the relationship between father and son, making the son more confident about taking a greater role within the family group and the father more defensive of his position. This may or may not be the case, but it is certain that the family structure will be fragile until their communal confidence in survival returns. Much will depend on their first crop following their return, if it fails for any reason they will need to sell livestock to survive and buy seed and fertiliser before the next planting. So they are dependent on the elements and, most importantly, their land.

Father and son will concentrate all their efforts on preparing the land and irrigation ditches which, after their enforced absence, will first require clearing of weeds and probably the removal of rubbish left by soldiers who will often have used the ditches as trenches. It is at this point that the family's future may depend on a decision or decisions taken by one or more, often junior, military commanders during the family's absence from their land as internal refugees. If their land was mined the following chain of events is virtually unavoidable and so common as to be almost unworthy of comment in a modern post-conflict scenario.

The Mine Incident

The eldest son is climbing out of a ditch and stands on an anti-personnel mine. One foot is torn off by the explosion and he is partially blinded. His father finds him, is lucky not to initiate a mine himself although he is not yet aware that the ditch contains more than 30 mines in the section which crosses his land and that his two fields have been sown with over 50 anti-tank and anti-personnel mines). He carries his son home and the mother and eldest sister treat the wounds and stop the bleeding as best they can while the father looks for transport to take his son to the hospital some 60 kilometres away in the nearest town. The owner of the pick-up is working for a group of farmers hauling rocks to the river where a new dam is being built to divert the flow into an irrigation system.

He will lose a day's earnings and, although little is said in the circumstances, the father understands that he must reimburse the driver and replace the fuel for the trip. Hasty instructions are given to the children and the grandmother takes charge while both father and mother join their son in the back of the pick-up; as a last-minute decision the second-eldest boy is also pulled on board. The small group in the back of the vehicle now focus totally on keeping the eldest son alive and as comfortable as possible. The remaining members of the family are traumatised, mechanically doing their chores and whispering but only having the vaguest impressions of what has happened.

The Hospital

At the hospital the son is rushed to surgery where his right leg is amputated just below the knee and a large fragment of metal, part of his axe, removed from his groin. His eyes are cleaned and examined. One eye is subsequently removed; the other is not damaged although the effects of dust and blast will make it painful and his vision will be blurred for several days. He will need to stay in hospital for at least three weeks, possibly more, after which he may be able to attend a prosthetics centre run by a foreign aid agency in a nearby town who will give him a false leg and teach him to walk. The doctor gives the father a list of medicines he should buy and explains that the hospital provides one basic soup and bread meal each day to all patients but that the family is expected to provide any other food and to look after their son while he is in the hospital. He is sympathetic to their plight but the hospital has few nursing staff and only minimum funding – their son is out of danger but needs constant care to ensure that his wounds do not become infected.

The three family members huddle at the bottom of the eldest son's bed and hold a whispered conference. They need to make decisions now – the pick-up driver is being patient but needs to start back to the village before dark. The mother wants to stay with her son but knows she can't, the father also knows he cannot afford to stay away from his land for long – he has all the money they possess in his vest pocket and most needs to be spent on drugs for his son. They decide then and there that the mother will return in the pick-up, the father will stay for one day to buy medicine and ensure the younger boy knows what he must do, and then will make his way home. The boy will stay with his brother, sleep by his bed, feed him and clean his wounds as instructed by the hospital staff.

The Impact

At this stage the family are on the edge of an abyss. It is important to understand the impact of this single landmine explosion:

1   The eldest son is totally lost to the family workforce for at least eight weeks, probably more.
2   The eldest son, partially blind and disabled, will be permanently limited in his physical contribution to the family unit.
3   The injury to his groin may have affected his ability to father his own children, his disability and possible facial disfigurement may affect his marriage prospects in any event.
4   The second-eldest son will eventually have to take the place of his elder brother at least in relation to physical work which will have three major implications:

    a   he will no longer be able to attend full time education
    b   his unavoidable promotion within the family group will be a serious blow to the morale and standing of his elder brother
    c   the boy's childhood is effectively curtailed.

5   Any financial buffer against hard times which existed will be eaten away by providing care for the eldest son and travelling to the hospital to visit him. (Funds which may have been reserved to cover funeral expenses for the grandparents may have to be used. Burial ceremonies are often important social status indicators and losing these funds may eventually be a further morale blow to the family.)
6   The family have effectively lost two members of their workforce for at least two months at a critical period. Other members of the family must take over the duties of the two boys. There will be no time for school and play. The baby will/must spend more time with the grandfather who, in turn, will feel more acutely that he is a burden on his family.
7   Although the trauma of events will not have given the father time to consider the full implications of the mine explosion itself he will soon be forced to recognise the risk attendant to any further work on his land and, paradoxically, accept that his next-youngest son must work the land in place of his injured brother.

The Future

I have listed only the inescapable implications – in practice there would be many more. The family face a difficult and defining period during which almost any decision will be critical, but one fact must be faced immediately – their land is dangerous and they have no way of knowing the scale or limits of the threat, yet they must work the land in order to survive. The irrigation canal must be cleared, regardless of the risk involved, the land must be prepared for planting, despite the fact that the family have no way of knowing if the mines are confined to the ditch or have been laid in their fields.

In a typical case the family would suffer at least one more landmine casualty. Their plight would be representative of the community as a whole – the humanitarian implications are clearly apparent, but the breakdown of the family structure also impinges on the community's traditions and the damage may be irrevocable. When war is over Third World rural communities facing the kind of problems described above have no time for looking backwards. They must work to survive, and culture is one of the unseen casualties.

Religion

The disparate roles which religion plays in many conflicts are source material for many books and learned papers; the cause, or perhaps excuse, underlying many wars can certainly be at least partially attributed to religion, but it may equally be religion to which people turn for stability when the war is over and they are faced with rebuilding their lives. This aspect of culture may seem remote from the very worldly and man-made affliction of landmines, but even here they have had their impact, especially in Buddhist communities.

Baseth village is situated in Sang Kee District close to Battambang Town in northwest Cambodia. The village has a long history as a place of religious significance due to the Pagoda and burial grounds situated there, it is a centre of pilgrimage for the area. The ruins of an older temple are strewn among the thick vegetation which surrounds the Pagoda, although many of the great stone remains were broken up by the Khmer Rouge to build bridges around Battambang Town. The community of monks who live at the Pagoda do so at great risk to their lives. Meksal, an 18-year-old monk who joined the order to study Dhama – the scriptures – was clearing undergrowth near the Pagoda when he stood on a mine and lost his leg. He is lucky to be allowed to remain since those who are 'unwhole' are normally not allowed to be monks in Buddhist society. The minefield which surrounds the monastery is now being cleared by a demining team; not, however, primarily for the religious significance of the site, but to allow villagers access to the nearby banana plantation and its valuable crop. But for the monks and many of the local people the freedom to worship and visit the burial grounds to mark the celebrations of the Buddhist calendar will have at least as much significance as the lucrative banana plantation.

The loss of a limb often prohibits Khmer men the opportunity to become monks, a denial which strikes at the heart of their culture, but not a consideration which would be readily associated with a landmine explosion.

Resettlement

The impact of landmines can be perverse as well as horrific. Displaced communities have frequently migrated several times during the course of the war, often leaving areas unaffected by mines to settle, through circumstances beyond their control, close to mined land. They may eventually move back to their homes, sometimes after years as internally displaced people (IDPs)[6] only to discover that their land has been mined in the intervening months or years. IDPs are especially vulnerable to the indirect as well as the direct impact of landmines because they are not afforded the international recognition nor the protection which are the rights of the refugee. It is small wonder that many of these people are suspicious when informed that their land is mined – they will have learned to distrust authority during their migration and come to the understanding that the term 'land rights' can be widely and imaginatively interpreted with a balance towards the richer man or the man who can afford guns to impose a personal definition of those rights. In the postwar period a failure to stake claim to productive land is a threat to existence. IDPs who remain landless will eventually find that food aid and other outside assistance decreases as the UN and international agencies begin their phased transition from a post-conflict aid response to a structured development plan. They stand in grave risk of becoming displaced in a different way, and while they may not understand the intricacies of the transition in which they only figure as a marginal statistic, they will certainly recognise the changing circumstances for which the key indicator is hunger. Desperation leads families to take risks which, to the observer, seem insane. The following field report submitted by a despairing field manager from the UK demining charity MAG is an example of how desperate IDPs can become in their attempts to become masters of their own future, to stake their claim to land from which they can make a living and feed their families.

The population of Tahen are building a village in a minefield. The dry season has left the ground baked hard and, for the moment, the risks are limited because pressure is not transmitted to the buried mines. The villagers appear casual, cutting wood, herding cattle. The mined areas are marked but people step over the marking tape while ox-carts pass through gaps made in the marking tape. The community is expanding into surrounding areas, undergrowth is being cleared for agriculture and there is little chance of curtailing this trend. Cattle wander everywhere, often pursued by children whose job it is to look after the animals. A child hoes the ground with an adze, striking from above his head to break the hard-packed earth, a drunken soldier wielding an axe is pushed over the marking tape into the undergrowth by a comrade. The minefield marking tape stretches for 200 metres along the road and behind it scenes of construction and expansion can be seen everywhere. These people are IDPs who, with the improved security in Bavel District, have been coming home since November 1997 and now the sparse land beside the main highway where they were dependent on food aid has been abandoned in favour of their home village. Families of locally stationed troops arrived first followed by villagers who had fled the area in the late 1980s, some are still afraid to return, but those who have say they had no choice. It is a last stand – a chance to regain their land or establish a new house, to grow rice and cultivate vegetables. They were uncertain of their land rights and afraid that their land would be stolen if they did not occupy it now. There have been no mine accidents yet but everyone is afraid the wet season will bring a crisis and then there is a danger that our teams will not be able to get access to the village if the road is flooded.

The soldiers at a small camp about 500 metres away have no doubt that the village is mined and are concerned for their families. The desperate circumstances in which these people have lived has pushed them into an even more dangerous relationship with mines.

It is dangerous for the deminers as well. They must be constantly aware of the activity around them, stopping work when people come too close or when cattle get in the way of their work. I have discussed the problems with the village authorities, to try to dissuade more people from moving in – there was nothing they could do. People are taking risks because of their need for land – they are coming back home. Now they have heard that the village is being cleared of mines more people are coming back and others are coming because they fear that their land will be taken if they do not stake a claim to it now. The villagers say they are happy with our work and listen to our warnings, but these people are living in a minefield, it is not surprising that they have a casual attitude towards the dangers.[7]

Refugees

A generally accepted definition of a refugee is a person 'distinguished from the ordinary alien or migrant in that he has left his former territory because of political events there, not because of economic conditions or because of the economic attractions of another territory'.[8] The United Nations High Commissioner for Refugees (UNHCR) is the international body charged with the welfare of refugees and for their eventual repatriation to their homeland voluntarily and in safety. But the UNHCR has for some years been, at best, forced to avoid the full responsibilities imposed by their mandate in relation to resettlement in safety when repatriation is to a mined region. It would be easy to criticise this failure but more problematical to offer realistic solutions. The solutions do exist, dealt with in later chapters, but they are not in the hands of UNHCR, although the High Commissioner certainly has a responsibility in this area to take far more radical action than at present.

Repatriation is rarely a totally voluntary process on the part of the refugees. Most commonly it is a combination of political and social pressures supported by toughening of attitudes by the host government and sometimes a phased reduction of rations. In such circumstances the definition of 'voluntary' is something of a movable feast. The attitude of UNHCR staff may also be instrumental in setting the tone at such times, for instance, comments such as those made by one senior UNHCR official, Zhia Rizvi, in Cambodia when talking about the possibility of a formal programme of repatriation from Thailand to Cambodia in 1980:

> the conditions prevailing in the country to which the individual wishes to return are immaterial [In deciding whether his return is or is not voluntary] ... UNHCR must assume that the individual requesting repatriation has given the matter due consideration. It cannot be UNHCR's role to provide information on the conditions in the country of origin.[9]

It is likely that Rizvi had in mind the enforced repatriations by the Thai army which took place less than a year before at Preah Vihear when nearly 45,000 refugees were forced into border minefields, a situation which the then UN Secretary-General's special envoy, Ilter Turkman, referred to as 'a delicate political matter requiring much prudence'.[10]

Cambodia and Afghanistan both illustrated the UNHCR's unwillingness to acknowledge the presence of landmines as having a direct relevance to repatriation. In Cambodia it was the publication of the human rights report *Landmines in Cambodia –The Coward's War*[11] and the persistent lobbying of the two UK demining NGOs the Halo Trust and the MAG, and the French NGO Handicap International, which eventually forced UNHCR to include a first-phase landmine survey in their plan. In Afghanistan, where MAG had already conducted a widescale landmine impact survey in 1990 funded by the Norwegian and Swedish committees for Afghanistan, the UNHCR were less open to direct involvement and, while offering incentives to refugees who repatriated, took the view that basic mine awareness lessons given by the IRC to refugees and the very limited amount of mine clearance being conducted was an adequate response.

These examples are not unrepresentative and certainly UNHCR has no reason to review their track record in this regard with anything but shame, for many returnees have died and been maimed, often within days of arriving at their homes. But this is a glass house which very few organisations or governments could throw stones at with any ease of conscience; certainly major donors involved in the funding of repatriation programmes were equally culpable for failing to recognise the gap in proposals submitted to them. Many NGO staff with years of experience in areas earmarked for resettlement failed totally to challenge the wisdom of repatriation to heavily mined areas. During a visit to Cambodia in 1991 I was criticised by some experienced aid workers for suggesting that landmines were 'the business of NGOs'. Happily some were blessed with greater vision and took a different view. But the complexity of the problem facing UNHCR and, ultimately, the returning refugees themselves, was well defined by Gavin O'Keefe, a member of the CONCERN team charged with setting up the Cambodian reception centres, in his testimony to the Human Rights Watch researchers who wrote *The Coward's War* report: 'The sites themselves are undoubtedly safe. The problem begins when the people return to their homes and fields.'[12]

In the end it was the UN itself, rather uncharacteristically, which took up the challenge of accepting a greater responsibility for the safe resettlement of refugees. In a decision which directly rejected Rizvi's remarks of 1980 the UNHCR took on not just the role of knowing what the conditions prevailing in the country of origin were, but also the responsibility for doing something to rectify the situation where it proved necessary. In 1995 the 46th session of the UN General Assembly called on UNHCR to 'strengthen its activities in support of national capacity building', a call which came as a result of what the 50th Annual Report of the UN termed as a recognition 'that the mandate of UNHCR to seek permanent solutions for the problem of refugees gives the organisation a legitimate interest in the prevention of conditions that lead to refugee movements by means of operational activities within countries of origin'.[13] That decision has enormous implications for UNHCR's capacity to resolve the landmine emergency which faces many returnees and there are indications that they are prepared to take the responsibility seriously. One such country is Angola where, had the return to fighting after the 1992 elections not effectively cancelled the repatriation programme, the UNHCR would have been complicit in a dangerous operation which would have risked the lives of thousands, despite warnings from some of their own field officers that the scheduled repatriation held unacceptable dangers. One UNHCR officer based in eastern Angola told me in 1992, 'The bridges are down and the roads are mined and we simply don't know what the landmine situation off the main roads is – repatriation in such circumstances is madness – or worse.'

During the intervening years wisdom has grown, and although much more could be done, at least the UNHCR repatriation plan recognised the landmine problem and, in the spirit of their wider mandate, had subcontracted the Angolan national demining organisation, INAROE, and specialist NGOs to undertake surveys, clearance and mine-awareness programmes in advance of resettlement. Paragraph 41 of the UNHCR repatriation plan was unequivocal in its language:

> 41. Returnees, especially those who return spontaneously, face potential dangers from landmines in Angola. Programmes to protect and inform refugees of this danger will be implemented prior to organised repatriation. *Mine Awareness Campaigns* will be implemented in all refugee camps in countries of asylum. In Angola, demarcation and demining teams will be requested to give priority to repatriation routes and agricultural fields in areas of major returns. Efforts should also be made to ensure that national mine awareness campaigns reach areas of concern to UNHCR.[14]

Angola could have been a landmark in building a working relationship between the key refugee agency and specialist organisations involved in mine-related work. Sadly there were far too many agendas being played out in Angola and few had the interests of the great mass of Angolan people at heart. Neither UNITA nor the MPLA government had a true commitment to peace while any possibility of total military victory remained.[15] The pontificating demands for peace by the United States was hardly likely to be taken without, at least, a large measure of cynicism by the government, who had suffered the consequences of the covert and overt US arming of and support for UNITA over so many years and, even more so, by UNITA itself who had learned from their partnership with the CIA that what the White House said was not necessarily even a vague reflection of its real intentions. Despite international posturing, both sides continued to amass arms. Meanwhile many nations and multinational companies were taking unofficial steps to protect their interests in Angola's natural resources – the term 'interests' took on a wide range of definitions in this context. (One company especially, De Beers, has profited massively from its willingness to buy gemquality diamonds originating in Angola with all the evidence available that their corporate greed was directly contributing to UNITA and, by definition, the death, maiming and continued exile of millions of Angolans.) However, despite the fact that UNHCR had recognised the need to respond to landmines as an integral sector of the repatriation process, it was the UN itself, through the failure of its national mine-action initiative, which effectively neutralised the foresight of UNHCR. It is not beyond the bounds of possibility that had Angolan and international agencies cooperated within a viable and well-managed national mine-action programme renewed war could have been averted, largely through the confidence in peace generated by a timely and safe repatriation of refugees and resettlement of IDPs. This integration of skills is a vital factor in ensuring that risks to returnees are minimised – it requires innovative thinking on the part of those responsible for the repatriation of refugees and a cooperative response from demining agencies.

Reconstruction

Perhaps the most perverse property of landmines is their ability as inanimate and comparatively simple devices to be the cause of so many complex problems completely unrelated to their stated military purpose. Almost every aspect of physical reconstruction as a sector of postwar response is adversely affected by the presence of landmines and UXO. There is a logical, if perverse, explanation for this fact, if one examines the underlying national motivations for reconstruction after conflict:

- social stability through access to land and homes
- access for peacekeeping forces, domestic police, justice and administrative officers
- reopening of telecommunications
- production of food, commodities
- capitalise mineral wealth
- trade – internal and export
- reopening of key community sectors of health and education services
- ensuring supplies of water, fuel and power.

Many of these factors are interactive and there are others which could be added to this list. But each of these peacetime priorities is mirrored by a reverse wartime priority – bridges are destroyed and roads are mined to damage the ability of the enemy to maintain a logistic chain. The primary military purpose may be aimed at the opposing army's transportation capability, but a secondary impact, intentional or otherwise, is the destruction of the civilian transport and communication system since this is perceived as giving support to the military. Stability in the enemy camp is anathema to warring parties – chaos and fear should reign for greatest effect, a 'softening-up' to damage morale and hasten defeat. All kinds of enemy production are targeted, anything which assists the economic wellbeing of the enemy improves their capacity to prolong the war and improve their military potential. Targeting food production is, from a military standpoint, common sense, although it contravenes international humanitarian law. Article 14 of Protocol II, 1977 to the Geneva Conventions of 1949 is very specific:

> Starvation of civilians as a method of combat is prohibited. It is prohibited to attack, destroy, remove or render useless, for that purpose, objects indispensable to the survival of the civilian population, such as foodstuffs, agricultural areas for the production of foodstuffs, crops, livestock, drinking water installations and supplies and irrigation works.

Of course, the people who negotiate the terms and terminology for international humanitarian law and the laws for the conduct of war are, at once, protecting their national interests in wartime as well as the interests of non-combatants – an often conflicting agenda which leads to the inclusion of those three damaging words, 'for that purpose'. Despite the cynical nature of such wording there still remains a practical test of military actions in such circumstances – that of proportionality. As a guide and practical legal reference for the military field commander this principle is straightforward and can be paraphrased thus: 'No military action is justified if its impact on non-combatants is greater than the immediate military gains.' It should be noted, particularly in relation to the use of landmines, that the impact on non-combatants is not time-limited, although the potential military gains against which they are measured are only the immediate and foreseeable gains.

In Afghanistan the Soviet and Regime forces took the targeting of food supplies to such an extreme through widespread mining of agricultural areas and destruction of irrigation systems that it was impossible to differentiate between the military target and the 'collateral' civilian victims. The truth was clear – no attempt was made consider the principle of proportionality or to distinguish between military and civilian in Afghanistan – if they were not actively pro-government they were *mujahideen*. (It is, of course, interesting that this inevitably becomes a self-fulfilling prophecy – farmers *do* become fighters when they are treated as fighters for long enough, especially when members of their family are killed, injured, mistreated or taken prisoner and the family's economy is destroyed. The inability of generals at headquarters to perceive what corporals on the battlefield can often clearly see is perhaps one of the most enduring and asinine features of large-scale warfare.)

Because every facet of reconstruction is a mirror of the destructive aims of the combatant forces it also follows that every action possible will have been taken to prevent reconstruction. The fact that this was a wartime aim becomes immaterial when the preventative means used were landmines, since their effectiveness is not adversely affected by the advent of peace. And so reconstruction must have an integrated element of mine survey and clearance and, given the time-consuming nature of those processes, the whole reconstruction effort is impeded. It is also worth noting that the presence of mines may totally transform the reconstruction plan. Faced by the need to integrate a costly landmine-eradication sector into the overall plan which will inevitably reduce the funds available for reconstruction the temptation to focus first on unmined areas is perhaps understandable, if not excusable. It is certain that such an approach can be rationalised in a manner which would overcome most objections, especially if mined areas are simply demoted to later phases of reconstruction.

It would be easy, although mistaken, to see this as a strategic issue to be remedied by ensuring that agencies, indigenous and international, responsible for reconstruction give equal priority to mined areas and integrate mine-action sectors into their programmes as a matter of policy. The root of the problem is funding and the uncertainty of timescale involved. The latter factor can be resolved by the introduction of widescale technical landmine surveys as a standard post-conflict strategy (see Chapter 3), but the former consideration requires a fresh line of thinking to identify adequate funding sources for mine action which do not reduce funds available in other essential response sectors.

INDIRECT IMPACT

The indirect effects of landmines and UXO are likely to be as widespread as the weapons themselves. No list could be inclusive;

however, some effects are so damaging that it is surprising that the cause is often not recognised.

Medical and Health Services

As soon as conflict ceases so the profile of the medical and health service is transformed. The military medical support infrastructure, although it may survive to some extent as a service for peacetime soldiers, will be drastically downgraded. These facilities have often given support and treatment to war-injured civilians, especially surgical, while the fighting continued. One of the most valuable wartime medical structures is provided by the ICRC, but a feature of the ICRC mandate, these surgical hospitals, medical aid posts and ambulance services, may be closed at any time following the cessation of combat. The timing of the withdrawal of these vital services differs from country to country and seems, at times, to be a somewhat arbitrary decision without apparent logic. (That the ICRC itself must leave when its mandate is deemed to be concluded is understandable, but there is a need for better planning to hand the facilities, especially of a surgical nature, over to either national bodies or international medical agencies.)

At the same time as, or soon after, wartime medical facilities are winding down, displaced civilians and demobbed soldiers are returning to their villages – often leaving unmined areas to live close to mined land. Their priorities will be food and income – for the majority this will entail clearing overgrown land, in urban areas it may be establishing a small vegetable plot or scavenging for valuable scrap on former military sites; for many it will mean falling victim to a landmine or an item of UXO at a time when evacuation and surgical facilities may have almost ceased to exist.

Even where the government and regional authorities give high priority to health services the emerging facilities must cope with an increasing flow of mine-injured patients who require complex and costly surgery and who will take up beds in hospital wards for at least twice as long as the average patient and subsequently require intensive physiotherapy and prosthetic treatment. Amputee children require new prostheses, ideally, at annual intervals until they stop growing. Those blinded by their injuries will be a constant charge against a comprehensive health service.

Since few hospitals at this stage are able to ensure sterile conditions the incidence of infection during and following surgery is high and adds to the workload faced by staff and the economic strain on the health infrastructure as a whole.

Transport and Trade

The basic needs of a country following a prolonged period of conflict may be expressed in simple terms of rebuilding an economy with priorities of feeding the population and exporting surplus production. Although this may seem, at first sight, an oversimplification there are no matters of more importance to a postwar government with the possible exception of maintaining peace and stability which, especially if the war has been internal, merely emphasises the need to feed the population.

Although statespersons, economists, bureaucrats and politicians may discuss these issues as affairs involving complex theories, they are, in fact, matters of pure logistics. The greatest economic theories are meaningless in a nation where a truck cannot drive from the production point to the market or the docks. A farmer whose usable land area is reduced by landmines may not take his surplus to market but may store it against future shortages. It may seem a small thing to those who see only the global view when the trader in the local *Suq* goes out of business as a result of many farmers making similar decisions, but the impact will be felt throughout the trading chain.

In Angola, due almost entirely to mined roads, the WFP was forced to maintain a vastly expensive airlift to feed cities and towns throughout the country. But this was free food aid – what was happening to trade during that period where peace had finally arrived but the movement of commodities remained virtually impossible? And if commodities cannot be traded, why produce them? The fact that Angola is rich in oil and diamonds hid this impact to some extent – there is never any shortage of funds and political will to ensure that commodities which affect the *world* markets can be extracted and transported. A country in the same predicament with no such natural resources would become totally reliant on aid and, without the means to build an internal economy or feed the population, a drift back into war or widescale lawlessness would be the almost inevitable result. Few would blame landmines for such an occurrence, and, of course, they might not be the sole reason, but they would certainly be a prime factor in the collapse because physical communications are central to any nation's economy.

The Impact on Development

Much of the impact which landmines have on post-conflict development have already been mentioned or are clearly apparent. However, there are two areas where landmines and UXO have a critical if largely unrecognised impact.

Planning

When peace becomes a possibility, especially if international intervention or diplomacy has been instrumental in reaching that phase, the UN and other involved agencies come under pressure from international donors to produce rehabilitation and development plans. In turn, the government of the country is pressured to accept and approve those plans so that funds can be released. This has become a well-practised procedure, almost a formula with many agencies who employ standard formats to design their programmes. Not only is it not coincidental that these formats often coincide with the layout of major donor's funding paperwork, it is considered, by some donors, to be an essential element of the working bond with the organisations they fund. The European Community Humanitarian Office (ECHO) developed a computerised format for NGO proposals which, while it clearly met the internal accounting and contractual requirements of ECHO, was remarkable in that it fitted the needs of no field programme that anyone I knew in the NGO world had ever experienced. While NGO programme staff were disparaging of the format between themselves, they were loath to be so scathing in direct dialogue with ECHO staff since this may have adversely affected future proposals – or, at least, that was the perception of the NGOs. It is my own view that they were unnecessarily cautious and that their concern regarding the content of the format was misplaced because very few donors ever read the details of comprehensive funding proposals. During the mid-1980s while I was working in the Sudan a colleague and myself spent our spare hours concocting a complex and detailed proposal to establish a ski resort based at Jebel Mara in Darfur Province, one of the hottest and most rain-starved places on earth, where even a mild frost would be a major event. To test our theory that donors only read the summary page and the budget of proposals we made no specific mention of skis or snow in the summary. Not surprisingly the proposal reached an impressively advanced stage with one major international donor before an alert financial officer questioned some of the equipment requested within the budget. It was a prank, but it amply proved our theory since the first paragraph of the main body of the document laid out clearly that the programme was reliant on the reintroduction of traditional rain-makers to change the weather patterns sufficiently to ensure annual snowfalls.

This focus on procedure to the exclusion of people is central to the problems relating to mine and UXO eradication. Development is about humankind, but actual human factors in developmental planning have been reduced to the inclusion of a selection from a list of approved terminology – 'developmentally sound', 'culturally sensitive', 'gender issues' – the list is long and as distant from the realities of life in post-conflict society as could possibly be devised. Rather similar to the endless and meaningless debates as to when the rehabilitation phase ends and the development phase begins, this Euro-American aid shorthand has no relevance to the problems facing real people in the country who are trying to salvage an existence from the remnants of war.

But the UN and other organisations must play the game – interested governments and donors demand a plan of action and that leaves no time for even a cursory survey of the national landmine and UXO problems. One of two things happen: either a wild guess is made, usually by a harassed field officer based in the capital with no relevant expertise, as to the cost of a mine-action element; or the whole issue is ignored on the basis that 'it's outside our mandate'. And so, for instance, agricultural rehabilitation programmes in heavily mined countries are designed and submitted with no consideration given to which land is mined and which is mine-free. This is not planning – it is criminal madness – but it continues because, despite the wide publicity of the past few years, very few donors have more than a superficial understanding of the landmine crisis, and even fewer comprehend the fact that survey and clearance is a sector of field engineering which can release land for community use when adequately funded.

International Confidence

Governments of mined countries are often caught in a trap as a direct result of the failure to include mine action at the planning phase of development programmes. They require urgent funding but, in mined areas of the country, funded programmes may be impossible to complete or, in some cases, even start. A government which finds itself unable to implement funded development programmes inevitably finds itself losing the confidence of the international community. This, in turn, will adversely influence future funding decisions.

1 PMN-2 anti-personnel blast mine exposed during clearance operations. Cambodia. (John Rodsted)

2 Landmines and unexploded ordnance. Bosnia. (John Rodsted)

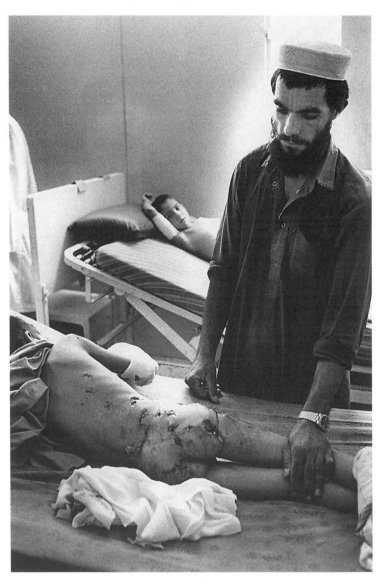

3 A young boy with fragmentation injuries. Afghanistan. (Sean Sutton)

4 Swords into ploughshares. But familiarity with the remnants of war may breed contempt – especially among children – for UXO, with the inevitable consequences. Laos. (Sean Sutton)

5 Mine victim Um Keltum Suleiman with her family. Kassala, Sudan.
(John Rodsted)

6 Level One impact assessment gives an overview of the problem facing
landmine/UXO-affected communities; those who survive explosions have
vital evidence about the location of risk areas. The author conducting
casualty interviews. Sudan. (John Rodsted)

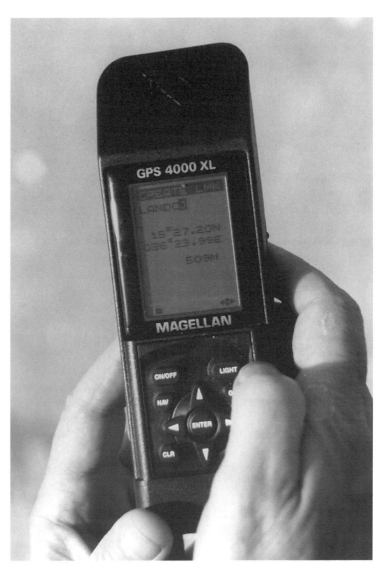

7 The GPS receiver is a lightweight and accurate survey tool.
(John Rodsted)

8 Anti-personnel mine prepared for *in situ* demolition. Mozambique.
(John Rodsted)

3
The Survey Process

'Now in the first place,' he said, 'you're looking at it all
bassackwards, you're going on the idea of the world as people say
it is, instead of as it really is'

James Jones, *From Here to Eternity*

MINE AND UXO ERADICATION – A TASK FOR THE MILITARY?

At a meeting in Cambodia in April 1991 I was told by a senior
UNHCR official that 'Mines will be cleared by people walking on
them but it will take a long time. The mines are an issue this country
must live with.'[1] Many people were shocked by that statement when
it was reported in the Human Rights Watch report *The Coward's War*,
but the official was merely stating what to many people at the time
seemed an unpalatable but unavoidable fact, not just in Cambodia
but in a growing list of countries. Most people had looked to the
military for answers on the reasonable grounds that landmines were
military hardware, but it soon became apparent that the soldiers had
no answers and, like everyone else, were bereft of solutions. What
made everyone despair was the sheer scale of the problem – what
seemed to be knowledgeable sources were talking of millions, tens of
millions, of landmines – where would one begin to eradicate such a
massive problem? The UNHCR official in Phnom Penh was simply
expressing the fears, more normally unspoken, of almost everyone
facing the problem.

And yet, even then, the solutions did exist and, to a large extent,
were known to the engineering branches of most European armies.
They had the tools for the job and simply did not recognise them
because, like almost everyone else involved, they were hypnotised
by the statistics. But estimates of the number of landmines in any
given minefield, district, nation or region are only of academic and
media interest when viewed in isolation, although they may have
some utility for assessing the lucrative activities of arms exporters.
The figures, in any event, range from inaccurate estimates based on
trade figures to wild guesstimates usually emanating from

intelligence sources which sometimes border on the insane. For instance, a recent official estimate of the number of landmines in Western Sahara gave the startling statistic of 'between one and ten million' – a crazed but clear illustration that the real problem is not so much the inaccurate nature of the assessments but the fact that officials feel it necessary to make them in the first place. The reason that the military were unable to respond effectively to the landmine emergency was due, in practical engineering terms, to their lack of vision. There was nothing which the early NGO demining operations incorporated which was unknown to military engineers. The oft-repeated argument that the military only breach minefields – that is, make lanes through them for purposes of offensive or defensive actions – is actually a statement of the limitation of their conceptual image of mine clearance rather than an assertion of their technical incapacity. The clearance of a minefield is simply a series of breaches using a field-engineering methodology which was proven, by the military, decades ago. The British army Pamphlet No. 6, *Detection and Clearance of Mines*, issued in 1947 for the use of Royal Engineers and Infantry Assault Pioneers[2] laid down detailed drills for the manual detection of landmines which differ very little from the procedures used by the best humanitarian teams working today. Where differences do exist they have developed as refinements of those original techniques adapted largely due to experience gained from daily operations incorporating safer working practices and the development of less bulky and more accurate detection equipment.

But the military were never a solution to this problem, not because they lacked the technical knowledge and capacity, but because there were overwhelming political considerations which limited their involvement. They were as follows.

Financial Considerations

Military budgets were never considered a relevant source of funding to resolve a humanitarian dilemma, despite the fact that the problem had been caused by military actions. Senior treasury and military staff in most countries were at least perceptive enough to realise that the clearance of landmines and unexploded ordnance was likely to be a long-term and high-cost undertaking and general commitments in that area made in haste would undoubtedly be regretted at leisure.

Risk Considerations

Most governments consider that the direct involvement of their military personnel in widescale mine clearance is too high risk to be contemplated except in very specific and limited operational circumstances. This is a more complex calculation than it may, at first sight, appear. The risks to which such judgements refer are not those faced by an engineer in a minefield, but those faced by a government whose soldiers may be killed or injured during mine clearance operations. The political implications of the media running headlines of the 'Our Boys' Lives on the Line to Clear Mines in Country X' type, are enormous, and governments who thought nothing of whipping up national hysteria to justify sending troops to the Gulf where hundreds or thousands of lives were placed at risk will always fight shy of risking votes for purely humanitarian purposes. Very few countries have allowed their soldiers to enter live minefields as part of a humanitarian initiative and even during peacekeeping operations most are only allowed to clear landmines to achieve a specifically defined operational objective.

These may seem cynical reasons for the military abrogating what is clearly a military responsibility, a viewpoint with which few would disagree, including many soldiers who would be no less willing to work in minefields than those civilian specialists who work for demining organisations, many of whom are former military personnel. But there are good reasons why the military should not, as a general rule, be involved in widescale mine and ordnance eradication. These are as follows.

Cost

There is no such thing as a low-cost military operation. It has become fashionable to criticise NGOs for excessively high operational budgets and it would be difficult not to question the cost/results equation of UN programmes. But the cost of deploying a military force of any kind is phenomenal, merely because almost everyone involved, with the exception of the country's treasury and its taxpayers, wants it to be so. Any military operation is an opportunity to test and prove new equipment and use up old equipment which will then require replacing – the obvious military benefits of doing so, substantial though they may be, are far outweighed by the interests of defence suppliers who will get contracts to replace the old equipment, modify the new equipment which is found not to work satisfactorily and reap the benefits in sales to new customers of equipment which is proven in action. Add to that fact the enormous logistic support without which the military is virtually unable to operate and the cost implications of importing a management and control element which, regardless of any existing indigenous or UN management team, is required because of the peculiar nature of the military control and administrative structure.

Suitability to Role

There is a certain contradiction in military thinking concerning their involvement with post-conflict landmine and UXO eradication. On the one hand they want to avoid the obvious and justified demand that the military should be held responsible for clearing up the contamination of war to ensure the safety of the civilian population in peacetime, while, on the other, they claim that they should be able to *choose* to be involved in humanitarian mine- and ordnance-clearance operations because 'it is a military matter'. The operative word, of course, is 'choose' – common sense dictates that the military should be forced by international law to ensure that all landmines and UXO are removed from the battlefield as an integral part of the peace process. Allowing the military to avoid that responsibility but retain the option to gain credit for being involved when it suits them is both illogical and, in some cases, unjust. The international community would, for instance, be justified in demanding that Russia and the former Soviet states at least pay the cost of eradicating Soviet-deployed and supplied mines and ordnance from Afghanistan. However, if the Russian government chose to despatch some military personnel to train Afghans in mine clearance and allocated one or two million dollars towards the cost of clearance operations that should be seen as minimal and, in the circumstances, derisory, reparation rather than a humanitarian gesture worthy of praise. This is exactly what has happened in the case of the Lao People's Democratic Republic (PDR). The US bombed and mined Laos for nine years without the formality of ever declaring war. They then imposed an effective trade blockade on the country in the years following the cessation of the bombing in 1973 on the grounds that

Laos was an 'enemy' of the United States. A recent survey of UXO and landmines in Lao PDR[3] found that 15 of the 18 provinces still have significant problems and 10 provinces have districts considered to be severely contaminated. In addition to the fact that UXO and landmine incidents involving death and injury occur, on average, every two days the report also concludes that UXO contamination 'is a major constraint to development and contributes to endemic poverty'. The survey goes on to report that the continuing presence of UXO has a significant impact in terms of 'loss of productive labour force, and adding a burden on the limited and over-taxed health care system. It also limits agricultural and forest-based activities and increases the cost of rural infrastructure projects.'

Real justice would demand that the United States pays reparations equivalent to the cost of clearing all US-sourced ordnance and landmines from Lao soil (some would also argue that the members of the US administration who ordered and kept secret the bombing of Laos should face trial for war crimes), however the only action taken to assist has been the deployment of some military trainers to Laos to train local staff in demining and ordnance-eradication techniques. This latter initiative was transparently mounted to counter increasing international attention on the problem caused by US unexploded ordnance in the country. Clearly the US military have 'chosen' the level of involvement and the financial commitment and, despite the clear legal and moral responsibility involved, the project is not a recognition of US responsibility nor is it on a scale which could be considered anything other than superficial. In fact, far from being embarrassed by their failure to respond to the devastation caused by US ordnance in Laos, the present US administration appears quite proud of what it clearly perceives as a charitable initiative to assist a developing nation.

In addition to the prohibitive cost of military demining involvement and the failure of governments to allow their soldiers to deploy on a realistic scale or as part of a problem-related strategy, the inability of military planners to grasp the priorities of post-conflict rehabilitation and development will always limit the utility of military participation. This is not a failing of the military – their training and priorities are designed to facilitate the efficient fighting of wars. The reputation which the military have for 'getting things done' is largely undeserved given that most organisations could also get things done if they were empowered to ignore the normal restrictions imposed by civil society and operate in a martial law environment. In fact, placed in a non-combat situation the military are no better at achieving results than any other organisation and are often far less efficient, excessively authoritarian and culturally clumsy. Their advantages lie mainly in tackling specific tasks of an engineering or logistic nature when they are involved in self-contained unit strength and are not reliant on local people or facilities, however such involvement is costly and clearly unsustainable as a programme resource. That is not to say that individual soldiers are not suitably qualified to be involved in development-related projects – in fact the great majority of NGO personnel working on mine-clearance projects are former soldiers – it is the system of which the individual soldiers are part which is unsuited to the task.

The Moral Perspective

There is an uncomfortable fact which must be faced whenever the military are involved in humanitarian operations of any kind, but especially in relation to landmine- and UXO-related programmes. The soldiers involved are receiving valuable training, nearly always paid for out of aid and development budgets, and although that fact may not be the primary motivation for countries who detach military personnel to work in humanitarian demining programmes, it would, none the less, be naive to believe that it is not a factor in the decision-making process resulting in such troop deployments. In a recent address to media and guests prior to a demolition demonstration at a military camp in Perth, a serving member of the Australian army stated that the work of military engineers involved in demining operations in Afghanistan and other countries was 'the best training available in the world, all paid for by the United Nations'. The statement was made in a positive manner, seeking to encourage continued participation by Australian forces in humanitarian landmine action programmes, but it was indicative of the naive perception held by many soldiers involved in such operations. The truth is even less palatable: the involvement of Royal Australian Engineers is paid for at *full cost* from the overseas aid budget by Ausaid;[4] the recipient of those funds is the Australian Department of Defense. In other words, the military are being paid to deploy soldiers on what are, in effect, advanced training exercises from public funds allocated for humanitarian purposes.

So although the removal of landmines and UXO is quite obviously a military responsibility it is equally apparent that the military are unequal to, and in some circumstances unsuitable for, the task. This conclusion, however, should not be seen as excusing the military from any responsibility – they can, in some circumstances, be involved in training and may provide logistic support to humanitarian projects during peacekeeping operations. However, the military can best respond by reviewing their use of weaponry and their training of commanders and soldiers to ensure that they do not increase the worldwide problem during future conflicts.

ERADICATING LANDMINES AND UXO – RESPONDING LOGICALLY

If we accept that the military, in the majority of cases, cannot, will not or should not be responsible for eradication operations there must be an alternative avenue; in order to define what may constitute a relevant response it is important first to define the task. Since no definitive version of what should properly constitute a landmine- and UXO-eradication programme exists, or, to be more precise, since there are many incomplete and unsatisfactory definitions, it is worth laying out the essential components and their rationale at this point. The essential elements of an eradication programme, as follows, are relevant regardless of the scale of the undertaking.

Surveys

Impact Assessment (Level One)

A field assessment through interviews and questionnaires conducted among the local population, authorities, former fighting forces and such institutions as hospitals and health centres to determine the impact of landmines and UXO on the community. An impact assessment may also identify the actual sites of landmine and UXO incidents. It is normally carried out in advance of a technical survey but may be incorporated, quite naturally, into that process. To avoid the confusion which has grown, largely as a result of differing terminology, I employ the term 'impact assessment' since this clearly explains the field process. Using – as many organisations do – the term 'survey' indicates a technical content which is not present at this stage of the eradication process.

Technical Survey (Level Two)

Confirmation of the location of minefields and UXO concentrations and determination of the physical extent of contamination. A technical survey includes the construction of a permanent benchmark at each minefield and the production of an accurate map. Comprehensive technical survey is, inexplicably, widely neglected, especially as an integral component of national mine-eradication programmes.

Mapping

The accurate mapping of minefields and UXO concentrations is a critical operational sector within the overall engineering response. Threat or Risk maps are also a major contribution to the reduction of casualties and should be made available to all relevant authorities and agencies, especially the UNHCR and organisations working with IDPs where repatriation, resettlement or major population movements are a factor. Most importantly, they should be made available to vulnerable communities.

Marking

In company with the technical survey, the physical delineation of mined areas is a neglected element of virtually all widescale eradication programmes. This is especially difficult to understand when consideration is given to the level of protection afforded to the community by the erection of markers which make danger areas clearly visible.

Minefield Reduction

Technical survey delineates the borders of minefields but often, by necessity, includes fringe areas which are safe or which are only lightly contaminated. The reduction of the area identified as mined to the very minimum is a critical factor, especially in subsistence agricultural and residential areas where every square metre of land released for use is of enormous value to the community. This key component of clearance operations has been developed to an advanced level in Afghanistan.

Community Mine Awareness

Although a vital element of any eradication programme it can be argued that awareness programmes are often afforded too high a priority within the overall response, sometimes to the detriment of other programme components which might achieve a greater reduction in the threat to the community and expedite the return of land for their use. The educational content of awareness programmes should be dependent on the overall eradication approach adopted in the target area. Mine awareness can be very effective as an integral part of the survey process as used by MAG mine action teams, which incorporate four response sectors within a single team: Level One assessment and Level Two survey; minefield marking; emergency clearance; community awareness.

Central Record Keeping

Any mine-affected region must establish a comprehensive and accessible record of risk areas. The information system employed must be flexible to allow for constant update to show the progress of various elements of the eradication programme and for retrieval by involved agencies at every level of government and community as well as those directly linked to the eradication programme.

Landmine and UXO Eradication

Quite clearly the eradication process is the most important element of the overall programme. However, it is also the most costly and time consuming and relies to some extent on the completion of other programme components, most essentially a Level Two survey.

THE BASICS – CHICKENS AND EGGS

Recognition

Undoubtedly the first obstacle to the eradication of landmines and UXO once conflict has ended is recognition. That is, *the basic recognition that a problem exists which requires a response*. Of course, there is a certain complexity involved because the degree of recognition varies at different levels and may often be less a failure to appreciate that a problem exists than an unwillingness, or even plain refusal, to acknowledge its existence. The paradox is often clear to see in retrospect – the community who are forced to recognise the problem every day due to their proximity to the minefields are least equipped to respond, while the majority of those who are in a position to take action have no daily contact with landmines and, therefore, little or no recognition of the need for response.

However, what has been most remarkable in recent years is the lack of effective response by governments, UN agencies and international donors which, at times, has bordered on institutional madness. For instance the failure to develop a sufficiently integrated situational view capable of linking widescale landmine infestation with the recovery of postwar agriculture has been commonplace. Taking the thought process a step further and forging the obvious link between mined agricultural land and post-conflict stability in rural areas has appeared to be beyond virtually all agencies – government, non-government and UN – whose defined roles are in the field of development, whether as donors or implementers. And yet many of those same agencies have been claiming credit for responding to landmines while doing almost nothing involving logical, or even workable, engineering-based response planning. There is a tendency to concentrate on the peripheral responses, thus the need for a comprehensive and coordinated approach *including* community awareness and victim assistance may result in *only* those latter sectors being addressed because donors perceive them as being uncontroversial and less risky than the engineering sectors. The most common justifications proffered by donors for the decision not to fund landmine and UXO eradication are illustrative of the actual reason – ignorance.

- 'Our fields are education, reconstruction and development – we don't fund engineering, it's out of our area of expertise.'

- 'Demining is too slow – we want to fund sectors which have an immediate impact on the community.'
- 'Mine and UXO clearance costs too much – we would prefer to use that money in traditional areas such as agriculture and education.'
- 'We will only commit funds to mine clearance when it has a direct impact on the work of our other funded programmes in the area.'

(The final statement all too often conceals a far more complex and, some would say, perverse approach – the donor may avoid funding projects in other rehabilitation, reconstruction and development sectors in areas which are believed to have a landmine problem.)

However, it is the ignorance which underlies the decision-making process which is most startling. It is evident at two levels – practical and conceptual. There is a complete failure to recognise the scale of impact of landmines and UXO right across the social and economic existence of affected communities, and also an inability to incorporate knowledge of that impact into the planning of response in other sectors. Treating the symptoms rather than the disease – educating schoolchildren how to reduce the risk of becoming a mine victim while accepting the continued presence of the mines, or fitting prostheses to farmers who have lost limbs while farming their land then sending them back to the same, mined, fields – incorporates obvious risks:

- few agencies will turn down such funding or even challenge the underlying logic, or lack of logic, involved
- funds earmarked for 'mine action' may be used for victim assistance, a sector which should be allocated a dedicated funding line
- since non-engineering sectors are classified under the generic heading of 'mine action' the impression may be given of a far greater response to actual mine eradication than matches the facts.

So how should the landmine/UXO sector be prioritised?

- Remove the threat?
- Treat the victims?
- Educate the potential victims?

It is not really a chicken-and-egg situation unless a lack of funding dictates the need for choice, always the case in reality. But when the cost of making war runs into billions it is only a lack of humanity which sets the price of peace so much lower. Given that landmine-UXO-related funding rarely, if ever, matches needs there is an unavoidable logic in concentrating on the only permanent solution – eradication.

Where to Begin?

There can be no response initiative without a plan and there can be no plan without an understanding of the problem. Landmines and UXO cannot be eradicated outside a field-engineering context and any attempts to respond in such a manner can only be viewed as dabbling – a fair assessment of the UN national mine-action programme in Angola – on a massive and costly scale. A 1997 UNDHA assessment report recognised the failures of the Angola programme, stating bluntly: 'This case study unfortunately shows that the UN lacked an overall vision and repeated many of the mistakes it had encountered in other settings.'[5] The report concluded:

> Angola is a text-book case of how not to initiate a mine action programme. In the future, the UN must act as one in the development of a humanitarian mine action capability. To do this it must have the long-term vision, commitment, and resources including appropriate staff and management mechanisms, essential for building a solid foundation for the development of a sustainable indigenous mine action programme.[6]

If the United Nations really can learn lessons then such honest and outspoken reports are invaluable, but all the indications are that UNMAS[7] is unlikely to heed the lessons of recent history with any greater foresight than did its predecessor, the UNDHA. However, the report, while accurate to a point and justifiably damning, fails to identify the most vital gap in the Angola programme and in virtually every international mine-action initiative so far undertaken – the complete failure to quantify the scale of the engineering task to be implemented. Technical survey is not an optional element – it is the essential precursor to successful eradication of landmines, the basis of minefield marking (the most effective interim lifesaver) and the key to programme planning. Of course, it goes without saying, it is important that the responsible agencies and individuals understand how to conduct technical surveys. Yet, if that understanding exists, it is difficult to see why only the Afghanistan programme incorporates comprehensive technical survey on a national scale. Part of the explanation undoubtedly lies in the fact that the Afghanistan programme has its roots in field engineering, launched at a time when there was little or no non-technical influence on programme design.

The survey element (now the Mine Clearance Planning Agency) was established simultaneously to the mine-clearance element and, from the very first deployment, worked in advance of clearance operations. MCPA's role was always the implementation of widescale technical survey and the tasking of clearance teams. Its capacity and experience in those fields has expanded dramatically during the past decade, however, although the agency is now fully computerised its beginnings were decidedly low-tech. The very first equipment purchases were a large map table and an engineers' pantograph. Surveyors, trained first as deminers, were taught how to use a compass, take bearings and read and draw maps. Because most available maps were out of date, inaccurate and of an unsuitable scale for survey purposes, MCPA staff began upscaling and reproducing the maps by pantograph retaining only unchanging natural features, boundaries and map data known to be accurate. These baseline maps were then added to accurately by survey teams in the field. The product of those grassroots beginnings, in addition to some of the most accurate maps of Afghanistan in existence, was the development of an expert core staff so that, when MCPA eventually computerised their operations, the software was designed to meet the agencys known needs rather than, as has happened in other countries, tailoring field reporting to match inappropriate software. There is an important lesson in this example which has a direct relevance to the establishment of credible national mine/UXO-eradication programmes – it can summarised in a single, deceptively simple, rule: begin at the beginning. And the beginning of any field-engineering process is survey. A programme of response to landmines cannot be formulated without a comprehensive understanding of the problem to be addressed.

THE SURVEY PROCESS

As mentioned earlier there are two levels of survey: impact assessment (Level One) and technical survey, also referred to as Level Two. It is unfortunate that the Level One process has been termed 'survey', which tends, among some non-specialist circles, to suggest a technical content, whereas the emphasis is actually on socioeconomic-based assessment. The two processes are linked, but Level One assessments offer no substantial or reliable prime data for the purposes of designing widescale eradication programmes, although valuable secondary data can result from well-conducted impact assessments. The latter are especially useful for determining prioritisation for Level Two survey, marking and clearance operations.

Establishing the Facts – Sequence

It is first worth examining who should establish a mine-action programme. The ideal situation would clearly be one where the government of the country concerned initiates, finances and implements the whole process. This could be the case for nations such as Egypt, Iran and Syria where the landmine and UXO infestation results from long-concluded conflicts and the economy can support the cost of the programme.[8] A more common contemporary scenario relates to countries emerging from wars which have crippled the national economy and often totally devastated the infrastructure – the government itself may have limited control beyond the main cities; landmines and UXO may be low on their list of priorities. The actual process of establishing an organisational structure is dealt with at a later stage of this book, but the initial priority must be to make an accurate situation assessment. *In fact, in all cases, the temptation to focus on formal management, logistical and implementation structures should be resisted at this stage.* UNMAS should especially pay heed to this advice: it may seem like a good idea to set up a mine action centre or similar structure on day one, the truth is that this style of management-oriented approach, inevitably found to be inappropriate but bureaucratically entrenched at a stage too late to easily make organisational changes, is at the roots of the UN's consistent failure to establish effective engineering responses to landmines and UXO. The weakness of this approach lies in the understandable quandary which the staff of such premature action centres find themselves; they must be seen to be doing something but, because adequate surveys have not been undertaken, planning is inevitably broad brush and conceptual rather than detailed. Mindful of the need to be *perceived* to be responding they invariably adopt a short-term objective of getting deminers on the ground in order to establish credibility with donors, UN headquarters and other agencies. This management-led impatience, while perhaps well meant, is short-sighted and sets the scene for a programme which must constantly justify its existence in order to access the next tranche of funding from increasingly sceptical donors. Preference should be given to a field-biased unit with a specific role limited to survey, assessment and reporting – *begin at the beginning*. Since a descriptive title can often help to define an operational undertaking it would usually be appropriate to adopt military terminology and call the survey staff a 'task force'. Since technical training will be a major component of any response initiative an advanced training element should be established as early as possible and may, for administrative purposes, be integrated into the Survey Task Force.

The Survey Task Force

Role

The Task Force has three key objectives:

- To undertake a Level One impact assessment designed to evaluate the impact of landmines and UXO on the population and to provide an overall picture of the geographical extent and comparative severity of the problem.
- To undertake a Level Two technical survey of mine/UXO-affected areas and produce detailed, accurate maps and reports of surveyed locations.
- To produce a comprehensive report to include recommendations for action in the fields of further survey, marking, landmine/UXO eradication and community education.

Composition

The Task Force composition depends on the scale of the proposed operation. Numbers will vary but the following must be considered essential staff.

Level One Impact Assessment

Team leader Must have a comprehensive expertise in the fields of community survey and data analysis. A general understanding of the direct and indirect impact of landmines and UXO would be an advantage, but is not essential.

Data manager Must have expertise in questionnaire design, data management and analysis and the training of field surveyors in household survey techniques. The data manager would also be responsible for organising any computer programming and software requirements of the survey.

Field supervisor(s) Will always be indigenous to the target country. Preferably experienced in conducting household surveys and with good supervisory skills. Each supervisor would normally be allocated to oversee and monitor the work of surveyors operating in a prede-termined geographical sector.

Surveyors Local staff who are experienced in, or can be trained in, the skills required to carry out household surveys using a purpose-designed questionnaire. Young graduates may be found especially suitable for this work. It is important that relevant cultural, tribal and gender balances are reflected in the make up of the survey team to ensure safe and productive access to all sectors of the target community. The number of surveyors deployed will depend on the planned scope and timescale of the assessment – clearly it will always be preferable to maximise the number of surveyors in order to access the

	maximum data for analysis within the minimum time window.
Data input staff	Computer operators with the basic skills to code and input data from completed questionnaires. The most experienced staff will be employed on collating inputted data and assist the data manager on primary analysis tasks.

Level Two Technical Survey

Survey manager	An experienced field engineer with a comprehensive knowledge of mine clearance, survey, mapping and technical reporting. Must also be a competent manager with considerable expertise in planning and implementing field-based operations. A knowledge of the target country and its language(s) and culture should be considered advantageous.
Survey teams	Each survey team will normally consist of the following staff, some variance may be dictated by technical peculiarities or working conditions prevalent in the target region.
Team leader	An experienced mine clearance engineer with a comprehensive knowledge of UXO and mine disposal. A competent manager with a high level of expertise in land navigation, mapping and the use of global positioning systems (GPS). If not recruited locally it would be a considerable advantage if the team leader had a working knowledge of the relevant language for the allocated survey area and of the local culture, although technical proficiency should be the primary selection criteria.
Minefield surveyors	Each team would normally consist of four surveyors, all trained deminers, the number however, while never less than four, may be increased as local conditions and operational planning dictate. Each surveyor should have attended an advanced first-aid course and at

	least one should be a qualified paramedic unless the team has dedicated medical support permanently in attendance.
Dog handlers	If mine dogs are incorporated into the survey operation two fully trained handlers and dogs should be attached to each team.
Radio operator/driver	A fully trained radio operator additionally capable of carrying out basic maintenance and repair on radio equipment and of correctly erecting and siting a full range of aerial configurations. Should be given a basic understanding of survey operations and be trained in land navigation and in the use of GPS. Should have at least a basic knowledge of vehicle mechanics and be well versed in maintaining the vehicles in use.
Other staff	Extra staff recruited to the team, such as interpreters and medical staff, should be given a basic understanding of survey operations and, where possible, should have a multirole capability. Interpreters should be made fully aware of technical terminology, its meaning and context. If an assistant to the team leader is nominated from within the team or she he should be trained in the necessary skills and be kept fully informed of operational planning. Where operational exigencies and funding permit, an assistant team leader may be an additional team member.

Planning and Deployment

The survey model presented here assumes operations on a national scale in the immediate post-conflict period, but can be adapted to meet the requirements of programmes launched in more stable environments and initiatives based on a lesser geographical scale such as may be implemented by NGOs or local government bodies.

The key is to allow overlap of operational build-up between Level One assessment, Level Two survey and training to maximise the potential for early response to incoming data. There will normally be known, assumed and unknown factors to consider as a basis for initial planning. Examples include the following:

Known Factors

1   Military forces known to have used landmines.
2   Credible reports of deaths and injuries due to mines and unexploded ordnance.
3   Landmines and UXO visible on some roads and airstrips.

Assumed Factors

1   UN and NGOs report some roads and tracks unused due to unverified community belief they are mined.
2   Areas of major battles and on some roads and airstrips military posts assumed to be mined.
3   Many locations with human and animal remains and military vehicle wreckage assumed to be mined.

Unknown Factors

1   Geographical scale of mine dissemination unknown.
2   No detailed knowledge of humanitarian, logistic and economic impact of mine and UXO presence.
3   No reliable knowledge of landmine strategies employed by combatants and the scale of any random dissemination.
4   Insufficient data available to establish operational priorities and funding, equipment and manpower requirements.

The result of balancing the known and assumed factors against the unknown in this way is to illustrate clearly the limitations placed on planning and action by the lack of specific data. A balance of knowledge better than the example given above would be exceptional. However, there is sufficient information to determine the following:

• a situation exists which will require a major eradication initiative

- there is a need for a better understanding of scale and impact and therefore a widescale Level One impact assessment is required
- there is insufficient technical data available for planning purposes which dictates the need for a nationwide Level Two survey
- since it is clear from available information that a major clearance programme will be required, the training process should begin without delay.

Training and Level Two survey will be ongoing throughout the life of the programme, Level One is a one-off assessment to establish baseline socioeconomic and impact data as an initial planning and response tool. Response must now be mobilised in three action areas, as follows.

Training – Key Considerations
Instructor selection, student selection, interim funding, school(s) setup, training aids, clearance equipment, curriculum, lesson plans, translation and printing of training material, status and salary of trainees, insurance.

Level One Impact Assessment – Key Considerations
Full funding, team selection and training, Hardware and software procurement, questionnaire design and printing, identification of geographical and demographic parameters of survey, logistic planning.

Level Two Survey – Key Considerations
Minimum one-year funding, management staff selection and recruitment, recruitment of minefield surveyors from training programme followed by intensive additional training for survey role, recruitment and training of additional staff, equipment procurement, team insurance.

Training, since its long-term existence is closely linked to landmine and UXO clearance operations, will be dealt with in detail later in this chapter. The role of the Survey Task Force, logically and practically the first step in the eradication process, must be examined first.

HOW TO CONDUCT A LEVEL ONE IMPACT ASSESSMENT

The Questionnaire

The assessment is based on a questionnaire which must be tailored to the operational area. The secret is to obtain the maximum relevant information through the simplest and shortest question-naire possible – it is inevitable that the result will be a compromise so design criteria are extremely important. It is helpful conceptually to think of the surveyor and the questionnaire as a unit – a good set of questions in the hands of a poorly trained or inept surveyor can be worse than useless while, conversely, the finest interrogator armed with the wrong questions can achieve little of value. A good exercise which worked well for me when designing the first Afghan impact assessment[9] is to make a list of all the questions, under subject group headings, to which it would be useful to have answers. The next stage is to meet with experienced survey managers who have a good knowledge of conducting surveys among the target communities, advisers (preferably indigenous to the target areas, who speak the relevant languages), the data manager and the Level Two survey manager. The first stage is to address each proposed question and as:

1   What do we expect the community to tell us in response to this question?
2   How will we use this information?

The results of this type of multidisciplinary consultative session are always useful and, inevitably, a salutary learning experience for the person or persons who compiled the original list of questions. The answer to each question must contribute substantially to the overall picture of the target area when analysed within the context of the whole survey, questions which would only produce information of general or peripheral interest should not be included in the ques-tionnaire. However, there is one factor beyond the obvious engineering response requirements for data which must be considered when deciding which questions must be included to illicit specific information – funding. It is a fact of life that donors need justification to support funding decisions and data from project-specific surveys is perfect for their purposes. A good Level One assessment can be an effective funding proposal in its own right.

It is worth examining some examples of questionnaires while emphasising that there can be no global pattern and each assessment must use a questionnaire designed specifically for the target area. It is possible that consideration should be given to the use of more than one questionnaire if there are broad cultural or occupational divisions within the survey area. For data input purposes most questions will be multichoice in order to predetermine input codes; for clarity and simplicity I have generally used simple queries in the examples below, which are taken from surveys conducted among predominantly rural agricultural communities.

Subject Headings and Questions

Location and Respondent Details
It is important to recognise the understandable resistance which may exist in a post-conflict community to giving names and other personal details. Even during surveys conducted in stable communities, especially in rural areas, there may be suspicion that the government will use information to assist tax collections or conscription. Anything which makes the work of the surveyors more difficult or, in some cases, dangerous, will reduce the accuracy and ultimate usefulness of the assessment. As a general rule there should be no requirement to record respondents' names – if they have specific information which may be of value to clearance teams their identity and contact details can be recorded separately by the surveyor. A focus on the household is widely accepted as the most effective approach and is assumed here.

01   Province
02   District
03   Village
04   How many families in village?
05   How many *farming* families in village?
06   Classify prevailing security situation in village:

    a   No hostilities for more than 6 months
    b   No hostilities for 3–6 months
    c   Occasional hostilities
    d   Regular hostilities

07   Household members:

	Male			Female	
number 40 yrs +	____		number 40 yrs +	____
number 20–40 yrs	____		number 20–40 yrs	____
number 10–20 yrs	____		number 10–20 yrs	____
number –10 yrs	____		number –10 yrs	____

08   What is the main family occupation?

Mines/UXO and the Community
This section determines whether the area is mine/UXO affected and seeks to assess the scale of the problem in general terms and basic community responses.

01   Do the community consider that landmines and unexploded ordnance are a major obstacle to their daily life? YES/NO

02   Do the community find the presence of mines and UXO a greater hazard at specific times of the year? (Classify in descending order of severity.)

a ☐   b ☐   c ☐

1 Summer 2 When snow has fallen 3 During snow melt
4 Rainy Season 5 Planting season 6 Harvest
7 Other (specify) _____

03   When a member of the community finds a mine or UXO what action do they normally take?
1 No action taken 2 Tell family and neighbours 3 Mark with stones
4 Report to civil authorities 5 Report to military
6 Report to village elders 7 Mark in other way (specify) _____
8 Other action (specify) _____

04   How many people have been killed or injured by mines or UXO in this village?

	Killed	Injured
1 In the last month?	_____	_____
2 In the last year?	_____	_____
3 In the last 2 years?	_____	_____

05   How many animals have been killed by mines or UXO in the last
      year?
      1 Oxen/cattle _____ 2 Horses _____ 3 Camels _____
      4 Mules/donkeys _____ 5 Sheep/goats _____

06   How many vehicles have been destroyed by mines or UXO in the
      last year?
      1 Trucks _____ 2 Tractors _____ 3 Cars _____
      4 Buses _____

Location and Severity Information
Although it cannot be taken for granted that the community has
accurate information regarding the physical location of minefields it
is possible to gain valuable data regarding affected areas through a
well-designed questionnaire. Although the surveyor should make
separate note of specific locations where mines and UXO are known
or thought to exist by respondents, the questions should not be
designed to elicit such area-specific information. This is extremely
important for several reasons, not least that first-phase assessments
may be conducted many months, or even years, in advance of any
eventual clearance initiative. It would be irresponsible to give any
community the impression that the questionnaire was an immediate
precursor to such work in their area by focusing questions too
narrowly. It is also, understandably, a fact that a household believing
that its answers will directly influence clearance operations in their
community is likely to respond in a manner which will prioritise
survey and clearance of its own land. However, the most important
reason for seeking a generalised rather than a detailed view of each
area's problems is that this is the most effective way to ensure the
usefulness of the final data – detailed minefield information only
becomes relevant when a Level Two survey begins.

01   Which activities are most seriously affected by the presence of
      mines?
      1 Work in Fields 2 Irrigation canal cleaning and repair
      3 Travel by vehicle 4 Travel by foot 5 House repair/building
      6 Grazing of animals 7 Collecting firewood
      8 Other activities _____

02   Are farming activities most affected by mines or UXO on:
      1 Arable land? 2 Grazing land?

03   How many houses have mines or UXO in or near them?

04   Are the mountains and/or hillsides in this area mined?

05   How many irrigation channels are out of use:
1 because the channel itself is mined?
2 because the channel cannot be reached for cleaning or repair due
to mines?

Clearance Information
It is important to know of any attempts which are in progress or
have been made in the past to clear landmines and UXO from target
areas. Where these attempts are high-risk community initiatives it
can be an indication of the desperation which exists and of a local
recognition that an engineering response is required.

01   Have any attempts been made to clear landmines or UXO in this
area?
02   Who organised these projects?
03   Do the community have confidence in the completed clearance
work?
04   How have the clearance projects been funded?

Technical Information
It is sometimes possible to interview military personnel and, most
often former, fighters who may be able to give useful technical data
regarding the types of landmines and ordnance they have used and
information about their tactical deployment. But here a serious word
of caution – asking questions of a military nature in a conflict region
is a dangerous occupation and surveyors should be given clear
guidance as to the circumstances when these questions can be put
and, more importantly, when they should be excluded. During the
collation of data for the Afghanistan mines survey in 1990 two
surveyors were imprisoned, one of whom was threatened with
execution for spying, by suspicious *mujahideen*. Happily both were
subsequently released following protracted mediation, but a positive
conclusion may not always result.[10] It is normally wise to formulate
and pose this group of questions in a way that they do not call for
the respondents to offer replies which they may feel are personally
incriminating.

01   What are the most common kinds of landmines used in this district? (By all combatant forces.)[11]
02   What types of ordnance have been used in this district which have regularly failed to detonate?
03   Which mines (if any) have anti-handling devices or other boobytraps attached?
04   What signs have commonly been used by each combatant force to mark the presence of landmines or boobytraps?

Background Issues

There are always many issues of a secondary nature which can stand in the way of the eradication process; many are unforeseeable but some can be forecast and may be addressed, at least initially, within the questionnaire. These questions are usually of the kind which can only usefully be put to local government officers, military commanders, or community committees or elders. It should of course be emphasised that clearance may not be imminent. Although questions under this subheading are categorised as background information they must still meet the basic criteria for inclusion – each must contribute substantially to the overall picture.

01   Will a policy of immediate destruction of all landmines and ordnance detected be supported?
02   Will it be possible for the community to make available accommodation for demining teams?

The assessment questions above are examples of a survey approach likely to result in quality data which, when analysed, will assure a good general impact picture. The specific questions used will depend on the circumstances prevailing in the target area.

Training the Survey Team

Perceiving the surveyor and his or her questionnaire as a unit is critical to the training process – lessons and exercises must emphasise that approach. The whole training programme should centre on the questionnaire – the surveyors must learn not just the meaning of the questions but also why each question is being asked, they must be able to present the survey to communities with an enthusiasm which conveys the importance of the project. The training team, ideally managed by the team leader and the data manager, must themselves spend some days working with the questionnaire to ensure that lessons are consistent, especially in relation to the interpretation of individual questions and the approach to be taken by surveyors in their introduction of the project to community leaders and individual households. This will be an easier task if the trainees have previous experience of conducting household surveys. However, that advantage should be balanced against the problems which may arise if some trainees have a 'know-it-all' attitude; if that problem arises it must be dealt with firmly, as must any lack of motivation. Far too many field assessments, regardless of the survey focus, suffer from poorly trained, underpaid and ill-motivated surveyors who learn quickly that completing questionnaires themselves in a teashop is far less demanding than trudging from village to village. Training must be dynamic and practical with only as much classroom work as is essential. An ideal curriculum would include the following.

Introduction to the Assessment Aims and Objectives and the Questionnaire

Although this will be a classroom activity the training team should avoid long, complex and, inevitably, boring lectures. This is the first look the trainees get at their new job – it is an opportunity to motivate and enthuse them or, if poorly presented, an equal opportunity to damage the effectiveness of the project at the very start. Lesson plans should be imaginative, making good use of visual presentations – overhead projectors with well-designed slides are an excellent and adaptable training aid.[12] The questionnaire must be dealt with comprehensively, each question dealt with separately. A good training approach is to tackle each question under four headings as follows:

- *Comprehension*: First, ensure that all trainees understand the essential meaning of the question.[13] Check comprehension by selecting trainees to play the role of respondents in given circumstances and answer the question in a realistic-to-role manner. Trainers should be patient in ensuring that each question is fully understood by all students.

- *Translation*: If surveyors will be required to work in more than one language or dialect any translation complexities or differences should be resolved at this stage.
- *Discussion*: This is an important element of building an interest in, and an understanding of, the questionnaire. Discussion should be free and unstructured with the training staff acting as facilitators rather than adopting an authoritative role. Criticisms and suggestions for the improvement of the questionnaire should be considered seriously.
- *Test*: The trainee surveyors should be rigorously tested to ensure that they have developed a clear understanding of the project in which they will play a key role. If results are unsatisfactory consideration should be given to extending this phase of the training.

Training Exercises

If time allows – and there is no good reason to rush the training since it is so critical to the effectiveness of the project – the trainees should spend four or five days on practical exercises. These should be increasingly realistic, beginning with closely monitored classroom work with some trainees acting as respondents while the others take the surveyor's role. If possible a video camera should be used to film students during training – this can be valuable as a training aid which allows trainees to review their own progress and better understand their strengths and weaknesses. Each of these exercises should be followed by a class critique with instructors playing the roles of surveyor and respondents to illustrate methods of dealing with complex or difficult situations. As the students improve their skills and become more confident the exercises should become increasingly realistic. During the predeployment training in preparation for the Afghanistan mines survey trainees undertook a realistic training exercise in refugee camps in Pakistan. This had the obvious advantage that the surveyors were faced with the kind of problems which they would experience in Afghanistan – some households were briefed to be unhelpful or give deliberately inaccurate responses while others were simply told to respond as though they were in their home villages. This kind of training is extremely valuable, not just for the trainees but also as a final check on the viability of the questionnaire. Obviously such realism will not always be possible, but every effort must be made to allow the trainees to develop survey techniques and personal confidence in an environment which closely resembles the target areas to which they will be deployed. This is not a sector of the project in which to be parsimonious with funding – expenditure on surveyor training is an investment which will add considerably to the quality of the assessment.

- *Final test*: Each trainee should undergo a final test. The format may differ but emphasis should be placed on the practical ability to interview one or more household groups and, in each case, accurately complete a questionnaire form and maintain good notes of any relevant information not covered by the questionnaire. Although it is probable that any unsuitable trainees would have been rejected at an earlier stage this is clearly a final opportunity to make such decisions. It is also the time to select field supervisors if those posts have not been filled, and training given as a separate process.
- *Target-specific preparation*: When trainees have been allocated to specific areas they should be given reasonable time and resources to study all relevant aspects of the area. If each surveyor is to have a role in target selection (see below) those decisions should be made at this time. Transportation arrangements and individual timetables should be finalised.

Aims, Target Selection and Assessment Methodology

These elements of programme design may have been completed prior to the training of the surveyors, but it is important that planning remains flexible in order to incorporate changes indicated during the training process. Since they will differ considerably from region to region I have not attempted to suggest firm guidelines but have instead reproduced the relevant programme design information from the Afghanistan mines survey which will serve as a useful template for other projects.

Extract from the Report of the Afghanistan Mines Survey 1991[14]

Aims
The primary aim of the survey was to obtain first-hand community information regarding landmine dissemination and its affects over a broadly representative area of rural Afghanistan.

Because such a high proportion of existing information regarding mines in Afghanistan had been collated from estimates based on generalised and often inaccurate reports, an urgent need existed for reliable data on which to base long-term mine eradication plans. With that aim identified there was an obvious requirement to conduct the survey at a level where respondents were communicating knowledge held personally.

Secondary aims of the survey were as follows:

- to collect data regarding current community practices relating to mine clearance and marking of minefields
- to identify occupations and seasons where a vulnerability to mine incidents appears to exist
- to collect information relating to categories of devices existing in survey areas.

Target Selection
Selection of target communities was designed to provide for a degree of random selection within a broadly representative total survey area. To achieve this target provinces were selected to include:

- areas where little information relating to mines was available to agencies in Pakistan (Farah, Baghlan, Urzghan, Lowgar, Helmand)
- areas where involved agencies believed that a medium to serious mines situation existed (Paktya, Ningrehar, Ghazni, Parwan, Kapisa, Kandahar)
- areas where the mines problem was believed to be of a limited nature (Badakhshan, Bamyan).

Having identified the provinces for survey, districts were divided into two categories:

- *Compulsory districts*: Selected for their importance as centres of refugee origin, as focal points for combat activity or for the assumed but unconfirmed existence of large concentrations of mines.
- *Surveyor-selected districts*: Surveyors were allowed to make a choice from the districts remaining for survey prior to deployment. Unselected districts were retained as reserve areas

to be targeted in case problems were encountered in surveying selected districts due to military action or similar obstacles.

Within each district surveyors were given freedom to select target communities as they wished, within the following strict guidelines:

- each questionnaire was required to relate exclusively to a single village or minor village group (the latter defined as physically connected villages with a common mosque, farmland and source of irrigation water)
- no more than two villages could be surveyed in any village group.

Methodology

The questionnaire was initially designed in rough form to include all the possible information it was felt would be useful to know for planning and clearance purposes. At a series of working groups this document was modified to reflect the need for specific fields of *useable* data and the necessity for an enquiry format that would be easily understandable by both surveyors and respondents.

Surveyors attended a ten-day training course culminating in a series of practical tests and assessments prior to deployment. This course was designed and run by the training department of the Agricultural Survey of Afghanistan, a section of the Swedish Committee for Afghanistan (ASA/SCA). Surveyors were instructed to select respondents in the following manner.

- Sections 02–05 inclusive: These sections were to be answered by a representative individual or group from within the target village. In general this meant that these questions were responded to by farmers.
- Section 06: Due to the technical bias of these questions the surveyors were instructed to identify the person in each target village who was generally accepted by the community to have the best knowledge of mines in the areas immediately adjacent to or connected with the target village. In most cases this meant that the questions were answered by local commanders or *mujahideen* or a group from the community who collectively were best qualified to respond accurately.
- Section 07: Question 071 was aimed at whatever local administration or representative body existed in each community.

(Question 072 was unconnected with the survey, being included to provide information requested by MCPA).

Each surveyor was extensively debriefed on return to Peshawar and each completed questionnaire subject to thorough checking procedures; we believe that the data presented in the report represents a fair description of the situation in the areas surveyed, subject to the observations in Para 4 (survey limitations) listed below. Within the constraints imposed by the prevailing security situation in Afghanistan and accepting the necessarily arbitrary selection of target villages we believe that the data can reasonably be said to present a realistic indication for planning purposes of the impact of landmines dissemination on a countrywide basis.

The Assessment Report

Although target selection and methodology may differ considerably between Level One assessments it is essential that they are well defined and fully explained in the final report. Government agencies, donors and involved organisations need to trust the findings of the assessment and must, therefore, be aware of the methods employed and inbuilt limitations. Information must be included to identify the respondent groups to each question where they differ since, as illustrated in the Afghan example, this, normally positively, effects the credibility of the data source.

Honesty in identifying the limitations, errors and weaknesses of the assessment do not make it less credible but serve to illustrate the serious and responsible nature of the project. Most people with a knowledge of field survey, especially in post-conflict situations, would expect that such an assessment would be subject to some limitations. Once again the Afghan survey can be used as an example of the type of observations which should be clearly presented within the final report.

Survey Limitations[15]
Data should be read and interpreted subject to the following observations:

- Lowgar: Data relating to farming families affected by mines laid on arable and grazing land (Tables 21a and 21b) are inaccurate due to the inclusion of refugee families in farming population figures. Data columns 3–8 inclusive should be disregarded for Lowgar in Tables 21a/b. No information was collected regarding the security situation in surveyed areas.

- Ghazni: It is felt that the survey in Ghazni is likely to be less representative of the provincial situation due primarily to the geographical concentration of the surveyed village groups and the comparatively limited population surveyed.

- Baghlan: Data relating to mined irrigation systems for Baghlan at Tables 24a and 24b has been omitted. The decision to omit these figures was made when it became clear that a considerable overlap existed in villages reporting mined canals, thus a high number of villages had reported the same canals as being mined giving an exaggerated total figure.

- Paktya: Extremely high casualty figures are a feature of the Paktya data which may be subject to some limitations in accuracy. These are discussed in detail in the analysis.

- Mining of villages: The overall response to Question 056 in the questionnaire was such that it was clear the question was badly framed. The resultant data was too generalised and ill-defined to be of use and is not included.

- Tables 11/12 (Fatalities by gender and age/Injuries by gender and age): Two cultural points should be taken into consideration when referring to these tables:

  - The indication that no male casualties belonged to the 10–20 year age group is plainly incorrect. It is clear that in Afghan society the male *teenager* is not seen as a distinct group. *Viz: a man is a man when he is no longer a boy.* Thus all *non-boys* are grouped in the 20–40 category by respondents.

  - The numbers of female casualties reported are likely to be far below the true figure. This is thought to be due to the cultural reticence that exists in giving details about female members of the family in many parts of Afghanistan. It is not clear whether women have been included in the male figures.

It can be seen that the survey information extracts quoted above, if not reported, could considerably distort the conclusions of the assessment and thus risk its acceptance as a credible body of data.

The main body of the report should be presented in clearly defined sections as follows:

- *Executive summary*: A brief and clear presentation in layman's terms of the major findings, conclusions and recommendations of the report.
- *Technical notes*: The aims of the assessment and clear explanations of the methodology employed, limitations and an explanation of the report layout, data presentation and analysis.
- *Written analysis*: By region. Each regional analysis should be laid out in the same format and must include:

  - demographic information
  - breakdown of surveyed areas within the region
  - data synopsis
  - a subsection for each key data heading, i.e. Casualties, Community action, etc.
  - regional summary.

- *Conclusion*: A detailed written analysis of the collected data for the whole assessed area and the implications for involved indigenous and international agencies.
- *Recommendations*: A concise list of key recommendations resulting from the assessment findings.
- *Data tables*: There are many ways to present data – a simple tabular format is probably the most suitable for this purpose. It is extremely important that all the data is presented since this is the supporting evidence for the written analysis, conclusions and recommendations of the report. The tables may be included in the main body of the report or as an annexed section.
- *Supporting information*: Where it adds to the reader's understanding of the situation presented within the report supporting sections may be included. These may deal with subjects such as conflict history, hospital admission figures for mine/UXO victims, UN agencies and NGOs operating in the demining and related fields in the assessment region, etc.

It is important that irrelevant data comparisons are avoided; for instance, there is rarely, if ever, any purpose in comparing the impact of landmines and UXO on one surveyed area with that on another area. However, it is easy to fall into the trap of including such meaningless data exercises unless great care is taken to validate each data-analysis exercise.

The Level One Assessment Report as a Tool

The Level One assessment report has two key functions:

- as a planning tool for Level Two survey
- as a fundraising resource.

Both functions are obvious, and the former is dealt with at a later stage, but for the report to raise funds it must first be read, understood and widely accepted by the right people – that demands a level of planning and media awareness on the part of those responsible for releasing the report. The circumstances will differ from country to country, but the following notes should act as useful guidance in every region.

- Never refer to the assessment as a 'survey'. Funds must be raised for the Level Two survey and many donors will question the need for two surveys of the same region. At best this will only serve to create confusion, in the worse case it could reduce the financial support available for technical survey and, inevitably, clearance operations.
- Use the media, both locally, in the affected country, and inter-nationally, especially in potential donor nations. This entails more than simply sending out press releases. A media strategy should be part of the project from day one and this should not need the services of a public relations or media agency, whose prime aim is to distort (a word often referred to in the prevailing vocabulary of new politics as 'spin'), whereas the project management should be seeking ways to educate the media and their audience in the facts about the impact of landmines and unexploded ordnance. This requires planning – it is wasted effort to focus on sections of the media which will not provide access to the right audience. The assessment report is a valuable media and funding resource as well as a project working document.

The Limitations of Level One Assessment

The report is, at one time, an invaluable information resource and a frustratingly incomplete document. The temptation to exaggerate the former while downplaying the latter is great, especially when dealing with donors, but the facts are unavoidably present – the assessment confirms the existence of landmines and UXO and gives some idea of the scale of their impact on the community. The need for a response is identified but, on the basis of the data available, cannot be quantified with even approximate accuracy. There is a need for implementing agencies, especially the UN, to be bluntly honest regarding the limitations of initial assessment and for major international donors to educate themselves in the survey and eradication process.

The simple fact is that the Level One assessment identifies three important things, no more, no less:

- the fact that a landmine/UXO problem exists
- the requirement for detailed technical information in order to design an effective engineering response
- the need to begin technical training in order that specialist indigenous manpower will be available for deployment within an eventual eradication programme.

The word 'eventual' will arouse an indignant response in some quarters: 'this is an emergency – we must get deminers on the ground, clearing land of mines'. It is certainly the kind of impassioned argument that is hard to challenge in the public or political arena, but it is, however, ludicrous nonsense in engineering terms. And an engineering response is the only one which will return land to the community and stop people and livestock falling victim to mines and UXO. A clearance programme unsupported by accurate survey data is, at best, misusing funds – on a national level it can mean wasting resources clearing low priority land while people die unnecessarily in other areas.

Donor response to an effective Level One assessment should be urgent support for, most importantly, a Level Two technical survey. This must be funded initially for at least one year. Second, since it is known that some level of national clearance programme must be mounted, funds should be made available to establish a training programme which will ensure the availability of indigenous specialist manpower to staff that programme. It may also be wise in most affected countries to fund international demining NGOs to respond immediately in urgent situations and in support of humanitarian operations. These initiatives, although limited in scale, have an important secondary value as pilot projects of enormous benefit to later widescale eradication operations.[16]

The most critical limitation of the Level One assessment must be recognised by everyone and every agency concerned: alone, it changes nothing – it saves no lives, releases no land to the community and serves no community need.

HOW TO IMPLEMENT A LEVEL TWO SURVEY

The UN defines Level Two survey as follows: 'The objective of a Level Two: Technical Survey is to determine and delineate the perimeter of mined locations initially identified by a Level One: General Survey.'[17] The definition is both right and wrong – the aim of the survey is to determine and delineate the perimeter of minefields, but this cannot be achieved by relying solely on information drawn from the results of a Level One assessment. If this were so it would mean that the initial process, what the UN terms a 'general survey', would have to be ongoing throughout the life of remedial operations and work in advance of technical survey teams. The concept, while plausible on paper, has nothing to recommend it in practice. It would, regardless of any other considerations, mean that every village in a country would need to be visited by the first-phase assessment surveyors, a ridiculously complex programme which, if it ever happened, would constitute an enormous waste of funding and resources.

A more accurate and realistic definition can be taken from the technical handbook of the Afghan NGO, the Mines Clearance Planning Agency – certainly the most practised and experienced survey organisation in the world. It says:

Technical (Level 2) Surveys are the detailed investigation of areas known or suspected of being contaminated by mines or other explosive devices. Such areas may have been identified during General (Level 1) Surveys or have been otherwise reported. The technical survey process aims to accurately identify, mark and record the boundaries of such hazardous areas. In doing so, the survey process:

a) reduces the risk to the local population by providing warnings of hazardous areas;

b) provides information for national, regional and local planning;

c) provides planning information for subsequent clearance or other related operations; and

d) expedites clearance operations by establishing safe areas, reducing boundaries (if possible) and providing perimeter 'safe lanes'.[18]

It can be seen that the technical survey process as defined here involves much more than perimeter definition, it is the first step in saving people's lives, a result which cannot be achieved by Level One assessment for all its value. And yet, on a global scale, technical survey is the most neglected and misunderstood of all the engineering processes which make up the overall post-conflict response to landmines and UXO.

Building a Picture – Sources of Information

The prime initial source of data is, obviously, the Level One assessment report since this will virtually always be the most comprehensive and accessible body of reliable data. However, the nature of the assessment ensures that many mine/UXO-affected areas will not be featured and, most importantly, those areas absent from the report may include seriously impacted communities. Neither does the assessment report record the physical location of mines and UXO. There are, however, a number of methods to widen the scope and coverage of baseline data which will ensure that information is available from all sectors of the target country.

Monitoring of Mine/UXO Incidents

'There is no such thing as a single mine – there are only minefields.' The deminer's working maxim, while not strictly accurate, is the basis for one of the most important and effective methods of identifying the existence and location of minefields. Whenever a person or animal falls victim to a landmine detonation it is an absolute indication that at least one mine existed, but a probable indication that a minefield can be found in the immediate vicinity. The essential factor, for the purposes of survey, is that an accurate record of the incident is retained and accessible to the survey organisation or authority. It is extremely rare for a mine incident to occur without witnesses, although they may not be present at the time of the actual explosion; unless the incident is fatal, the victims themselves are the prime witnesses. It should be said, however, that people do fall victim to mines alone and without anyone being aware of their fate, inevitably these doubly unfortunate victims will die even if not killed by the initial blast. Hill shepherds, woodcutters and nomadic herders are especially vulnerable in this respect. However, in the great majority of cases, incidents, both fatal and otherwise, are recorded.

Gaining access to those records is the challenge which faces the survey organisation and one source is more reliable and accessible than all others combined – the hospital. In almost every case the casualties from a landmine explosion will be taken to some kind of medical facility, perhaps a local clinic or a traditional healer in a nearby village, but, except in the rare cases where injuries are superficial, the casualty will eventually arrive at a hospital. What is critical for survey purposes is that the hospital includes details of the cause of injury in its records – this will make it possible for researchers to go back through admission records to extract information about mine victims and where they can be located for interview. Unfortunately this task is not straightforward – many hospital administrations, understandably, see no reason, especially during a war or in the immediate aftermath, to differentiate between one cause of injury and another. Perhaps surprisingly, however, many do. An obvious and urgent task for the national authorities and involved organisations is to ensure that hospitals and clinics begin recording landmine and UXO casualties separately and include in those records details of the incident location, the nearest village and the name and contact details of the patient. The ICRC and Red Crescent have for some years maintained such information at their field hospitals as a matter of policy. It may even be possible in countries where the communications infrastructure allows, to introduce a casualty reporting system where the survey organisation is informed of each relevant patient as a matter of course.

Since a high percentage of mine victims lose limbs or sustain eye damage they will often become resident or outpatients at prosthetic workshops and eye clinics. These are important information source centres since they normally maintain contact with their patients over a long period. Prosthetic facilities are especially productive because such a high percentage of amputees are mine/UXO casualties.

The aim of the Level Two survey team will be to build up a 'cluster map' showing the locations of every reported landmine and UXO explosion.

Military Information Sources

Many mine victims are soldiers and fighters[19] who may often be interviewed through medical facilities in the same manner as civilian casualties. But they also lay mines and, in many cases, have a good knowledge of the types of mines deployed and the tactics employed by their own forces and those of their enemy. This is invaluable information and should be sought as soon after combat ceases as possible,[20] although it is worth bearing in mind that information from senior officers is likely to be theoretical in nature and may have little relationship with the actual situation, whereas information from experienced fighting soldiers will nearly always be accurate, although perhaps harder to obtain. While researching the Human Rights Watch report on landmines in Cambodia[21] I was able to obtain some of the most important information on the soldiers' own attitudes to the anti-personnel mine and its use during the course of a long conversation with a group of soldiers drinking at a marketplace bar – it certainly had its risks but the soldiers were more willing to speak openly to a former British soldier over a beer than to a human rights researcher in a formal interview setting.

At a higher level, normally the relevant defence ministry, it may often be possible to obtain copies, or at least be allowed to view, minefield maps and plans if such records exist. Their veracity will vary and each document should always be treated with extreme caution until proven accurate. Both the MCPA and the Halo Trust have had some success in obtaining and making use of such maps with varying degrees of practical advantage being gained.

Building Dialogue with Farmers and Nomads

Farmers know their land and are commonly a prime source of quality information regarding land made inaccessible due to mines and UXO. This is hardly surprising – the land gives them their livelihood. But what should be borne in mind is that farming is one of the most landmine/UXO-vulnerable occupations, primarily because many of those affected are subsistence farmers who have little or no choice – they work the land or go hungry. For every human who falls victim to a landmine there will be several animals killed. Livestock must graze and all too often traditional areas of pasture have been the site of battles and defensive positions and are mined and heavily contaminated with unexploded munitions. Farmers do not forget when and where they lose animals, especially when draught animals such as oxen, horses and camels are involved. This is important since grazing areas are often on the edges of villages and small towns, land which will only be used for other purposes when displaced communities return and the security situation stabilises. Establishing dialogue and trust with farming communities must be a priority objective of all survey teams.

Nomadic and semi-nomadic communities cover substantial distances during their migrations. They are reliable and knowledge-able witnesses because not only do they travel over the land but they develop a detailed knowledge of the geography along the way. They are often, although not always, uninvolved in war and may be treated with suspicion by combatants on both sides while normally managing to maintain, at least a nominal, neutrality. In such cir-cumstances they must develop the ability to avoid minefields during migrations and will pass their knowledge between groups. They are among the most important of all information sources and, if it is possible to build a good working relationship, will reward the effort with excellent and reliable data. It is worth remembering, though, that nomads have often boosted their incomes by carrying war salvage to scrapyards. This deadly commodity may often include fused and unstable ordnance – care should be taken.

Mapping Packs

I offer this method with some reservations. I believe it has only been used on one occasion and was not a great success, but the concept is good and the idea is my own and I am stubborn enough to continue promoting the idea. The idea is not complex – each mapping pack contains several sheets of blank white sketching paper (A3 size is probably ideal), an example map, a good-quality B or 2B pencil, an eraser, a single-sheet questionnaire and an instruction sheet. The whole pack is contained in a strong envelope preaddressed to the survey unit and, in countries where postal services are operational, prepaid. The instruction sheet contains simple directions for the recipient to draw a basic map showing the areas known or suspected of being mined in the immediate area of his or her home. Suggestions are given for symbols to show the location of key reference points (churches, mosques, rivers, bridges, etc.), different land types and minefields. All relevant languages are included both on the envelope and in the instruction sheet. If no postal service exists respondents are encouraged to hand the completed pack in at a local government office, UN agency, NGO or medical facility – the envelope should have instructions on it for returning the pack to the survey unit via organisations with whom prior arrangements have been made. When the concept was piloted in Afghanistan during 1990 using the umbrella of Operation Salaam, the UN humanitarian programme, the recognition of the post-conflict impact of landmines was in its infancy and the project had a poor response. However, the quality of those maps which were returned was excellent and it would be a worthwhile exercise to test the concept again in a different country.[22]

The essential difference between the collation of data for Level Two survey and the Level One impact assessment is that, unlike the first-phase assessment, all areas of the target country must be covered in order that the technical survey can be prioritised; it is effectively the first stage of the engineering process. How this widescale information gathering is implemented depends to a large extent on the physical scale of the country or region involved – the most common method is to integrate a general survey element within each technical survey unit. However, it is worth emphasising that many priorities are not decided by reference to the community but as a result of governmental policy and the urgent requirements of humanitarian aid and post-conflict rehabilitation and reconstruction. Government-imposed priorities are often, naively, viewed by aid agencies and some donors as a negative factor, largely because the government agency involved is inevitably following a different track than those dictated by purely humanitarian and developmental considerations. Perversely the government may well be responding to priorities dictated by other external forces such as the International Monetary Fund; none the less there is a tendency for international agencies to label any purely economy-based or commercially orientated policy as 'uncaring'. In some cases they may be correct but, for practical purposes, the government's motives are immaterial, they cannot simply be ignored and this applies just as much to landmine eradication as to any other sector of rehabilitation.

Establishing Priorities

The prioritisation of operations must, by definition, begin with the technical survey process since no planned clearance work on a wide scale can begin until surveys have been conducted. The first priority policies were established by demining NGOs based on humanitarian, community and donors considerations. Probably the very first such policy was incorporated into the demining conducted in Chamkani, Paktya Province in Afghanistan during the late 1980s.[23] Since there was no precedence to which the team could refer, rules were made in response to developments within the programme, inevitably those responses were often to problems – prioritisation was no exception. Initially the rules were straightforward, mines were cleared which were an obstacle to the wider programme objectives. So, for instance, access to *karezes*[24] were cleared of mines to allow project teams to repair them and when a destroyed bridge over the River Laza was rebuilt the road which crossed it and took traffic up the Solaymankhel Valley was cleared of anti-tank mines. Inevitably the local farmers began to ask the team to check their fields; given the agricultural nature of the programme it would have been difficult, if not impossible, to refuse – but which farmer first? And what if all the land was mined – how would clearance be prioritised? The situation was fraught with difficulties and potential unfairness, yet this was just two intersecting valleys with a large percentage of the population still in exile in the border refugee camps of Pakistan – even then it was apparent that prioritising survey and clearance at provincial and national level was going to prove a major problem.

Since those early days there have developed two ways to deal with the priority issue; by far the most common is to pay lip-service to the principle while ignoring all priorities other than those which fit predetermined plans. It is not always the implementing agency who should be blamed in these circumstances, major donors often impose restrictions on the use of funds which ensure that prioritisation is a meaningless exercise. To their credit some organisations have taken on this challenge of prioritisation with some success. A pragmatic recognition of the competing interests rather than concern for political correctness works in practice, especially when there is a high level of indigenous management. This latter point should not be surprising, dealing with prioritisation issues, whether at government or village level, requires a toughness and cultural understanding which most foreign managers would find extremely difficult.

The survey prioritisation policy adopted by the MCPA illustrates how far things have progressed over the past ten years in Afghanistan.[25]

Allocated Priority

In order to select mined areas for survey and clearance the area should be prioritized according to the needs of the local people, government authorities and other involved agencies. MCPA allocate the following five priority types:

1 Priority One

a) Agricultural land, roads, villages, canals and other irrigation systems requested by UN agencies and NGOs. The requesting agency must provide proof that funds are available for rehabilitation tasks to begin immediately that demining is completed.

b) Agricultural land, roads, villages, canals and other irrigation systems requested by local *shuras*.[26] The *shura* must provide evidence that refugees or internally displaced residents will return to the area not more than one month after demining is complete.

c) Areas where residents are frequently affected by mine incidents.

2 Priority Two

a) Agricultural land, roads, villages, canals and other irrigation systems requested by UN agencies or NGOs where plans for operations have been completed but funds are not yet available.

b) Agricultural land, roads, villages, canals and other irrigation systems requested by local shuras but where the return of refugees and displaced residents is unlikely to occur within 12 months.

c) Grazing lands in areas affected by frequent mine incidents and the main source of income (more than 40%) for the residents is from grazing.

3 Priority Three
a) Areas requested by the local shura which will assist rehabilitation in the medium term (1 to 2 years).
b) Areas where temporary alternatives have been found (e.g. roads, housing, irrigation etc.) which will prove unsuitable in the medium to long term.
c) Grazing lands in areas where some income (10%–40%) is from grazing.

4 Priority Four
a) Areas requested by villagers or individuals where proof is given that other families (11 or more) will also benefit from the clearance.
b) Areas where permanent alternatives exist but clearance will strengthen the economic structure of the area.
c) All grazing areas not covered under priority two and three are priority four.

5 Priority Five
a) All hillsides and mountains where the presence of mines does not affect the normal life of the villagers.
b) Areas where a low number of families (10 or less) will benefit from the clearance.

The system seems complex but also clearly leaves many potential circumstances unclassified, this is probably inevitable and the important issue is that a policy based on the situation which exists on the ground, in mine-affected communities, is in use by the agencies who are implementing technical survey and eradication programmes. The Afghan example is probably more advanced than others for the important reason that the community is very involved in all aspects of the clearance process. There are cultural reasons for this, but they have been accepted as a beneficial reality by the involved organisations rather than resisted.

There is an urgent need for the international agencies involved in mine and UXO eradication to deal honestly with prioritisation in real partnership with affected communities. Donors, as well, should ensure they do not impose requirements on demining organisations which make effective prioritisation more difficult. There is a need to recognise the full vista of genuine interests across the whole spectrum of involved society – from individual farmer to central government. It is ludicrous to make simplistic demands of implementing agencies or to formulate policy which recognises neither the realities nor the complexities of a situation. For instance, many international agencies state their priorities in terms of this nature: 'survey and clearance will be prioritised to first meet the needs of mine-affected communities'. It sounds fine, but is as meaningless as stating a preference for soft over hard water in a desert – you may prefer it but you will take whatever is on offer. In fact, priorities are virtually always determined by the authorities and communities of the subject country, it is difficult to see why this might be considered not to be correct, but indigenous influence is constantly challenged and resisted by international agencies. Of course, when the agency develops a good understanding of, and rapport with, the society in which it is operating it may seem as though it is determining priorities unilaterally. It is more likely, however, that the authorities and community see no reason to interfere with a policy which is meeting their own priorities.

One area where implementing agencies can very effectively determine priorities is as a sector of a wider rehabilitation or development programme. Unfortunately, very few agencies in other disciplines bother to coordinate effectively, if at all, until their programmes stumble, sometimes literally, into a minefield.

Practical Survey Techniques

It is in the detail that technical survey seems such a difficult or impossible undertaking for most laypeople to grasp, and here it must be said that many individuals, well regarded for their apparent knowledge of widescale landmine and UXO eradication, display a layperson's ignorance in this regard. It is therefore worth explaining the process in some detail to illustrate both its practical nature and enormous value.

Baseline Information

A technical minefield survey begins with information indicating the presence of landmines in a given location. This may be a formal report as a result of a Level One assessment or accessed from military sources, minefield maps or interviews with combatants. The information could also be informal, a request from a community or an individual farmer to check or clear an area suspected of being, or known to be, mined. Commonly the latter type of information originates as a result of one or more mine incidents involving persons or animals and is especially valuable because first-hand witnesses are often accessible who can identify exact locations of incidents and describe the sequence of events leading up to each incident.

Whatever the source of information it is essential that it is available in full to the survey team leader, especially the details of local contacts and incident survivors and witnesses.

The Survey Team

The survey team must have all the capacity to enable them to undertake surveys within the target region. In practice this means that they must, first and foremost, be a demining and UXO team incorporating all the knowledge and skills required to perform in that role. Individual members of the team should have considerable practical experience of landmine eradication and at least one member should be capable of dealing with unexploded ordnance, requirements that will often dictate the need for expatriate specialists to be incorporated into survey teams during the early phases of a programme.

The team may include mine dogs and handlers and extra staff depending on the local approach and policies, but the ability of team members to employ to full effect all technologies available to them and, importantly, the capacity to revert to basics when technology fails. So, for instance, surveyors must be trained to use a map and compass, take accurate bearings, recognise geographical features both on the ground and on a map and be capable of drawing accurate sketch maps and minefield plans.

Each team must be capable of working as a self-contained unit for long periods since, even where there is no absolute operational necessity for such capacity, a tight team with pride in its abilities and a level of independence tends to produce high-quality of work and maintain enthusiasm in adverse conditions to a greater extent than is otherwise the case. A level of competition between teams is healthy, but care must be taken that this does not become a negative factor. Where it exists it should focus on quality of work rather than, for instance, the number of minefields surveyed; it is then unlikely to encourage exaggerated or inaccurate reporting motivated by competition.

One consideration for programme management should always be to identify especially gifted or skilled surveyors who may be earmarked as future team leaders, but also who may be transferred to strengthen other, weaker, teams. This process of ongoing personnel assessment is an essential factor in ensuring the eventual establishment of truly indigenised programmes. A word of caution, or perhaps warning, here, based on my personal experience during my tenure as director of the NGO Mines Advisory Group;[27] this kind of assessment reporting should be formalised and monitored closely. Asking expatriate staff to identify those who will take their jobs imposes a requirement for dispassionate objectivity which even the most purely motivated person may find a less than straightforward undertaking. My experience in some country programmes, largely because I failed to recognise the problem and, for some time, failed to monitor such reporting, was that either individuals were not highlighted as exceptional or, more commonly, were promoted to hold supervisory posts but were given little or no actual access to the management and planning process. The latter response was undoubtedly the most negative in effect, since it gave some impression that a level of indigenisation existed whereas that was, in reality, far from the case. It was also common for expatriate staff to comment that exceptional local staff were 'not ready' despite the fact that those same staff had often developed an expertise that outstripped the, albeit more experienced, expatriate staff.

It is not by coincidence that I have raised the issue of indigenisation in relation to Level Two survey – there is an unavoidable logic involved. Technical survey lies at the core of the eradication process and is the sector which requires the highest quality of staff at all levels, if indigenisation can be established here it will follow naturally in other sectors.

The Field-engineering Process

In simple, non-technical, terms the process is conducted as follows.

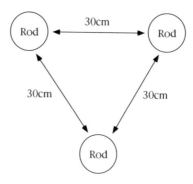

Figure 3.1 Bench mark

The bench mark is a permanent reference and navigation point ensuring that a minefield can be accurately located. It is always sited in a safe area at least 50 metres from the minefield and should be clearly visible, consisting of the following information painted on a substantial artificial marking post or an immovable natural feature: a red triangle 15 cm high below the letters 'MF' and the minefield reference number. The letters 'BM', the date of the survey and the survey team reference should be painted below the triangle. To be sure that the bench mark can be located even if the marker is removed or the paint wears away, three 30 cm metal rods are driven into the ground forming a triangle with the top of each rod flush with the surface, as shown in the illustration. This enables a mine detector to be used to confirm the bench mark location.

- The team assembles at a known safe location close to a suspected mined area.
- A *bench mark* (BM), either natural or manufactured, is established and its location recorded. This permanent mark will be used as the basis for all future measurements and bearings in relation to the minefield. (See Figure 3.1.) The exact position is recorded as an eight-figure grid reference. The BM must be in a safe location – the surrounding area must be thoroughly checked to ensure no mines or UXO are present.
- A *start point* (SP) is marked from where all operations will begin and from where *turning points* (TPs) will be measured. The route from the BM to the start point will be checked and clearly marked.
- A series of exploratory *breaches* are made into or through the suspected area. A breach is a cleared lane, normally a metre wide or a combination of 1-metre breaches. The lane, which begins at a known safe location and enters or traverses the

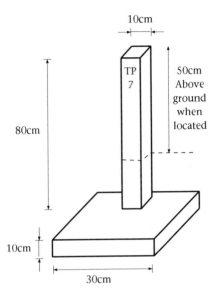

Figure 3.2 Permanent minefield marking

A pattern for a permanent minefield marking pole constructed of concrete based on the type used in Afghanistan. The base and approximately 30 cm of the pole are below the ground once the marker is sited. These markers can easily be mass produced at low cost and are unlikely to be removed from the ground due to their lack of intrinsic value and the effort involved, especially in firm ground. The portion above ground is marked and painted to local specifications. The *safe* side will normally be painted white and the *minefield* side red.

suspect area, could be explained in lay terms as a 'sample drilling'. The team, using detectors and probes (and sometimes dogs) locate, expose and destroy any mine found within the breach but, having located a mine, have no operational requirement to extend the breach further since their prime role is to define the minefield boundaries.

- The series of exploratory breaches combine to indicate the depth, length and perimeter of the minefield (or, of course, indicate that the area is clear of landmines) and provide data as to the device types and their density within the minefield.
- In practice, where previous minefield markings have survived, or where local information due to mine incidents and through interviews with combatants gives a reliable indication of the physical extent of the minefield, the survey may be confined

to confirming the veracity of the existing information. In such cases breaches may be confined to those undertaken to obtain information regarding the device types present.

- The perimeter of the minefield is recorded as follows. An SP at a clearly defined bearing and distance from the BM forms the entry to the minefield. The extent of the minefield is delineated through marked TPs at every location where the perimeter changes course, recorded by bearing and exact distance from the SP, in the case of the first TP, and subsequently from the previous TP. The SP and TPs are marked physically on the ground and drawn on a detailed scale plan and are recorded as eight-figure grid references. Two other location types may be recorded. Reference points (RPs) may be any prominent or easily recognisable and permanent feature which will clarify navigation in and around the minefield – an RP is recorded as an eight-figure grid reference. Intermediate points (IPs) are used as a check location where the distance between BM, SP and TPs is extended or where the landscape is complex and may lead to confusion. An IP should be recorded in the same manner as a TP. The exact location and details of each mine located and destroyed and of any known incidents are recorded.

The Minefield Plan

This plan, or map, on which all the above information is recorded, will be the baseline document for all subsequent work in relation to that specific minefield and, as clearance progresses, it will be updated. This is an important element of the whole eradication process, because the minefield plan performs two key roles:

- it is an accurate working reference for all technical staff who carry out subsequent work in that minefield
- it forms the basis of any centralised depository of minefield information.

The map should include key information – north indication, scale and legend – but also whatever additional information is considered essential. This will vary depending on the local situation but should always include the following.

1   Name used by local community for minefield.
2   Allocated reference number of minefield.
3   Name, distance and direction of nearest village or town.
4   Area in square metres of minefield.
5   Date of survey completion.
6   Map sheet numbers of relevant map(s) and BM coordinates.
7   Survey team number and name and signature of team leader.

The two minefield maps drawn by MCPA survey teams in Afghanistan (Figures 3.3 and 3.4) show clearly the quality of information that can be made available to clearance teams. Note the use of bearings and distances to indicate accurately access, boundaries and key information. Also note the indications of adjacent safe and mined land and areas which have been reduced following survey.

Area Minefield Maps

These maps, referred to by a variety of names, record the exact location of all located minefields within a given area – they would normally be kept as master maps at the survey headquarters, updated constantly, but may also be used as working documents for technical teams and community information maps, for which they may be produced, for instance, to cover specific village or district areas.

Master Maps

The regional or national headquarters of any demining operations must maintain master maps which are updated after each stage of operations – survey, marking and clearance – is completed. These may be computerised, in which case fully qualified staff must be employed to update records accurately. If hard copy master maps are used an 'overlay' system may be employed. This low technology system, where the base map has three transparent 'talc' overlays, is updated by recording survey, marking and clearance progress, each on separate dedicated overlays. When the three overlays are in place operational progress can be illustrated and monitored very effectively.

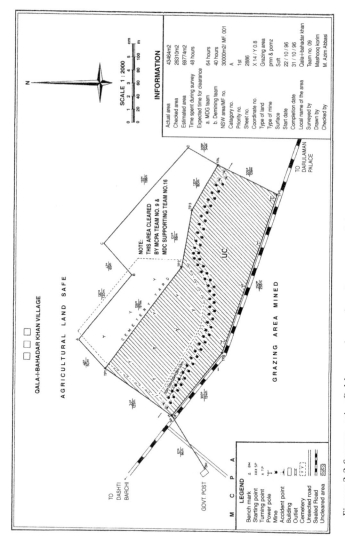

Figure 3.3 Survey: minefield maps (reproduced courtesy of the Mines Clearance Planning Agency, Afghanistan and redrawn from MCPA original)

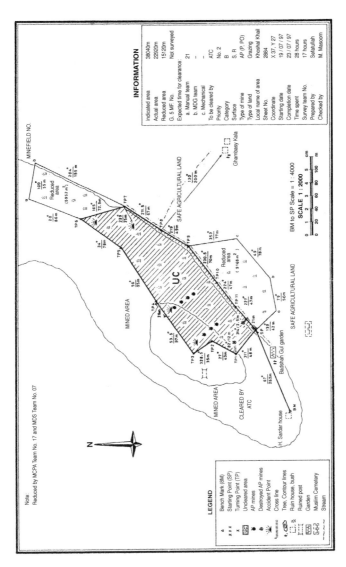

Figure 3.4 Survey: minefield maps (reproduced courtesy of the Mines Clearance Planning Agency, Afghanistan and redrawn from MCPA original)

127

Global Positioning System

GPS receivers use the 24 satellites of the *Navstar* system, originally developed for use by the US military, to give an accurate location anywhere on the Earth's surface. The system is capable of pinpointing a location to within 3 metres but, presumably due to US military paranoia, such accuracy is denied to non-military users through the incorporation of something known as 'selective availability'. In effect the satellites lie to the civilian GPS receiver and reduce the horizontal position error to over 100 metres no more than 5 per cent of the time and 300 metres no more than 0.1 per cent of the time. The practical effect of selective availability is that horizontal accuracy will randomly vary between 15 metres and 100 metres without the user knowing the extent or direction of the error at any given time. For general purposes this is more than adequate accuracy, but is insufficient alone for the purposes of bench marks, start points and individual devices which must be recorded to an accuracy of +/–10 metres.

Happily there is a way around selective availability which should be considered by any widescale survey operation. Differential global positioning system (DGPS) can give an accuracy of between 5 centimetres and 15 metres and is accessible to non-military users. There is, however, a considerable cost penalty involved and some geographical limitation may make the system unavailable to some programmes.

The other option is for direct negotiation with US authorities in order to make use of the military system for humanitarian operations which, if the US government's commitment to global landmine eradication matches its rhetoric, should present no obstacles. However, a White House policy directive issued on 29 March 1996 stated that selective availability should be kept in use for between four and ten years.[28]

There are some regional considerations when using GPS. A decision must be made as to which grid system will be employed, in practice one of three:

1 Latitude and Longitude, the most common coordination system, available on all GPS receivers.
2 Universal Transverse Mercator system (UTM). UTM is a metric coordination system designed for ease of use, and is available on most receivers.

3 Military Grid Reference System (MGRS). A form of UTM relevant when using US Defense Mapping Agency maps.

It should also be noted that by far the most common reason for errors using GPS are a result of mistakes made by the user. Comprehensive training in the use of the system must be incorporated into the training curriculum for all staff who will use GPS at any operational level.

Survey Reports

The survey report provides the baseline data for operational planning purposes. The information contained in the report may vary from country to country but the opportunity to maximise on the survey as a way of amassing data covering all useful operational aspects should not be underrated. A good example of this approach is the survey report format used by MCPA in Afghanistan:[29]

1 Minefield Code Number
2 Location (Province, District, Village)
3 Survey Date (Start and Completion dates)
4 Survey Team Number and Team Members
5 Minefield Category: Reason:
6 Type of Land
7 In case of agricultural land, what will be cultivated once area is cleared?
8 Coordinate in 1/100,000 scale maps: X: Y: Sheet number:
9 Priority
10 Types of Mines and UXOs
11 Any indication of boobytraps. Give details
12 Impact of mines and UXOs on the daily lives of residents
13 Proposed clearance method (manual, mechanical, by MDGs).[30] Give reasons
14 Land surface
15 Route from MCPA office to the area:
    a Type of vehicle most suitable
    b Stop point for overnight stay and re-fuelling
16 Area of the minefield:
    a Indicated by locals
    b Actual mined area marked

17   Estimated clearance time (for 30 man manual team, mechanical unit, MDG)
18   Basis for the above calculation
19   Requesting source for clearance
20   Number of beneficiaries
21   Number and types of mines destroyed during survey operations
22   Have you briefed a clearance team? If yes, include team number and agency of the team leader briefed and date and time of briefing
23   Documents provided to the clearance team leader during briefing (map, brief report etc.)
24   Are there any mine action operations other than the UNOCHA Programme?[31]
     If yes,
     a   Who is supporting the programme?
     b   When did they start operations?
     c   Where have they operated so far?
     d   How do you assess their performance?
25   Was this minefield covered in the National Survey?
     If yes,
     a   National Survey Minefield Number
     b   Area in square metres indicated in the National Survey
26   Local contacts (sources of information)
     a   Mujahideen Shura (name and parties)
     b   Name of Commanders and their parties
     c   Government offices and personnel
27   Any other sources that might be able to provide information about mines?
28   Do local authorities support mine action? If yes, what kind of assistance can they provide?
29   Aid organisations working in the area
30   A brief introduction to the village:
     a   Pre-war population
     b   Number of migrated families
     c   Number of families returned
     d   Present population
     e   Number of people killed by war and by mines (indicate separately)
     f   Number of people disabled by war and by mines
     g   Number of people missing
     h   Indicate total number of houses in village
     i   Destroyed ____% Partially damaged ____%

j   Houses presently inhabited _____%
k   Number of vehicles destroyed by mines and by war
l   Number of livestock lost due to war and mines (give details of animal type)
31   Main industry of the area
32   Climate of the area
33   Months when demining operations cannot continue due to weather conditions
34   Security situation
35   Prior to Soviet withdrawal who occupied the area?
36   Is there electricity in the area?
37   Is safe drinking water available?
38   Is accommodation for demining teams available?
39   Are fuel, oil and lubricants available in the area? Where and how far?
40   Is there any local vehicle repair facility?
41   Any communication means other than mine action radios?
42   Any special considerations?
43   Provide details about the location and type of any medical facility
44   Any common diseases in the area?

At first glance this may appear like an almost random list with some questions having no obvious relevance to mine clearance. But a more detailed examination tells a different story, the questions have developed from long experience of running mine clearance operations in a difficult and often dangerous environment. The report covers every aspect of operations, giving good background about the social and political situation in the target community – essential to enable the mine clearance teams to establish good working relations on site and ensuring that any social protocols are correctly observed. Any field engineer understands the essential nature of what most academics and bureaucrats would perceive to be mundane logistic details and that awareness is recognisable in the MCPA report format. When there is a need to recharge mine-detector batteries on a 24-hour basis, for instance, it is essential to know if there is an electricity supply in the operational area. If there is no electricity then generators must be purchased with attendant budgetary and logistical implications. Similar importance can be placed on medical and climate data in the report – the former, particularly, is a key planning consideration. The level of surgical and clinical support available locally will determine the need for dedicated medical staff and evacuation facilities which may include contingencies for the hire of commercial helicopters, for instance.

The survey report in conjunction with the minefield plan should provide a comprehensive overview of each individual clearance operation; combined with progress reporting the information needs of all involved agencies should be adequately met. If the 'pen picture', as in the case of the Afghan programme, is detailed and relevant it should be possible to provide donors not just with details of proposed operations requiring funding, but with accurate achievement forecasts over several funding periods.

Summary Survey Report

It may be that the information required by the teams who subsequently mark and clear the minefield require different, and possibly less detailed, information. For that reason a separate report may be prepared. The example below is also an MCPA format used in Afghanistan.

1   Prepared by (survey team number):
2   Minefield number:
3   Location (province, district, village):
4   Sources of information (local population, *shura*, former military personnel):
5   Information about minefield:
    a   Type of land:
    b   Category:
    c   Land surface:
    d   Type of mines:
    e   Any indication of boobytraps:
    f   Priority:
6   Any factors having negative impact on mine clearance operations:
7   Proposed clearance method (Manual, Flail, MDG). Why?
8   Total area of the minefield (in square metres):
9   Estimated clearance time in team hours:
10 Security situation:
11 Local contacts:
12 Logistical requirements: Are the following available?
    a   Accommodation (distance from minefield in hours/kilometres):
    b   Drinking water:

c   Electricity:
d   Foodstuffs:
e   Fuel for vehicles (where, and distance from base camp):
f   Vehicle repair facilities (where, and distance from base camp):
13   Medical facilities (location and type):
14   Communication facilities (telephone, fax, sitor, telex):
15   Any special considerations for the clearance of this minefield:

COMPARATIVE VALUES OF LEVEL ONE ASSESSMENTS AND
LEVEL TWO SURVEYS AND POLITICAL INFLUENCES ON THE
PROCESS

This is a comparison which, in a sane world, would never need to
be made, but if the world's response to landmines cannot be fairly
termed insane, it is most certainly not logical and the comparison is,
in my view, justified, if unwelcome or, perhaps more accurately,
uncomfortable.

Level One assessment, if well conceived and implemented, can
afford a valuable impact overview and give some good indications of
the scale of response which may be required and provide a justification, based on humanitarian aid and developmental criteria, for the
allocation of funds by donors. Very importantly the assessment will
also show the impact overlap into various parallel response sectors
– repatriation, food aid, reconstruction, agricultural rehabilitation,
for instance. It may, in some circumstances, point to areas of clear
priority which must be addressed urgently and should also form the
basis of a contact – point data base for affected communities.
However, the Level One assessment is not, in any engineering sense,
a survey. It is worth using a somewhat simplistic but, none the less,
relevant comparison.

Take the case of a subsistence agricultural community formed by
a group of villages sited on the banks of a river which is subject to
annual flooding. For various reasons the flooding has become more
widespread in recent years and takes longer to return to preflood
levels. The bridges which used to enable villagers to cross the river
in flood have been washed away and neither the government nor
the community itself have the necessary resources or expertise to
resolve the situation. It now falls to a humanitarian NGO, let us say,
which is operational in the area, to alert the international
community to the problems facing the community. In order to

produce a comprehensive report capable of achieving a good response from suitable organisations and, very importantly, international donors, the NGO undertakes an impact assessment of the affected communities. It can easily explain the impact the floods have on its own sector of assistance but sensibly seeks to give a much wider perspective. The usefulness of this assessment and report process is to alert, inform and encourage relevant response. But no one would seriously suggest that the NGO's assessment could be used as a technical basis for bridge construction. Certainly the report might indicate the need for a new bridge and may even offer some opinions as to where the bridge should be sited and the volume of traffic which would use it. But no donor would consider releasing funds for construction to begin until a technical survey had been conducted by qualified engineers and plans were drawn up for the bridge. It is, therefore, a source of some amazement to many involved engineers that funds for mine and UXO eradication are released on the basis of impact assessments and, by definition, *guesswork* projections of manpower, equipment and funding requirements. It would be charitable to argue that this situation has evolved as a consequence of an urgent response by the international community to a comparatively new problem, and this excuse might be justified if it were not for two indisputable facts.

- The very first international humanitarian response to landmines and UXO was in Afghanistan and, since January 1990, this programme has, under the auspices of the UN and through implementation by indigenous engineering NGOs, adopted a logically sequenced approach: assessment – technical survey – clearance – confirmation. It is the programmes which have followed in other countries which have ignored, in whole or in part, the essential nature of technical survey.
- Rather than rectifying the lack of Level Two survey within the response process, involved agencies are institutionalising Level One assessment as the prime survey process while largely ignoring the need for widescale technical survey.

For these reasons I will risk the displeasure of those who promote this reversal of logic by being less than charitable and suggesting that the evolution is a result of inexcusable ignorance or political pressure. It may also, as in the case of Angola, be a combination of the two. It is worth, in this regard, examining the situation evolving in the Balkans as I write.

Viewing the situation from a purely technical standpoint there are two well-defined problems to be resolved.

1 A landmine clearance programme, probably of limited scale, is required in Kosovo to eradicate landmines laid by Yugoslav forces (regular and irregular) and the Kosovo Liberation Army (KLA). It is likely that this will require teams to respond to two situations:

   a) Defensive minefields in the vicinity of military strongpoints, key installations such as communication centres and bridges, and in border areas to deter infiltration by the KLA and NATO special forces. Any teams responding to this problem will be required to deal with unexploded ordnance within mined areas as a result of NATO bombing. A high percentage of UXO will be failed submunitions from cluster bombs. Teams may also be required to deal with demolition charges placed on key installations.
   b) Indiscriminate use of mines and boobytraps by Yugoslav forces and the KLA. Given the nature of the conflict these are likely to be predominantly concentrated in and around abandoned dwellings and business premises.

2 A widescale battle area clearance (BAC) initiative or, in practice, a series of BAC programmes in response to the high percentage of failed ordnance following the intensive NATO bombing campaign. The response area should cover all target areas in Yugoslavia and Kosovo and include some ancillary response in locations where NATO aircraft have dumped bombs following aborted missions. An example of the latter requirement is for underwater clearance of bombs dropped in the Adriatic off the coast of Italy.

This requires a major engineering commitment and funds to match, but presents no major problems in comparison with responses in, for instance, Laos and Afghanistan. All the mines and UXO are the result of recent combat, good sources of intelligence are available and, although supply and communications, especially in Kosovo, may be difficult, high-quality logistic support is available from Western European countries. Even the ethnic tensions between Serbs and Kosovons are unlikely to cause a major obstacle to a well-planned response, certainly no greater than have been faced by teams in North Iraq, Cambodia and Afghanistan for instance.

This, unfortunately, is the situation only if no account is taken of international politics. The actual situation will offer little opportunity for engineering priorities to be given their rightful place in the order of things. The gap between engineering reality and the surreal world of international politics is, quite simply expressed, the difference between fact and fiction. The vast anomaly inherent in the position of NATO begins with the illegality of the bombing – undertaken without the licence of a Security Council resolution and, therefore, regardless of motive, illegal. How does this effect the subsequent requirement for clearance operations and the need for assessment and survey? The answer is either complex or simply crazed – depending on your viewpoint. In Western European political terms the NATO bombing must be seen as successful which, if its only aim was to halt Serbian aggression in Kosovo, it was (although a reversal – ethnic Albanian aggression towards the remaining Serb population – seems a likely result). However, if the aim of the bombing was, as stated repeatedly by President Clinton, Prime Minister Blair and others, also to allow displaced and refugee Kosovons to return to their homes in safety, to end ethnic conflict in Kosovo and to bring President Milosovic to trial in the Hague, it can only be perceived as a campaign which failed in all but one of its objectives. In order to make Kosovo safe for the returning population it must be cleared of landmines and UXO, and the latter, as a consequence of their indiscriminate dissemination, are likely to present the greatest and most long-term threat. But the UXO are a consequence of the NATO bombing and, politically, cannot be seen as an obstacle to resettlement and a threat to the lives of the people of Kosovo. Therefore emphasis must be placed on the *Serb landmines* and as little as possible must be said about UXO. Unfortunately, within a short time of NATO troops entering Kosovo, two British soldiers were killed by a NATO submunition – these were the first British forces to lose their life in the conflict and few, even among those who wholeheartedly supported the campaign, could miss the irony that they should die as a result of an exploding BLU-97B dropped by a US aircraft.[32] The situation places the politicians and their media teams in a quandary; the UXO must be cleared – it is unthinkable (politically) that NATO-deployed ordnance continues to take a toll of life in Kosovo in the same manner as has bombing of a similar intensity in other countries. But in order to launch the scale of UXO clearance required it would be difficult for an – already sceptical – public to avoid arriving at the conclusion that the NATO bombing campaign had been counterproductive and lacking in foresight given the careless attitude to post-conflict consequences shown by NATO planners. The political emphasis on landmine eradication over the equally urgent need for UXO clearance is complicated by the division of the NATO target area. Leaders of NATO countries have repeatedly warned Serbia that no reconstruction assistance will be forthcoming while President Milosovic remains in power and it must be assumed that this embargo includes technical assistance related to the location and destruction of unexploded NATO ordnance. It is, to be realistic, hardly a new discovery that governments who lay claim to the moral high-ground and wage war in defence of democracy and human rights or some, less clearly defined, 'better way of life', are willing to place at risk the lives of those least able to influence societal change. So in the case of the Kosovo situation there are strong political reasons in favour of a selective socioeconomic assessment of landmines over the need for widescale technical surveys which would, for technical reasons, throw a spotlight on the need to respond to unexploded air-dropped munitions. Of course, if the concentration is on landmines then there is no reason to conduct any kind of assessment or survey in Serbia where the problem is exclusively related to UXO from the NATO bombing campaign.

Such political reasoning is likely to be short-lived, if only for the reason that European and US commercial interests are enthusiastic to obtain reconstruction contracts in Serbia. The clearance of UXO may well be undertaken in Serbia as a piecemeal operation in response to purely commercial engineering priorities rather than any humanitarian dynamic. This will inevitably mean that rural areas are neglected.

However, the major damage caused by political interference, intentional or otherwise, is that the requirement for, or the results of, a purely technical situation assessment is obscured and when a response is finally launched the political emphasis shifts to calls for 'urgent action'. This is a trap to which the UN, especially its hastily established mine action centres, may find itself especially vulnerable. Under pressure from donor and other governments to begin 'getting mines out of the ground' there is an obvious temptation to dispense with the time-consuming Level Two survey and use a Level One assessment as the basis for a clearance programme. The trap closes

firmly once the programme has been running for a year or more –
how can the management then admit that they have no clear picture
of the problem to which they have been responding; no method of
accurately forecasting their future requirements for manpower,
equipment, funds; no way to estimate the area of ground requiring
clearance or of prioritising their response? And so it is the charade
rather than the technical process which increases in sophistication
as time passes.

The real tragedy of the failure by many eradication programmes to
afford survey and assessment their proper place within the field-
engineering process is that the emerging expertise of indigenous
clearance teams will often be misemployed and, inevitably and most
seriously, people will die and lose limbs as a consequence.

The strongest argument for prioritising Level Two survey can be
based on the facts available in the one country which has
implemented technical surveys throughout the ten-year life of the
mine-action programme – Afghanistan. The following are a selection
of those facts.

- MCPA returns almost 4 million square metres of land to safe
  and productive use every year as a result of the combination
  of Level Two survey and area reduction.[33]
- Based on recent costings, area reduction in Afghanistan costs
  less than 8 cents per square metre, compared with mine
  clearance which is costed at approximately 60 cents per square
  metre.
- 98.93 per cent of civilian mine incidents in Afghanistan take
  place in unmarked areas. Only 1.07 per cent of civilian
  incidents happen in areas marked by Level Two survey teams.
  Since roughly 25 per cent of the total mined area in
  Afghanistan is now marked the value of technical survey
  followed by marking is clear – only 1 in 32 accidents occur in
  surveyed and marked areas.[34]

4.1

Eradicating Landmines and Unexploded Ordnance

There are tens of millions of landmines around our world – no one knows how many and it simply does not matter. What matters is that we eradicate them.

'A Matter of Justice and Humanity',
ICBL Nobel Lecture, Oslo, December 1997

PHYSICAL ERADICATION OF LANDMINES AND UXO –
THE PROCESS

Level Two surveys allow planned programmes of mine clearance to be implemented. Demining may be separated into three component steps:

- detection
- exposure
- destruction

Manual Clearance

In its simplest manual form a deminer, using a pointed metal probe and trowel and working within a predetermined 1-metre-wide lane, pierces the ground at an angle of approximately 30 degrees to a minimum depth of 15 centimetres in maximum increments of 5 centimetres, although local conditions may determine that search depth is extended to greater depths. The horizontal and forward progress intervals between each insertion of the probe should never exceed the minimum surface area of the smallest mine or UXO likely to be discovered in the clearance area. In any event the interval should never exceed 3 centimetres, ensuring that the smallest mines would be contacted by the probe. The spoil is removed carefully with the hand or trowel before the depth of excavation is increased.

Whenever the probe makes contact with an object the ground is carefully removed using the probe and fingers until the object is exposed. If it is a mine the deminer carefully checks for any attached tripwires and particularly for other devices buried below the exposed mine.

The procedure following exposure may vary, but the mine will normally be destroyed *in situ* either individually or collectively with other located mines by sympathetic detonation. This method of destruction involves placing an explosive charge adjacent to each mine. A detonator is inserted in the explosive which is crimped to a length of fuse or, if an electric detonator is used, connected to a charge generator. If more than one mine is being destroyed the explosive charges are interconnected. The charge is detonated once the area is declared clear of people and animals and team members are under cover at a predetermined safe distance. If the mine discovered is damaged it is always destroyed *in situ* immediately to avoid a premature detonation.

As the clearance progresses the deminer will mark each metre of forward progress by inserting pickets at each side of the 1-metre lane. Manual clearance teams normally work in two-person teams (traditionally military teams consisted of three members, but this was found to be wasteful of manpower in widescale clearance operations) with the second person acting as an observer with the primary responsibility of checking that the deminer carries out their work correctly. The second person is also responsible for ensuring that the 1-metre clearance lane remains straight. The two exchange tasks at regular intervals which will vary depending on local conditions. Teams who have worked together over long periods usually become extremely proficient and provide mutual support, although managers need to ensure that teams do not become careless or begin taking short cuts through familiarity. Manual clearance is the fallback procedure – the simplest, and slowest, but most effective method of detecting mines in any given area. In areas of heavy vegetation which would make other approaches dangerous, the manual method remains reliable, the overgrowth being painstakingly checked and removed and the ground below probed section by section. In rock-hard ground water may be used to soften the ground in advance of clearance. The process, described by one journalist as 'zen gardening',[1] is the method which most experienced deminers would choose if they were called upon to clear land which their own family would use.

Electronic Search

This, the most common clearance technique, employs a combination of electronic search and manual clearance. This speeds up the operation without unduly detracting from its reliability. As with manual clearance the military traditionally used a three-person team and a procedure which involved constant exchange of positions within the 1-metre lane; however, demining NGOs with teams working a 48-hour week in minefields found that the inherent dangers of the military procedure were unacceptable. Most electronic search teams now consist of two members, the first operating the mine detector and, on receiving an indication from the detector, using a probe in the same way as a manual operator. The second team member performs the same task as in a manual team and, in addition, performs sensitivity checks on the detector. The two members exchange roles at regular intervals.

The actual electronic search procedure will differ to some extent depending on the machine in use, but essentially the operator sweeps across the 1-metre lane ensuring that the search head does not *rise* at each end of the sweep and that the previous sweep is overlapped. The detector will transmit a signal when metal is detected below the search head and, having isolated and marked the centre of the signal source area the operator places his detector aside (in a safe area) and probes in the same manner as described above until the source of the signal is located. In most cases the signal will be the result of extraneous metal fragments in the ground or metal-bearing minerals – these are stored in a container to avoid redetection and the area is rechecked with the detector before the search continues. Mines are dealt with in the same manner as for manual clearance.

The key safety and reliability factors in electronic search are:

- well-maintained and serviced detectors
- an efficient and observed battery-charging and maintenance regime
- regular sensitivity checks carried out throughout working day
- regular supervisory checks to deter operator short cuts
- operator confidence

The confidence of the operator in the detector is critical, and some features can be instrumental in improving that trust. One, incorporated into most good detectors, is a audible or visual confidence check – a regular clicking noise or a flashing diode are common – showing that batteries are charged and the machine is fault-free. Although all detectors have headsets (normally single ear, since the operator must also be able to hear extraneous sounds) through which the operator can hear detection signals and the confidence tone, some also have an option of a small external speaker. This has points for and against – it is obviously a very effective method of monitoring the operator's response to signals but, especially in a minefield where a large number of detectors are in use, there may be a confusion factor to consider.

Guide or Base Stick

Most responsible demining organisations use some form of physical guide to determine the demarcation between cleared and uncleared areas within a clearance lane. The recommended dimensions are $120 \times 4 \times 2$ centimetres; the extreme 10 centimetres at each end are painted white while the centre 1-metre section is painted bright red. At the beginning of clearance in a new lane the start line is checked and cleared of any metallic fragments and the base stick is placed centrally along the start line. The search sweep of the detector then begins in front of and adjacent to the stick and ends with the centre of the search loop over the white section of the stick. This procedure ensures an adequate overlap between lanes which avoids the danger of narrow, uncleared sections. The normal procedure is for the operator to make three sweeps, each moving forward and overlapping the previous sweep by half the diameter of the search head. Any signals are dealt with as explained above. When three sweeps have been completed and all signals investigated the base stick is moved forward a distance equivalent to the diameter of the detector search head. This procedure continues throughout the lane clearance. The built-in failsafe due to a continuing overlap and the visible demarcation between safe and unsafe areas is a very effective way of reducing accidental straying into uncleared sections of the lane and avoiding 'underlapped' clearance.

Safety Distances and Minefield Management

A basic rule of all mine-clearance operations are that the number of personnel exposed to risk in the event of an accidental detonation is reduced to the absolute minimum. This requires that the actual risk involved in such an explosion can be quantified which means, in practice, that the type of mines likely to exist in the area under clearance must be known. This information should be available from the Level Two survey report but, if no report is available, exploratory breaches are made to ascertain the mines present prior to establishing a full clearance operation.

There are conflicting management priorities involved in the clearance of any minefield:

- the maintenance of safety distances between teams and individual deminers
- maintaining the most effective use of available manpower in order to complete clearance in the shortest possible timeframe
- ensuring that any accident casualty can be safely evacuated from the minefield.

To the uninitiated observer a large area under clearance may have the appearance of a totally uncoordinated operation, with teams working in different directions in apparently randomly located clearance lanes. That perception is inaccurate, if understandable. Before tasking the teams the manager will draw up a minefield plan designed to maximise employment of the available teams, taking into account administrative information. Perhaps, for instance, one of the teams is due time off, or others may need to attend for medical examinations or trade testing – a good manager will take all these factors into consideration. He (or she – female deminers are increasingly common in some countries) must now prepare on the plan a series of interlocking 1-metre-wide clearance lanes which will ensure that no member of any team breaches a minimum safety distance. There is a generally accepted safety rule that the maximum length of any lane is 10 metres based on the realistic limitations of safe evacuation of an unconscious casualty along a 1-metre-wide lane. This limitation must be observed by the manager when drawing up the plan. The manager must also allocate dedicated areas for the medical point, rest areas, toilets, vehicle parking, an ambulance point and a visitor briefing area. If helicopters are in use or available for emergency evacuation a landing site would need to be selected and marked. Explosive stores require to be sited in two blast-proof bunkers for the separate storage of high explosive and detonators. All these sites have safety distance considerations which must be considered. The bench mark and start point must be accurately shown and distances recorded exactly.

Within the minefield there are two sets of safety distance which must be observed:

- distance between working teams
- distance between team members.

The distance between the operator and his teammate is less than the distance between working teams because the second team member must be in a position and at a distance from where he can observe his colleague. There is also an unspoken consideration that, in the event of an accidental detonation, the operator will normally mask his teammate from the full effect of the blast. The widely accepted safety distances are as follows.

Mine type	Between teams	Team members
Anti-personnel blast mine	20 metres	10 metres
Anti-personnel bounding fragmentation mine	50 metres	20 metres
Anti-personnel fragmentation mine	50 metres	20 metres
Anti-tank mine (all types)	50 metres	20 metres

Of course, in minefields where different types of mines are present, the relevant safety distance will always be that required by the mine with the greatest safety distance requirement.

Clothing

Demining teams require special clothing to protect them, not simply from the obvious risk of unplanned detonations, but from the environment in which they work. When the minefield is your workplace, your office, for eight hours a day, six days a week (the average working week for deminers involved in humanitarian operations) life can be harsh and physically unforgiving. Clothing requirements vary depending on prevailing conditions and climate, but in most countries there will be a need for winter and summer clothes. Cotton coveralls with long sleeves are a good general purpose basic uniform – when issued by the organisation they can be procured in bulk with logos. It is useful to add the team number and the deminer's name. They should be a generous fit and of two grades – lightweight for summer and hot climates, heavyweight for winter and cold climates. Knee and elbow reinforcing patches are a sensible option if available and will avoid overregular replacement. Loose-fitting military-style shirts and trousers make ideal basic clothing. Strong boots with a tough treaded sole are essential; once again, bulk purchase of military surplus footwear will keep costs down but modern hiking boots which combine lightness with strong construction are preferable if budgets allow. Most demining organisations do not permit gloves to be worn by staff when actually carrying out demining operations and preparing demolitions, however, they should be available to staff involved in other tasks in cold climates. In extreme conditions consideration should be given to the use of fingerless gloves for use by staff when demining and setting up demolitions. Suitable hats should be available for wear by staff when not wearing protective headgear.

Protective clothing for use by deminers is a compromise between utility and protection. A full bombsuit as worn by bomb disposal specialists would provide maximum protection, but restricts mobility and vision to an extent that makes its use for demining impractical. Standard protection for deminers consists of a ballistic jacket or waistcoat and helmet fitted with a full-face visor which can be swivelled up over the helmet when not in use. The jacket should be side fastening with a rear-facing overlap; fasteners should be of the velcro type. The jacket should have a high protective collar and, especially when deminers are working in areas where working in the prone position is not possible, a crutch extension should be included. The helmet should be as light as is compatible with protection[2] and incorporate a harness fastening system with a chin strap; when fastened the helmet should be a firm and comfortable fit. The visor fastenings should be capable of holding the visor securely in the raised and protective position – the latter is especially important to limit the possibility that the visor may be thrown upwards in the case of an accidental detonation.

Extended visors, some of which are fitted to a headband and offer head protection in place of a helmet, are used by some organisations and have been tested to their satisfaction. However, some organisations provide no adequate protective clothing for their deminers – this is simply unacceptable on both moral and professional grounds. Even from a purely operational viewpoint it makes no sense to place at risk staff whose training has required a major input of funds and resources and whose death or injury will damage the morale of colleagues and make it more difficult to recruit new staff. But the real fault lies at the door of donors who fund these programmes either in the knowledge that their safety procedures are inadequate or in careless ignorance of the fact. This is no major investment when considered in the context of the global problem – a deminer can be equipped with protective jacket and helmet for not much more than $1,000, the clothing will last at least two years, more with care, and only the visor may require replacing during that period. No more justification should be required – if protecting a deminer's sight or life is not worth $1,000 then international aid is a nonsense.

Mine Probes

I have a non-ferrous mine probe which can be adjusted for use in three different lengths and screws neatly inside its handle like a sword stick for transit. It costs around £70 and is as much use in a real minefield as a brown paper bag in a rainstorm. The shiny round pointed probe section bends easily and would wear quickly if used in stony ground. There is no hand guard to protect the deminer's hand in the case of an unintentional detonation. But, most importantly, it is an unnecessary expense. Most demining operations arrange manufacture of probes in the operational country, which ensures that the design meets local conditions, contributes to the economy and, on average, costs no more than $3 per probe.

Mechanisation

Most Westerners involved in mine-clearance programmes have long ago developed an automatic response to the most commonly asked questions – by far the most asked of those is: 'Why don't you drive a big roller through the minefield or just use one of these chain flails?' I suppose the inference that you are too stupid to have even considered such ideas is what becomes so annoying about that question after it has been asked a few hundred times. There are actually several good and valid responses.

- Flails and rollers do have some utility in some situations, however, they also have some considerable disadvantages, perhaps most importantly that the land must be checked by manual teams after the machine has finished work. There are, however, many situations for which heavy mechanised machinery is simply not suitable.
- The cost and overall utility of the mechanised approach must be balanced against the potential to use such funds to train, equip and deploy indigenous clearance teams.
- Especially in poor countries with minimum logistics support and services, mechanised clearance may prove unsustainable. In programmes where sustainability is a key factor there must be a serious question mark over large-scale mechanisation.
- It is common for mechanisation to be perceived as an alternative means of clearance – it will never be that. Some relevant mechanised approaches will be an additional tool in the clearance toolbox.

A lot of energy and funding has been expended on developing new methods of mechanised clearance and certainly one of the reasons that many of these inventions are never taken up for use by demining organisations is that the designers have not spent enough time understanding the physical nature of clearance operations before beginning work. There are very few, if any, field engineers calling for a one-shot solution to landmine eradication for two reasons:

- they are confident that no such solution exists
- if such a solution did exist it would not be available to the great majority of mine-affected communities who have in common their low income and their inability to influence national authorities sufficiently of their needs to ensure any response on an adequate scale.

There is also another reason which determines the lack of relevance of much of the research undertaken – it is undertaken by arms manufacturers funded by, at best, naive funding bureaucracies. The Esprit research programme funded by the European Commission is a classic example of an initiative which will never result in the deployment of any technology of prime use to humanitarian mine eradication. The arms companies who take a key role in the Esprit programme have no track record in human development – their expertise is in devising means of destruction, and among the commodities they have designed, manufactured and sold are, somewhat perversely, landmines. The logic, if such exists, for their inclusion appears to be that their expertise in manufacturing landmines might somehow especially qualify them to find a means of detection better than anything already in existence. Rather like asking the mad scientist to design a trap to catch the monster he just created. While there may be arguments in support of this strategy there are two overarching arguments against.

First, arms companies are central to a sector of industry which specialises in manufacturing commodities at the most inflated cost which they believe the target market can sustain – not only do they maximise profit margins, they boost costs at every stage of the process from research, through development and production to after-sales customer support. Such companies are institutionally incapable of producing detection technology which could be afforded by mine-damaged communities or NGOs and, in fact, these would not be seen as target customers for any product which might be developed – they are simply on a different economic level. The aim would be to produce a detector with a unit cost at least ten times higher than the existing equipment – say in the $35,000 bracket – and sell it direct to donors. In practice this would probably restrict sales to the European Commission and, of course, the military. Any restrictions placed on military sales as a result of the initial research and development costs coming from funds earmarked for development and humanitarian projects could be side-stepped by using 'peace-keeping', 'humanitarian intervention' and similar terminology to justify sales to the military.

The second argument, which tends to counter the first to some extent, is that the arms companies involved in such humanitarian-based projects are not really interested in developing any new detection technology. They are simply grateful that bureaucracies like the European Commission are financially underwriting one or more of their research departments. It is perhaps no coincidence that some of the most popular areas of research in relation to landmine detection, such as thermal imagery, have considerable and, it could be argued, far greater, military potential. There would be no way that a donor could know that the funds allocated for developing new mine detection technology, probably without success, actually paid for the development of new, perhaps lethal, military hardware.

I have resisted the temptation to include the argument that companies who have profited once from the sales of the landmines and ordnance which now blight our world should not be allowed to profit a second time from the process of clearance. This is an argument based on morality – you either agree or you don't.

Arms manufacturers have been widely involved in the development of heavy mechanised clearance machines – often no more than converted battle tanks. In post-Cold War Europe there is a much reduced demand for tanks and many existing stocks are being destroyed or decommissioned into storage; the sudden discovery of new clearance technologies based on battle tank chassis should therefore be treated with some caution and healthy scepticism by everyone involved. It hardly seems credible, for instance, that anyone who understands the nature of rural mine clearance and the climate and terrain of Cambodia should consider shipping a clearance machine based on a heavy battle tank chassis to that country. But they did. Even if the machine had worked it seems unlikely that it could operate without causing great harm to the environment, to say nothing of irrigation systems, paddy, bridges and roads. Happily the project was a failure and the Khmer people have been spared the ravages of this mad Swedish project – although the funds expended were, of course, not available for use in other, engineering- rather than profit-based, mine-clearance initiatives. That is simply one example among many – and more are being developed, often by arms manufacturers.

This very negative view may be dismissed as the ravings of a Luddite – that would be a mistake. I fought hard, and eventually successfully, to introduce mine flails into the Afghan clearance programme and, although the use of those flails has not been trouble-free, they do have a utility on the fringes of clearance operations, but they are a small part of the solution. It is worth commenting that flails are being used for minefield reduction in Angola, especially in areas where the probability of a high density of mines is low, it is possible that this approach may prove itself and increase the use of flails in widescale operations in the future.

By far the greatest need for mechanisation is to reduce risk to manual clearance teams in specific operational situations. The two most common scenarios are where thick vegetation or jungle has overgrown a minefield and, in urban areas, where collapsed buildings contain unexploded ordnance. The solution in both cases, particularly the former, probably lies in the adaptation of existing machinery such as backhoes. It is interesting that none of the arms companies, despite their much-vaunted commitment to developing mine-clearance technology, have shown interest in this low-cost type of response. Perhaps because it is also low profit? Most of the work has been carried out on an *ad hoc* basis by NGOs operational in the field, although some good work has been done in this and other areas by university-based research in the UK.

Dogs

Dogs which are trained to recognise the scent given off by certain explosives have been an integral part of humanitarian mine programmes from the very beginning. However, a short-sighted and inexplicable policy decision was made by the United Nations Office of the Coordinator for Afghanistan (UNOCA), that, due to a belief that animals should not be placed at risk for the benefit of humans, no UNOCA funding would be allocated to integrate US-trained dogs and handlers into the Afghan mine-clearance programme. This decision was not simply a grave misjudgement, it was grounded in inexcusable ignorance – the dogs were not placed in any grave risk by their detection role, being carried by humans in vehicles was, in fact, the greatest peril in which the animals were placed,[3] along with the risk of disease. Eventually the engineers involved on the ground in Afghanistan resolved the problem through informal arrangements between the US dog programme contractors, Ronco, and the Afghan NGOs involved in the UNOCA-sponsored programme whereby they 'coincidentally' worked and, therefore, coordinated their activities in the same locations. But the damage was not undone by this pragmatic field approach – the failure of UNOCA to fund and give visibility to the contribution of the dog teams considerably delayed the wider acceptance of a technique which has since proven itself of great value in many countries.

As with mechanised clearance technologies, dogs are not a replacement for manual demining; they are, however, a hugely valuable asset within any programme. Most of the original concerns about their cultural acceptability in countries where dogs are not tra-ditionally kept as pets and may be seen as unclean animals seem to have proved unfounded. A comprehensive report on the use of dogs in mine-clearance operations concluded, referring to their use in Afghanistan:

Conventionally, the Muslim faith dose not give dogs respect or status. Generally humans do not have relationships with dogs and, while they are sometimes kept as guard dogs, they are generally neglected and despised in Afghan and Pakistani society. This has also been an issue in Africa and Asia. In 1989, when the dog program began, many considered this to be an impossible barrier to its success. It was hard for Ronco to initially persuade Mujahideen leaders to contribute men to the programme. The results of the MDC [Mine Dog Centre] program, the level of commitment of the trainers and the visible bonding that exists between dog and handler illustrates that MDC has overcome whatever barriers that existed. Some operators may still talk about the difference between their 'professional' attitude to dogs and their private feeling (which may remain negative), but many others speak of the great love and friendship they have for their dogs, and how the relationship has to be built on mutual trust for survival in the minefield.

There clearly are cultural differences in relation to the acceptance of working with a dog, but the Afghanistan example appears to illustrate that they can be overcome, even if most MDC staff would still not consider having a dog simply as a pet. They are respected as working dogs.[4]

Dogs have proved most effective in well-defined operational situations where they can work more quickly than normal clearance teams, such as road and track sections containing widely spaced mines, areas with exceptionally high levels of extraneous metal fragments, and as a method of conducting minefield reduction operations. It is, however, important to recognise the nature and limitation of the dog team's involvement – the animals are, in effect, a detection tool, they cannot expose or destroy the devices they scent. Therefore dog teams are supported by a manual clearance element who respond to each mine indicated by the dog. Of course, in ground which is heavily contaminated by metal, such as battlefield impact areas which are slow to clear by normal means due to the high level of shrapnel, each piece of which will be detected by a normal detector, work can be speeded up dramatically because the dog detects explosive rather than metal.

There are limitations on a dog's ability to operate although, in good conditions, most dogs can work between four and six hours per day. Wind is a key factor – dogs work best in a low, steady breeze, while higher velocity and gusting winds will decrease the animal's ability to indicate the location of a mine. Disturbed ground following mechanised clearance can also prove a problem although, if dogs are to be used in a checking role following mechanised clearance, they can be trained to operate effectively in such an environment. One of the greatest positive factors about dogs is their ability to operate in areas which are difficult and possibly dangerous for humans – this is especially true on steep inclines where the difficulty in maintaining a regular sweep with the detector and the danger of deminers losing their balance places teams at great risk and makes 100 per cent detection assurance uncertain. The Horwood report quoted from above notes that resistance to the use of dogs and mistrust of their ability is most common among engineers who have not worked in operations including dog teams. However, the majority of those who have experience in such programmes tend to have great confidence in the abilities and utility of dog teams. It is my own experience that the animals are effective and, importantly, their integration into a national programme can be sustainable, but a tendency to exaggerate their contribution within the overall landmine response sector does nothing to promote an increase in their use.

MINEFIELD REDUCTION

Also sometimes referred to as 'area reduction' this technique, developed over the past seven or eight years, falls between the completion of Level Two survey and the subsequent marking and clearance of minefields. Different country programmes and organisations tend to define the process somewhat differently but, in general, the concept is based on two operational objectives:

1   To exclude from within the perimeter of a surveyed minefield those areas with no mines or very few mines.
2   To clear of mines those sections of a surveyed minefield which are of immediate and urgent importance to the community, leaving the rest of the minefield for later clearance.

The evolution of minefield reduction is interesting and important because its roots lie entirely in humanitarian-based demining and there is no equivalent military engineering technique. In essence this is demining growing as a branch of development engineering, taking on the challenges which face post-conflict communities and coming up with practical field solutions.

Similarly to other prioritisation considerations, reduction is most effective when there is a good understanding of community needs matched with a good overview of the funds and resources available for demining in the immediate and medium future. In this way it is possible to determine how minefield reduction can best be used to release valuable land for immediate use while other areas are clearly marked to reduce the level of risk for the community during the period – which in some cases may be measured in years – it is awaiting full clearance of the land.

The benefits of minefield reduction are most often referred to in terms of its micro-impact but, logically, its macro-effect is substantial and should be influencing national planning and prioritisation in countries where the technique is well developed. Since reduction is most effectively carried out at the same time as, or soon after, Level Two survey it becomes, quite naturally, part of the global picture which emerges as survey progresses. This is valuable national planning data, first because of the natural separation between communities which have benefited from reduction and those which have not – there are obvious implications for short- and medium-term prioritisation in such information. Second, the negotiations with local communities in order to agree areas where reduction is most urgent provides a valuable insight for planners into grassroots priorities which often differ substantially from those expressed by central government and from the perceptions of development and economic advisers.

It must be emphasised that minefield reduction without a fully developed marking programme is of limited value and, in some circumstances, may increase the risk to the community by encouraging confidence in safe areas which border closely on uncleared minefields which have not been marked or are inadequately demarcated.

MINEFIELD MARKING

It is worth re-examining for a moment the reasons for widescale landmine clearance. The *only* reasons that landmines and their eradication are of interest for humanitarian, developmental and economic purposes is as a consequence of their threat to non-combatants during and following conflict and because of their wide postwar impact. Landmines in themselves have no intrinsic interest other than for the military and the arms trade.

Given that fact, it follows that clearing mines is never, in itself, a priority. There must be a justification based on the impact of the mines and the response should be measured and designed to resolve the problem rather than its cause. There are three areas of response now generally accepted as of direct assistance to the community:

- mine clearance
- mine awareness
- minefield marking.

I have placed the three responses in the order they are normally seen, although minefield marking is often omitted. Not only is this perception of response priorities illogical, it is so obviously wrong that it is hard to imagine how anyone could find it credible. I will deal with mine awareness in detail separately; however, the comparative value of each response should be examined here.

- Mine clearance is the ideal response. It removes all risk to human life and livestock and releases land for normal use by the community. All obstacles to other sectors of post-conflict rehabilitation and development are removed. The quality of response is fully verifiable through resurvey.
- Community awareness has no impact on the physical risk present, although members of the community can be encouraged to adopt safer practices to avoid risk. Children can be effectively taught to avoid risk areas and unsafe practices. There is no reduction of risk to livestock and no land is returned for use by the community. Community awareness impact is largely unverifiable.
- Minefield marking has a direct impact in reducing risk to the community by making risk areas clearly visible. Danger to livestock can be indirectly effective because herders can clearly identify risk areas – when marked areas are fenced livestock risk may be removed entirely or reduced substantially. When used in conjunction with minefield reduction techniques marking can return valuable land for immediate use and increase community confidence in demarcation areas

between safe and mined land. Minefield marking and its
impact is fully verifiable.

Common sense would, therefore, indicate that minefield marking
should follow mine clearance on a list of priority response. This is
not only not the case but many donors and agencies simply do not
recognise minefield marking as a valid response at all.

What is minefield marking? There is a tendency to visualise First
World War scenarios with barbed wire strung between angle-iron
uprights. It is certainly a fine thought, but unfortunately only
military funding stretches to such comprehensive marking – saving
lives in peacetime attracts less lucrative budgets. What counts in
marking is that the community recognise the perimeter of a
minefield and understand the consequences of crossing the markers.
In Afghanistan and some other countries markers can be as simple
as red and white stones – red is the danger side, white the safe side;
simple and very effective. In other countries painted wooden or
metal poles are used although, while perhaps more easily visible than
coloured stones, any kind of marking with an intrinsic value may be
a problem. Wood has value beyond the understanding of anyone
who has lived life in the world of central heating and gas cookers –
wood is warmth in the winter, wood is fuel on which to cook. It
would seem an exaggeration to say that wood is life, but to a
displaced family living in a rotting railway wagon in Angola, for
instance, wood is just that – life. In such circumstances there is a
need for considerable thought and community consultation before
choosing marking materials.

Level Two survey provides all the information required for
accurate marking – this can be refined and reduced through
minefield reduction, the ideal scenario would be where the three
operations work in close coordination. In programmes where this
happens minefields are neutralised very effectively, although it may
be a considerable time before they are actually cleared.

BATTLE AREA CLEARANCE

Bombs, mortars and shells are not laid in predetermined areas or
patterns. Although they are fired at targets or into areas which have
a relevance in combat, a relevance which may last only for hours on
a single day, if they fail to explode as designed their presence in

peacetime is random and indiscriminate. The generic term, unexploded ordnance or UXO, refers to any explosive projectile, designed to explode after deployment, which fails to detonate. Failure rates, especially from aerial bombardment, can be extremely high and whereas mines are usually laid in some discernible pattern or within a definable area, UXO may be scattered randomly over huge areas. As mentioned earlier, Laos is probably the most horrific example of widescale UXO contamination – the result of a nine-year bombing campaign by the United States during the Vietnam War – but any country which has experienced war this century has suffered from UXO. From a purely technical standpoint the major problems facing clearance agencies are the wide range of munitions involved and the problems involved in safely transporting UXO to demolition sites. The threat to the community is, for the most part, different than that associated with landmines, although some UXO, primarily the submunitions from cluster bombs, can be considered *de facto* landmines which will explode on contact with a person or vehicle. With that exception the threat from UXO is greatest when items of ordnance are moved or, most commonly, attempts are made to salvage ordnance or component parts for its scrap value. The latter is another example of how economies damaged by conflict result in the poorest communities taking extraordinary risks to raise pitiful amounts of money. Two common, and horrendously dangerous, practices are the removal of copper driving bands from shells, a task often carried out by children using hammer and chisel, and salvaging aluminium fuses from bombs and shells.

Because of the wide dissemination of UXO structured survey is a difficult and, in some areas, impossibly random task in that it would require a search over a whole landscape with no guarantee that UXO existed on the surface or at an easily detectable depth. In such situations, where contamination is light, response must be realistically confined to actual incident or sighting reports of UXO. However, some obviously contaminated areas will exist which may be surveyed in the manner prescribed, for instance, by the MCPA in Kabul. The approach adopted by the MCPA for urban Battle area clearance (BAC) survey is based on 400 × 400-metre battle area clearance blocks (BAC Blocks). The following extract from the MCPA standing operational procedures for BAC survey[5] is self-explanatory and a useful guide:

3 *Aim*

The aim of BAC survey is to:

a Identify, mark and map areas highly likely to contain large numbers of UXO

and

b Discriminate between areas containing UXO only and those that are likely to contain sub-surface mines and booby traps.

[...]

5 *Task Sequence*

The task sequence remains flexible and is the choice of the survey team leader, the following is provided as a guide only:

a Before commencing any physical check gain as much information from local people/authorities as possible about the battle area. The main aim of this research is to determine the likelihood of buried mines.

b Develop a survey plan based on a map study.

c Establish and check/clear the boundary of the target area.

d Clear/check all access routes (ie: streets/roads/tracks/paths) within the target BAC Block using the survey team dog set.

e Mark and record all items of UXO found.

f Mark and Survey Blocks

g Prepare a map of the area.

h Prepare a Task Briefing.

i Hand over task to demining agency.

[...]

9 *Action on Location of mines*

In case of a location of a mine the survey team is to:

a Destroy the mine.

b Record the location of the device.

c Advise the Supervisor of MCPA Kabul.

d Reduce the area of the BAC Block to that area highly unlikely to contain mines.

e MCPA (normal team) to carry out survey to establish extent of the minefield.

[...]

11 *Marking*
BAC Blocks are to be marked as follows:

a   Start Point:
(1) The task Start Point is to be marked with a yellow disc/spot of 1000mm diameter. The marker should be painted on a wall at between 1 metre and 1.5 metres above ground level.
(2) The BAC Task Number is to be painted above the Start Point marker.
(3) The letters 'SP' are to be painted below the Start Point marker. For example:

BAC No. 001

SP

This marker indicates the Start Point of BAC task number 001.
b   Turning Points:
(1) Task Turning Points are to be marked with a yellow inverted triangle. The triangle is to be 100mm high.
(2) The Turning Point number is to be painted below the triangle. For example:

▼
TP1

c   Boundary:
(1) The boundary of a BAC Task will be marked with a yellow dash. The dash is to be 100mm in length.
(2) Dashes are to be painted along the distance between Turning Points every three metres.
d   Checked Areas:
All checked/cleared areas in the BAC task are to be painted with white tick marks as – '✓'.

12 *Mapping*
BAC Maps are to:
a   Be produced to a scale of no greater than 1:5000.
b   They are to indicate:
(1) The boundary of the task.
(2) The internal access routes cleared during survey.
(3) Any areas cleared/checked during the survey process.
(4) Information regarding adjacent areas in minefield, cleared land, future BAC task, unknown etc.
(5) Task area

(6) Local name for area.
(7) Boundary street names.
(8) Survey start and complete date.
(9) Survey team number.

Surveying and clearing ordnance over large rural expanses of countryside is, however, more difficult and less certain. It is normal to classify a given area of land according to an estimate of the density of UXO present arrived at by a visual and instrument sample check. The density classification generally accepted is as follows.

Very light	1–5	UXO per hectare
Light	6–12	UXO per hectare
Normal	13–49	UXO per hectare
Heavy	50–125	UXO per hectare
Very heavy		Over 125 UXO per hectare

Three types of search are used in order to find UXO:

1 *Visual*: This type of search seeks to locate UXO items above the ground or partly exposed. Since even those items of ordnance are likely to be overgrown this kind of search becomes less effective as time passes. However, an experienced team which has learned to recognise the profile of different UXO found in the region will normally locate a high percentage of items missed by less experienced teams and the local community.

2 *Shallow instrument search*: This search is conducted in a similar manner to normal mine clearance operations and employs a standard mine detector.

3 *Deep instrument search*: This search technique is conducted using a specialised search instrument known as a locator, which is capable of detecting ordnance at considerable depths. A deep search is always preceded by a shallow search.

Ordnance eradication: The disposal of large items of UXO such as bombs and missiles is a specialist task and cannot be carried out by mine-clearance teams. In countries where UXO is a widescale problem the training of specialist local teams must be considered and is recommended. Shells, mortars and other projectiles may be dealt with by mine-clearance personnel following suitable training.

Technique Summary

The most common search pattern employed is based on a 50-metre 'block' or 'square' sectioned into 1-metre search lanes. A number of adjacent blocks will be established (a block is normally allocated an identifying letter and each lane within the block is allocated a number), normally with one team working. Each detector or locator operator is accompanied by a second team member whose responsibility is to expose each item detected. Each UXO is classified either 'safe to move' or 'not safe to move'. The latter items are marked and destroyed *in situ* at the end of each working day. UXO classified as safe to move is removed to a predesignated demolition area for destruction. Obviously the safety distances involved when destroying large items of ordnance are considerably greater than for the demolition of landmines and demolition *in situ* may involve evacuation of nearby dwellings and protection of structures from blast effects. It is sometimes possible to disrupt the fuse mechanism of a bomb avoiding the need to detonate the high explosive filling.

There may occur situations where there is no perfect solution. For instance, a large bomb in a village where an *in situ* detonation would destroy or severely damage the village but where removing or defusing the bomb is unsafe and may result in the same damage with additional loss of life – a situation which has arisen in both Laos and North Iraq. In such circumstances the community must have the situation and the dangers explained to them and be left to make a decision whether they continue to live with the bomb in their midst or to opt for demolition with the attendant damage. In a small rural hamlet it may be possible to find a source of relocation funding if the residents are willing to consider that option.

QUALITY ASSURANCE

In 1990 when we finished the first ever UN-sponsored humanitarian mine-clearance task – a section of road on the route from the Nawa Pass to Chagaserai Bridge in Kunar Province of Afghanistan – we called together the *shura* and other representatives of the community from Chagaserai to tell them that the road was now cleared for use. They expressed their thanks but, when we asked them to join us in a walk up the road, they refused. Disappointing it may have been but it was hardly surprising – though the people of the town had watched our progress with interest they had no way of judging our proficiency and were quite sensibly in no rush to test it with their lives. It was a critical test, and the deminers were equally understandably disillusioned at this lack of trust and felt that there was little point continuing to clear Afghan minefields if no one had sufficient confidence in us to use the land when work was completed. I climbed into a project vehicle, drove it to the start point and then through the cleared section, swerving from side to side. When I reached the end of the section the demining team climbed into the back of the vehicle and we repeated the drive several times until, eventually, some members of the *shura* joined us. The road has been in use ever since. Question: was I foolhardy? To the layperson perhaps it may seem so, but had I chosen not to *prove* the road my position would have been, in my view, untenable on two counts. First, I was asking the local community to use the road. How could I do that with any conscience if I lacked the trust in our work to use it myself? Second, the team deserved my support and confidence at a time when the quality of their work was being questioned. There may never be a 100 per cent guarantee that every single mine has been located and destroyed in any given area of land, but if there is doubt based on something more than that statistic alone the land should not be released for use by the community. There is a great difference between saying 'one can never be absolutely certain' and 'in this case I am not certain'.

In Afghanistan the practice has continued – each completed minefield is handed over to the community only after the demining team has demonstrated its own confidence in its work by walking the minefield as the people who will use the area watch. The newly cleared land is then signed over to representatives of the community. This is quality assurance by the people who matter, the people for whom the whole international response to landmines is designed to assist – those who are deprived of their land and their right, in the words of the Universal Declaration of Human Rights, to 'security of person'.

However, it is not always in this context that the term 'quality assurance' is used – it is common, I suspect more so, to hear it employed to describe a method of assuring the donor that the work has been completed satisfactorily. My own view is quite clear on this point – if the community are satisfied with the quality of clearance and are willing to back their trust with their lives why then should the donor be less confident or need further assurance? But the truth is that, all too often, the community's opinion is not even a consideration; in fact the position is effectively reversed – if the donor is satisfied why should the community need any further assurance? The answer should be obvious. There is no correlation between a donor's satisfaction that funds have been expended in line with contractual agreements and, for instance, a parent's confidence that their child can safely play on the land in question. A studied response from most donors would be that they wish to ensure that the operation they have funded has provided safe land for the community. A more honest answer would be that quality assurance is commonly an institutional process seeking no more than confirmation that contractual agreements have been observed by the implementing agency.

In fact, quality assurance only became an issue for donors to humanitarian projects when commercial companies became involved. Those companies were possibly more anxious to define a point at which their responsibility for clearance ended in contractual terms. What, for instance, would be their legal position if a person or persons were blown up on a road after they had cleared it? Would they be legally liable? Would the donor seek the return of all or part of the funding on the basis that the company had failed to meet its contractual commitments? The commercial contractor had a different view to NGOs because, while the latter saw their prime commitment as being to the beneficiary community, the former, understandably, viewed the contract with the donor as the paramount consideration. The UN response was extraordinary and damaging – an arbitrary decision was made and it was announced that the United Nations saw 99.6 per cent as 'acceptable clearance'. I say damaging because this statement undermined the widely accepted principle that only 100 per cent clearance could ever be seen as 'acceptable', while recognising that many factors might lead to less than that being achieved in practice. However, the steadily improving team skills which have emerged in the past decade, the use of high-quality mine detectors and the introduction of dogs in certain situations make it probable that most clearance by responsible agencies is total. The 99.6 per cent figure was introduced to resolve a contractual obstacle for commercial companies and offers no benefit to mine-affected communities – it is not for UN employees or advisers to afford commercial pragmatism precedence over the interests of the poor and disenfranchised who make up the greatest proportion of those affected by the presence of landmines.

I have often wondered if the UN expert who came up with the 99.6 per cent figure ever bothered to consult, for instance, parents of children who must walk to school in mined areas for their opinion of an 'acceptable' clearance rate of less than 100 per cent. While it is certain they would recognise the difficulty of achieving total clearance, I strongly doubt they would have approved *aiming* for less.

By arguing against quality assurance as it is widely perceived at present I do not deny that any donor has the right, indeed the duty, to ensure that funds are correctly and effectively expended. However, when viewing the implementation of mine-clearance operations the beneficiary community's satisfaction (or, of course, otherwise) should be given due weight in arriving at conclusions. In all humanitarian mine-eradication operations the prime consideration should be the contract – written, verbal or assumed – with the community. Where that contract is satisfactorily met the legal contract between donor and implementer should, in all practical engineering terms, be met also.

ACCIDENTS – BEING PREPARED

There will always be situations where the very highest standards of evacuation and medical support will not be available to mine and UXO clearance teams. That fact is hardly surprising and the reason is clearly apparent – war destroys all sectors of infrastructure and places surgical and medical facilities under a greater strain than most. It is a paradox that most armies in battle have a level of evacuation, surgical and medical support that is rarely, if ever, available to civilians in peacetime. An additional factor is that minefields are often in comparatively remote areas and, in some cases, such as some parts of Angola for instance, seriously injured casualties may only be evacuated by aircraft and surgical assistance may be several hours from the site of the accident. However, the aim should always be to make the best level of support available as close to the minefield as possible.

Advanced first aid, preferably from a doctor, but at least from well-trained and regularly practised and tested paramedics, should always be available on site whenever anyone is working in a risk area. It may not always be possible to have an ambulance at every minefield, although that is the ideal situation, but an ambulance should be available within a reasonable distance of each minefield.

Evacuation drills will vary depending on the local situation but they must be written and understood by everyone involved. They must also be practical and should be practised regularly – key people and their responsibilities must be well defined. One of the most important factors in preparing for the evacuation and reception of seriously injured casualties is ensuring that key personnel can be contacted – in most cases these should include lists of out-of-working-hours contact details and, wherever possible, contact should be via dedicated emergency means such as portable radio or telephone.

The lives of even very seriously injured casualties can be saved by prompt and well-planned action in the period immediately following an incident. However, minefields are high-risk areas and mistakes or failure to observe drills can easily lead to further accidents. The immediate response must be understood by everyone involved – the following are the key actions which must be taken in every case.

Immediate minefield drills following an accident

Accident in a Cleared Area

1   All work stops immediately – the senior person present takes charge.
2   All deminers leave the minefield by safe routes and return to the designated rest area.
3   A full roll call is made of all personnel and visitors.
4   Two deminers are nominated as stretcher bearers.
5   An experienced and senior deminer is nominated rescue team leader and approaches the casualty via a known safe route followed by stretcher bearers, marking the route as they advance.
6   The doctor/medic must not enter the minefield.
7   The rescue team leader approaches the casualty alone and checks for mines around the casualty. Only a sufficient space should be checked on the far, uncleared side of the casualty to allow safe evacuation.
8   As soon as the area is checked the casualty is evacuated to a pre-determined safe area by the stretcher party guided by the rescue team leader along the marked route used to enter the minefield.

9   The casualty is then examined and given first aid by the doctor or medic before immediate evacuation begins.

10   Assuming serious injuries the casualty should be accompanied by two personnel of the same or compatible blood group to the nearest medical facility capable of dealing with the casualty's injuries.

11   Wherever possible direct communications should be established with the hospital to which the casualty is being evacuated, especially if an extended evacuation distance/time is involved.

12   Once the casualty is evacuated the accident site and approaches to it are sealed off. All witnesses are interviewed and make written statements. This process should not be delayed – witnesses should be reminded that accurate information is sought primarily to avoid further accidents and to learn from any mistakes made.

Accident in an Uncleared Area

The following is the basic procedure for rescuing a casualty who has strayed into an uncleared area, not necessarily as a result of clearance operations.

1   The senior deminer present details a two-member extraction team, equipped as for normal detector search, to clear a safe lane to the casualty from a known safe area.

2   The team maintains an increased safety distance of 20 metres.

3   Working with the detector set to the highest sensitivity the operator must not take risks in order to speed access to the casualty.

4   Each detector contact is marked 150 millimetres in front of the contact location but not investigated; the operator changes direction at each contact and continues work.

5   Consideration should be given to the best route to the casualty, which may not always be the shortest distance. Areas of thick vegetation and obviously suspect areas should be avoided.

6   If electronic search is not possible hand clearance should be undertaken using the shortest distance to the casualty. Wherever a mine is located it should be neutralised or disarmed if possible.

7   Where the mine cannot be disarmed or neutralised the lane should be closed and marked at that location 0.5 metres in front of the neutralised/disarmed mine. The deminer then changes direction and continues clearance.
8   When the casualty is reached a 2-metre safe working area is cleared and marked.
9   If the casualty is conscious and moving he or she is removed by stretcher along the cleared lane.
10 If the casualty is unconscious or dead a rope should be attached to him or her and the team then retire to at least 50 metres, from where the rope is pulled sufficiently to move the casualty several feet. This action will expose or disturb any mines or devices which may threaten the lives of the rescuers during the casualty extraction.

Planning

The key to all lifesaving response is not simply, as is often claimed, good planning. The key factors are ensuring that everyone involved is aware of the plan and that the plan is regularly practised and tested. Practise and test serve a similar purpose but are separate and essential elements in ensuring that response in the case of a demining accident or when a team is called to help rescue a member of the local community.

- Practise is a planned exercise where everyone is aware in advance that training is to take place. Realism should not be abandoned but instructors may offer advice or criticism while the exercise is in progress.
- Testing should be unannounced and as realistic as possible. The test should not be interrupted but a full debrief must follow and retesting take place wherever necessary.

INSURANCE FOR DEMINING OPERATIONS

A man or woman who goes to work every day in minefields deserves the protection of a good insurance policy. This should be taken into account by donors when allocating funds for mine-action programmes. But where do you go to insure yourself if your job involves being nose-to-nose with primed explosives designed to kill anyone who disturbs them? Obviously a specialist insurer, but an organisation which may employ hundreds of mine-clearance engineers needs to know what level and kind of insurance they need before deciding who will provide cover.

Imagine the worst case: a vehicle loaded with cleared UXO is being moved to the demolition area when it is involved in an accident and explodes. Staff are killed, others lose limbs and local buildings are damaged. The probable insurance implications are:

- compensation for death and loss of earnings to families of those killed
- funeral costs
- evacuation, treatment, loss of earnings compensation and ongoing medical costs for injured staff
- third party liability for damage to buildings
- replacement of truck and equipment lost in explosion.

It is no time to discover that insurance is inadequate after such an accident. Apart from the moral and legal issues involved the implications of having inadequate or inappropriate cover at such a time could destroy the organisation's ability to continue its work.

It is imperative to have a comprehensive understanding of the legal insurance requirements of the operational country. Where, as is sometimes the case in post-conflict situations, there is no governmental or legal structure in place the pre-conflict legislation should be assumed to still apply.

The most likely insurers, given the potential for loss, are a Lloyds syndicate and that can mean that there is very little direct contact between the insured and the insurer since the policy will be arranged through a broker. The best advice is as follows:

- ensure that the broker understands fully the nature of operations being undertaken
- take advice from different sources and have any policy proposal checked independently before acceptance
- arrange to meet members or representatives of the insuring syndicate if possible to ensure that they understand the humanitarian nature of the work being undertaken.

Although policies with host-country companies may be the most convenient way of insuring local staff it is important to check that cover is adequate and will provide, for instance, for the possible need to evacuate local staff to a third country for treatment. It is certainly worth examining the comparative costs and benefits of insuring all staff, local and expatriate, with the same insurer.

Care should be taken when organisations work, or individuals travel in, mined areas who are not covered by the kind of policy covering demining staff. At least one US-based insurance company has argued that injury sustained as a result of a landmine explosion some time after the end of hostilities, although the device was probably buried some years before the accident, invokes the war exclusion clause and that the insurance was invalid. This case was settled out of court and so the arguments remained legally untested. It is probably best that any individual travelling in a mined area looks for specific cover for that risk.

4.2
Sustainable Management Structures for National Demining Programmes

There is no single formula which can be recommended as the model management structure for the fairly obvious reason that each national situation is exclusive and what works in country A is unlikely to have more than a general relevance to the situation existing in country B. This is not to say that transferable lessons cannot be learned and used, nor that a growing number of successfully managed national programmes will not build a body of experience that will make the introduction of new programmes a more exacting process. However, neither the United Nations, international donor agencies nor involved national governments have, to date, shown any great capacity to learn from either positive or negative lessons from the recent past. But the damaging failure of each of those controlling entities in instances such as Angola and Cambodia could have been avoided had some basic ground rules been observed.

CONTRASTING APPROACHES

The primary responsibility for the establishment of a national demining programme is vested in the relevant government. The government may also, and would almost certainly wish to, retain a veto over any structure established by the UN or other international body and may disallow all or part of what it perceives to be an inappropriate intervention. But the fact is that most governments in the immediate post-conflict period or with a continuing war or internal insecurity situation to deal with have, rightly or wrongly, far greater priorities and may choose to maintain a virtually *hands-off* stance. In situations such as existed in 1989 in Afghanistan there may be no government or effective administration but a need to respond on a wide scale. Both scenarios impose a huge burden of responsibility on the organisation and individuals setting up and implementing the national programme who, in effect, take on a governmental role. However, there are undoubted logistical advantages to such a situation, where the inevitable bureaucracy which comes with the involvement of even the most motivated and enlightened government department is absent and where, if the opportunity is taken, engineering considerations can be given priority. But despite the fact that a response with no governmental involvement may, as in the case of Afghanistan, offer advantages, these are not factors exclusive to such programmes. It is worth recognising that the failure of operations in situations such as Angola and Cambodia have not been a result of government involvement, but the direct consequence of the involvement of inappropriate staff in ill-conceived organisational structures.

Two principles should be central to whatever response structure emerges, regardless of the players and whether government is involved or otherwise: operational effectiveness and sustainability. It is, in reality, the observance of those two key principles which have made the Afghan programme successful, against all the odds, rather than simply the lack of government involvement. That this is an operational approach which transcends the organisational detail is illustrated by the development of the national programme in Laos. The initial engineering response to possibly the greatest single UXO infestation anywhere in the world was a joint response by two NGOs, the Mennonite Central Committee (MCC) and the MAG. The MCC had many years of experience in Laos and understood the often complex workings of the government, and the MAG had the technical and engineering skills to respond. But, unlike Afghanistan, not only was there a government in Laos but one which would insist on approving the relevance of, and having direct involvement in, any such initiative. There were operational and administrative difficulties to overcome and some involved staff were better at their job and more appropriate to the cultural situation than others, but these were the roots which grew into the present large-scale, government-administrated, UXO-eradication programme.

Some have suggested that the success in establishing the programme in Laos was actually a direct result of the non-involvement of the UN demining bureaucracy. But, while it is true that the UN had shamefully ignored the desperate situation which faced communities throughout the country and prevaricated on the issue of funding because Laos had a UXO rather than a landmine problem, that perception is a not-to-be-missed political statement rather than a serious prognosis. The reasons for the credibility and effectiveness of the programme in Laos can be matched to those also central to the success of the Afghan programme, thus:

- the existence of a working document based on specific humanitarian and engineering needs and objectives
- the involvement from day one of appropriately qualified and experienced engineering personnel
- a commitment to sustainability in defined terms.

There has also, it must be said, to exist the ability of all sides to speak openly and, where necessary, disagree to the point of argument without the mealy-mouthed political game-playing which blights diplomatic and political circles. This is an area where the UN consistently fails to succeed: confrontational honesty. (I refer here only to mine-related programmes, but feel sure that this institutional weakness blights all aspects of the UN role.) This form of dishonesty breeds mistrust and, since it is endemic in most government bureaucracies as well, can be considered the greatest reason for the failure of so many national demining programmes to achieve or, in some cases, even adequately define, their goals. So, what is confrontational honesty?

SOME RELEVANT PRACTICAL MANAGEMENT SKILLS

Confrontational honesty is a term I use to describe a basic management requirement which is often absent, or, more commonly, discouraged when establishing and implementing complex national response programmes. The principle is quite straightforward: any manager who identifies a weakness or failure within the project he or she is managing must be, and feel, obliged to address that problem openly with colleagues, whether they be of senior, junior or equal status within the organisational structure. This should be a natural systemic process without any real or implied threat to the career or credibility of the manager involved, and this kind of questioning should be happening constantly. I would look with great suspicion on any complex programme, especially within the context of a country emerging from years of conflict, which was not in a state of regular self-examination and revision. Having received report of a problem the management team should determine the following:

1   Is it a problem?
2   What caused the problem? Could it have been foreseen or identified sooner?
3   What are the full effects and implications?
4   Has there been a management failure? Who by?
5   How can causes and effects be rectified?
6   An action and review plan.

It is important to recognise that this should not be a rare or necessarily negative procedure. Project management is about programme development and that demands a learning and adjustment process – review should be ongoing and unremarkable. Very few problems begin as big problems, they start small and, unrecognised or unreported, they grow in effect and complexity. It is very rare that problems go unrecognised, that it is, however, common for them to go unreported or for reports not to be acted upon. This is especially a problem where an organisation discourages criticism on the basis that it undermines confidence in a programme – the United Nations is such an organisation and, because it discourages recognition of its small failures which then, inevitably, become big failures, it is almost constantly in a state of crisis and thus consistently fails to build credible programmes. It is a fact that few international donors would give any funds to the United Nations for specific response programmes were it not for the political pressures to do so.

But why *does* the UN manage its programmes so badly? One overriding reason is the belief in a culture which identifies *system failure* with failure *per se* – so, something is wrong with the system therefore someone must be to blame therefore the first response is denial followed by camouflage rather than rectification. At that stage, of course, the prophecy is self-fulfilling because rather than dealing with the problem the system responds instead to the report of the problem and, in covering the problem up, becomes guilty of the fault which it seeks to avoid, etc. The UN could, overnight, be reformed if its staff could be taught to recognise the fact that every crisis is constructed of a mass of unaddressed, largely mundane, day-to-day management problems. The UN Lessons Learned Unit, within the existing organisational context, is the equivalent of an airline cutting back on routine servicing of aircraft and concentrating on crash investigation. The temptation is to see the very fact that the unit actually exists as a solution in itself and point to publications such as the hard-hitting and critical study report *The Development of Indigenous Mine Action Capacities*[1] as a proof of response to system failure, when such reports are, in fact, only the first step: identification of programme problems. This institutional comfort with identifying failure and carrying on blithely in a virtually identical operational vein is well illustrated by the foreword to the above-mentioned report. Here was an internally commissioned study which even the blindest UN *aficionado* could not have considered to be any less than damning. Had the UN been a commercial operation those members of the senior management who had retained their jobs would have felt obliged to assure the shareholders and customers at least that operations were being urgently reviewed and revised. And yet the emergency relief coordinator, Yasushi Akashi, chose to see the report itself as part of a successful response to landmines and almost totally avoided mention of the negative nature of the content which followed his foreword; the strongest tones he adopted were in the opening and concluding paragraphs:

> This report captures many of the insights and lessons which have been learned in recent years. Its findings, and the experiences documented in the four country case studies, add to an expanding reservoir of knowledge on the true nature of the landmine problem and how it can be effectively addressed.
>
> [...]
>
> I welcome this important study. Its recommendations will help the UN to improve its performance in addressing this key humanitarian responsibility.

Hardly a *mea maxima culpa*: it would surely have been appropriate for the coordinator to recognise that there had been damaging failures and to dedicate the UN to an urgent revision aimed at ensuring that things changed for the better in the immediate future.

The rot goes deeper, however, because all too often donors do not wish to hear that problems exist within programmes they have funded and may actively discourage openness when they are made aware. NGOs become party to covering up failures in national programmes because they feel that criticism may adversely effect funding, a particularly unforgivable stance since NGO staff are commonly closest to the communities who suffer the real impact of such institutional dishonesty.

And what is it all about? In some cases it may be self-protectionism by inadequate, negligent or, in the extreme, corrupt staff. But most commonly the failure to adopt a system of confrontational honesty, where each weakness or failure in a project is reported and dealt with head-on and with absolute openness, is due to the belief that reversing a decision is a sign of weak management.

THE DECISION-MAKING PROCESS IN MANAGEMENT

The decision-making process is often portrayed as a matter of great complexity, perhaps because some management academics make a living out of training managers in the process and long courses pay better than short ones. My own working definition of the process could be paraphrased thus: 'Examine the facts – make a decision quickly. If it doesn't achieve your aim your second decision should be to change your first decision. Examine the facts and make another decision quickly.' Challenges to my formula are largely from those who believe that changing a decision shows weakness and, in my view rather oddly, management indecision. I cannot speak for management in industry, although I see no reason why it should be different, but in field-engineering terms this concept of management 'strength' is pure nonsense. A manager must be judged by his or her success in using available resources in the most effective way to complete the job in hand.

In the uncertain environment of a post-conflict society with the task of establishing a response to landmine and UXO infestation it is certain that managers at every level must be afforded leeway to test workable approaches, and revision of plans should be actively encouraged rather than viewed as signs of weak or indecisive management. It follows, however, that this concept of the reversibility of decisions must extend to such areas as key staff hirings (which has obvious implications for the length of probationary periods) and clearance prioritisation procedures. This is also an area where donors, most notably the European Commission, need to review their policies. While it is a proper procedure that funding to implementing agencies should be subject to contract there should be sufficient inbuilt flexibility within the contractual terms to allow for revision of an operation during the funding period.

Of course, the reality for expatriate managers with an overview responsibility for local management staff may be that they are faced with indigenous managers who are inappropriate, negligent or dishonest, not an easy subject to tackle in the age of political correctness (all too often an excuse for doing nothing in a difficult situation), but one that must be dealt with none the less. Accepting lesser standards from local staff than from expatriates is potentially insulting to the government and all indigenous staff since the inference must be that criticism of local staff would not be acceptable. The response should be based on the relevant guidelines, regardless of personalities involved:

- Has there been a management failure? Who by?
- How can causes and effects be rectified?

If rectifying the situation is diplomatically or otherwise impossible or difficult then another decision must be made because clearly the interaction between the local agencies involved and the expatriate managers, advisers, capacity-building staff or whatever role is being undertaken is, at best, inadequate. Inevitably that decision must involve a renegotiation of cooperative modalities between the local and expatriate elements involved in the programme based on an understanding that *everything is up for discussion*. There are many arguments, based largely on diplomatic niceties and northern concepts of cultural respect, which would recommend forcibly against such an approach, but the facts are clear and unavoidable, unless there is mutual honesty at all levels an effective large-scale engineering initiative is unlikely to succeed.

One phenomenon which I have personally experienced is that a bluntly honest approach in such circumstances is more likely to meet opposition from expatriate than from indigenous sources. I was once criticised in Afghanistan for openly disagreeing with a policy introduced by a senior Afghan manager on the grounds that it was 'culturally insensitive' to express my opinion. This viewpoint went largely unchallenged by expatriate staff while causing some bemusement among Afghan colleagues. Of course, anyone who had witnessed and understood the confrontational nature of a *jirgha* would recognise the ridiculous nature of the criticism.[2] The fact is that, however disagreeable such duties may prove, the consequences of not addressing them are likely to be seriously damaging and, in the context of a mine-action programme, may well cost innocent lives.

KEY STRUCTURAL CONSIDERATIONS

- While it has become widely accepted that humanitarian mine and UXO programmes are most effectively developed outside the military infrastructure this view may not meet with much official sympathy or support in a country emerging from conflict where the military are likely to maintain a dominant position within government circles. A good start is to lead by example and reduce to a minimum the number of foreign military personnel involved within the UN operational response. It is essential that potential civilian trainees are not discouraged from taking part in the programme because they feel intimidated or discomfited by what may be perceived as a military-biased programme.
- The transfer of skills as part of the indigenisation process should not be delayed. Every key expatriate post should have a suitably qualified local counterpart from as early in the programme life as practicable.
- Expatriate staff should not be the sole arbiters of when their local counterparts are ready to take over the prime role, the obvious danger being that the expatriate is asked to decide on his or her own redundancy and, perhaps unconsciously, may prolong the skills transfer process unnecessarily. Two possible approaches are, first, to emphasise the capacity-building role within the expatriate's job description and make the timely handover to the local counterpart a positive measure of success and therefore of future employment, and second to retain the expatriate manager in an advisory role for a period following handover.
- Military-style titles and terminology should be avoided since the most effective national programmes are likely to be integrated into the civil administration rather than the defence department at both national and regional level. The introduction of military phraseology may encourage the notion that post-conflict demining is, by its nature, a task for the

national defence department which may lead to confusion and, in the wake of conflict, understandable suspicion and mistrust.

- There is no reason to delay the recruitment of women and disabled trainees to the programme now that this is an accepted practice in a number of national programmes. It will be necessary to examine the cultural relevance of such decisions but this should not be seen as a solely negative investigation – opportunities to push the boundaries and recruit from ostracised, minority and disabled groups should be actively pursued.

PROFILE AND OVERSIGHT OF NATIONAL PROGRAMMES

It is worth keeping in mind what is hoped to be achieved by the establishment of a national demining programme or, the UN preferred title, mine action centre. The ultimate aim must be to eradicate all landmines and unexploded ordnance and, during the process, to take practical action to limit the direct and indirect impact of landmines and UXO on the community and, it should always be remembered, the economy. Those are not vague ambitions but concrete aims which can be achieved primarily through the implementation of a practical, responsive and carefully planned and targeted engineering process. I would argue that involvement should be limited to those who can contribute to those aims, practical people rather than political figures. However some programmes, most notably the Cambodian Mine Action Centre (CMAC), have involved both high-level national figures and politicians and non-technical senior management. The thinking behind this approach appears to be that this would encourage a high profile, and therefore priority, being afforded to mine clearance at government level. The strategy does not stand up well to close examination however, since the government was, in the case of Cambodia, offering nothing of substance to the programme and actually contributed to the national problem by allowing its forces to continue laying mines. In such circumstances a strong argument can be made for a low profile rather than the opposite. There is certainly no need for such a response centre to have a high-level board of governors – if a board is required at all it would be more relevant for its members to be drawn from a practical engineering or rural development background. It has already been explained that pressure to *get the mines out of the ground* is a major factor in encouraging national initiatives to forgo a logical engineering approach, to the eventual detriment of the programme. The introduction of extraneous political factors can only increase that risk. The involvement of high-profile individuals with nothing of direct relevance to offer the programme other than perhaps the doubtful and uncertain benefits of political influence, and who are certain to have external interests and perhaps political ambitions must be considered, at best, a totally unnecessary complication with few positive and innumerable negative implications.

The profile of a national mine/UXO response body must be task oriented with links to relevant development, medical and educational agencies. It must obviously have the necessary government approvals but there is no more need for the direct involvement of senior statespeople or individuals of similar status than would be the case with any international humanitarian response. In fact, it will be almost certainly to the detriment of the engineering process, the practical and urgent work of eradicating mines and UXO, for the body to develop a high political profile since this can offer no great benefit and will almost certainly attract attention from the wrong people for the wrong reasons. Inevitably funds will be expended on irrelevant social functions in the capital city and will encourage the involvement of non-specialist staff at international seminars and conferences. Over the past five or six years international conferences, seminars and workshops dedicated to the eradication of landmines and UXO can be placed in two categories: those which have been of no value or benefit to the international eradication process at all, and those which have incorporated a relevant and useful agenda. The former are simply a waste of valuable funding, the latter are all too often attended primarily by non-specialists who, if they contribute anything of value at all, can only offer field experience from second or third hand and who, by definition, can take nothing of value *back* into the field. There will always be a few field-qualified attendees – it sometimes seems invited only for credibility purposes in order to avoid just the accusations I seek to make here – but they will be greatly outnumbered by non-specialists. In this way the managers and engineers who do the job are distanced from the donors and policy makers and are replaced by an intermediate category of 'expert' who, to use a phrase often heard in this context, talk the talk but are unable to walk the talk. In other words, they have picked up an impressive technical vocabulary and a selection of anecdotes while having little or, more often, no real understanding of the technical realities, concerns and priorities which should be heard and addressed by international policy makers and donors. There is also, I am certain, a social element at work here, because this strata of quasi-experts *do* understand the etiquette of the international conference circuit whereas field managers and deminers may often appear clumsy and unimpressive in such surroundings – although perceptive observers may find such a lack of smoothness in presentation welcome when it is, none the less, underpinned by actual knowledge of the facts and perhaps a refreshing level of undiplomatic honesty. This damaging phenomena can best be reversed by international donors making it known that they prefer the bald truth from management and engineering staff rather than a second-hand version from professional conference goers. This will be a first step to good oversight of national programmes.

SUSTAINABILITY

It is essential to define the sustainable elements required in a successful national landmine- and UXO-eradication programme because some are not readily apparent. I believe that the key sustainable elements are as follows.

Organisational Sustainability

The national programme organisation must contain all the elements which will ensure the ability of each of its integral components to survive and operate effectively, in most cases, through the emergence of a post-conflict society which may include periods of unrest or further conflict. So, ideally, the programme must have governmental approval but be sufficiently independent from any specific political faction, which can best be achieved through a wide acceptance of the neutral nature of the programme. This will naturally preclude the involvement of personnel in key management roles who are identified strongly and exclusively with one faction. Where staff are drawn from the military they should be publicly released from their military obligations and, preferably, not wear uniform. It is too easy, in this regard, to confuse 'impossible' with 'difficult' and fail for lack of trying hard enough. In North Iraq the MAG gave a high priority to convincing the main Kurdish political/military parties that all locally recruited deminers should be excused from conscription to military service and be seen as neutral in all interparty conflicts. They succeeded and, with few exceptions, the agreement has been honoured through all the factional disturbances which the region has suffered since. What can be achieved by an NGO in negotiation with non-state actors should not be beyond the abilities of the UN working in partnership with established government. The programme should be seen not as an international imposition but as a humanitarian requirement and, therefore, the scale of the problem and the response process should be well disseminated and transparent. Most importantly the organisational plan should allow for a flexible but unquestioned integration of the response programme into the indigenous administration whenever that becomes possible without placing at risk the humanitarian priorities associated with the clearance of mines and UXO.

Structural Sustainability

The programme must be designed in response to the problems facing the country in question and the structure should reflect that rather than be based on any preconceived notions. For instance, a mines action centre may not always be a relevant or operationally sensible approach. The alternatives could range from the indigenous NGO structure of Afghanistan to, perhaps, largely autonomous mine action centres in different regions of a country. It is important that lessons are drawn from experiences in other countries, but it is a mistake to believe that a generic national mine-action pattern capable of being parachuted into new response areas can be identified. It is important to emphasise the fact that a final programme design cannot realistically precede a widescale situation assessment.

Manpower Sustainability

The sustainable nature of the national landmine- and UXO-eradication initiative depends, above all else, on the availability of trained demining engineers. It is not uncommon to hear this vital element of the programme referred to almost as if their contribution was peripheral to the 'important' work of the mine action centres or the educationalists designing new mine-awareness literature; unintentional though such inferences may be they are a symptom of a conceptual malaise. The men and women who detect and destroy landmines and UXO are not just the lifeblood of the programme, they are also the indigenous pool of growing expertise which will sustain it through its life. There must be an internal process of advancement for those engineers whose skill and expertise identifies them as potential trainers and managers. Planning based on Level Two survey will identify manpower requirements and ensure that the support elements required to maintain the workforce – especially adequate funding – are guaranteed in advance.

Sustainable Technology

Available detection and destruction technology covers a wide range of equipment but the key consideration must be to ensure that the whole operational scope existing in the country is capable of being addressed by the range of equipment procured. It is short-sighted, for instance, to invest a large proportion of available funds in mechanised equipment for road clearance which cannot be effectively deployed in rural minefields. A balance must be struck which addresses urgent national priorities without abandoning the localised, but equally vital, priorities of individual communities. Imported equipment should, wherever possible, be purchased subject to local service and repair agreements, buy-back of unserviceable equipment and bulk-procurement discounts.

9 Gardens can be minefields too. Urban warfare may leave complex problems for clearance teams. Bosnia. (John Rodsted)

10 Play is recognised as a vulnerable occupation in many communities. Angola. (Sean Sutton)

11 Minefield scene. Angola (Sean Sutton)

12 Minefield scene. Bosnia (John Rodsted)

13 Minefield scene. Bosnia (John Rodsted)

14 Minefield scene. Bosnia (John Rodsted)

15 Minefield scene. Angola (Sean Sutton)

16 War victims need support and equality of opportunity, not pity.
Afghanistan. (Sean Sutton)

17 Subsistence agriculturists are the most common victims of landmines. When safe land is scarce the boundaries between mine clearance and food production are often dramatically reduced. Moxico Province, Eastern Angola. (Sean Sutton)

5
Responding to the Needs of Mine-affected Communties

I watched her, balanced on the edge of the bed, her two young sisters sat, a little scared by our presence, beside her on the mattress, the mother and elder sisters gathered closely and protectively around her. Um Keltum Suleiman was with her family but, with her two emaciated stumps dangling, her eyelid sown badly over the empty right socket, she was so alone, so isolated, she could have been in a different room. She looked out from her eye through the fringe of hair, answered my questions, ticked off her fingers to count her age – but she wasn't there with us. This teenager was inside her head and we were outside unable to imagine her thoughts. I realised then what a sham it was to call this kid a 'landmine survivor' because it made us feel less guilty, less helpless than the blunt but truthful 'mine victim'.

Trip notes, Sudan, July 1999

MINE VICTIMS – SOME OBSERVATIONS

It is only comparatively recently that the term 'landmine survivor' was adopted as a more suitable term than 'victim'. I can remember at the time, probably influenced by the fact that the terminology was coined by two survivors of landmine explosions from the United States,[1] being in agreement and began to refer to survivors rather than victims myself. Now I am not so sure – it certainly has a politically correct ring to it, but where does it link up with reality for those who do not have access to antiseptic hospital wards, whose anaesthetic during amputation may be aspirin, and who cannot claim against an insurance policy or aspire to high-technology prosthetic support? It doesn't. The fact is that an African, Asian or Central American who steps on a mine is a victim and survival may merely be a consequence of not dying – we may wish to put a positive spin on that harsh reality, but let us at least be aware that this type of word play stops above the poverty line. I would hate to think that, while attempting to respect the victims in this way, we inadvertently serve the interests of the arms industry by making having flesh torn from bone and being pebble-dashed with shrapnel sound like it has less than a horrifying, obscene and dehumanising impact on the victim.

I am against landmine manufacturers and former landmine manufacturers profiting from clearance contracts, but I do believe they should be forced to contribute to the cost of humanitarian response. What better and more appropriate way than by contributing to the treatment and rehabilitation of the victims of mines? This should not be a non-taxable perk nor should there be any burden of proof on the victims to show that a company's own mines were used in any particular country – after all, the farmer who steps on a mine has no choice in his fate, so why should a company which profited from the trade fare better? The precedent for such a charge against manufacturers already exists – oil tanker companies, for instance, which are found to be negligently responsible for oil spills, must pay vast sums to repair the environmental damage they have caused. What possible argument could be put in defence of companies whose product has plagued not just the environment but human survival, and not by accident, but by design? I can see no good reason why, to take a UK company in order to show no national bias, Royal Ordnance should not be taxed against past profits made on the sale of Mark-7 anti-tank mines which are to be found in almost every theatre of war in Africa and Asia – they are a blight on civilian populations from Afghanistan to Somalia, from Eritrea to Angola. It would be no great financial loss for Royal Ordnance, or perhaps British Aerospace, the parent company, to build, equip and staff a prosthetic centre in every country where those mines have been found and support the running costs for, say, ten years. Using a more contemporary example, the use of BL755 cluster bombs in Kosovo, it would seem that residents in that country who fall victim to, or whose land is made unusable by, these British submunitions have a fair claim against the manufacturers, Hunting Engineering. It seems likely that a legal action based on product liability would have at least a fair chance of success, since the damage is a result of the product, the cluster bomb and its submunitions, not performing as designed. I wrote to Hunting Engineering in April 1999 and asked them how they would respond to such legal actions. Although they gave no written answer they did respond by telephone and said that, while they had every confidence that the BL755 would not have an unusually high percentage of failures, they felt that any recourse would have to be addressed to the government. This seems a remarkable response and one that would hardly constitute a viable defence. In such cases it is always worth forgetting the deadly nature of the product in order to view the potential for legal recourse in unambiguous terms – the fact that a weapon is designed and procured with the express purpose of killing, maiming and achieving maximum destruction is irrelevant, the manufacturer still has the same responsibilities of care and is subject to the same laws as any other producer. If a vehicle manufacturer, for instance, made a car which regularly malfunctioned in such a way that the driver lost control, the producer could expect to be held liable for deaths, injuries and damage caused. It would hardly be a reasonable defence to say, as Huntings appear to argue, that the car has been sold and so it is no longer the manufacturer's responsibility, especially if the maker had prior knowledge of the potential for their product to fail. Of course, ultimately, this would hit the shareholders' pockets, but why not? If they went without premiums for a couple of years it would hardly begin to match the suffering of a family who loses a wage earner to an exploding Mark-7 or can't farm their land because it is covered with unexploded cluster bomblets. While the loss of return from their shares may hurt a little it would surely be balanced by the knowledge that they were contributing to putting right some of the wrongs from which they have profited albeit, perhaps, unknowingly. Now multiply that input by the number of landmine and cluster bomb manufacturers – why not a Belgian clinic, a German trade training centre, a Chinese wheelchair manufacturing facility, an Italian ambulance fleet, a Russian evacuation helicopter service? It only sounds unrealistic to those who do not understand the scale of the problem; equally it probably only sounds unfair to those who have investments in the arms trade. A real response to the plight of victims and mine-affected communities on a realistic scale to match their needs requires imagination and acceptance of responsibility, especially by those who have profited and those who have stood by and watched the damage done.

COMMUNITY MINE AWARENESS – A LESSON TOO FAR?

During my time as director of the mine-clearance NGO, Mines Advisory Group, I watched with some astonishment the growth of what can only be termed a 'development cult' – community mine awareness. I say 'astonishment' because the growth of what began as an attempt to warn Afghan refugees of the potential dangers which would face them when they eventually returned home,[2] has fast become a multimillion-dollar operation. I soon found that donors who were unwilling to grant funds to mine-clearance programmes or, even more difficult, minefield-marking initiatives, were falling over each other to provide funds for mine awareness. With the United Nations Children's Fund, (UNICEF) presented agressively as the 'lead agency' for landmine awareness it would take a very foolish organisation to state the unforgivable: *mine-awareness programmes on the scale and in the format presently employed by many organisations are a damaging misuse of funds which could be put to better use surveying, marking and clearing minefields.*

The problem has not merely arisen because donors are willing to fund these programmes but because they provide an opportunity for many organisations and individuals, with none of the engineering skills necessary to respond directly to landmines, to be involved in one of the major issues of our time. That is understandable and has, to some extent, been driven by the success of the ICBL and the involvement of high-profile figures such as the late Diana, Princess of Wales. But understanding why the mine-awareness phenomenon happened does not change the fact that it is, in general, an inappropriate, wasteful and, often, paternalistic and culturally insensitive response. Certainly part of the problem is that mine awareness tends to operate parallel to other landmine responses, rather than in an integrated manner. But many of those involved in awareness work have no realistic objectives and few meaningful indicators by which they can measure their achievements. If any reader doubts my argument that mine awareness is given an inflated value within the overall international response to landmines they should consider the fact that there is now a standing committee of experts based in Geneva, chaired jointly by the ambassadors of Mexico and Switzerland, which has the title 'Standing Committee of Experts on Victim Assistance, Socio-Economic Re-Integration and Mine Awareness'.

When the same status is afforded to the lowly skill of placing coloured stones or poles around the perimeter of minefields the world will be far closer to stopping vulnerable people being blown up by landmines. If I share with some of my colleagues the cynical view that painted stones and sledgehammers are as out of place in

Geneva as are ambassadors in minefields I should be forgiven – the cost of maintaining the standing committee would survey and clear many minefields and mark many others.

Why Mine Awareness?

No one can argue with the fact that some members of mine-affected communities will benefit if they receive some level of education about landmine-related issues at some times; the extent and seriousness of the impact is explained in detail in Chapter 2. But there is nothing to be taught that requires the present level of external input. It is worth reviewing the reasons that mine awareness is needed.

1   Everyone living and working in a mined or UXO-affected community needs to be aware of the nature of the threat in relation to their daily lives.
2   Some sectors of a community may be especially vulnerable as a consequence of their age or occupation.
3   Refugees need to be aware of the situation which exists in their country and, most importantly, in the specific areas to which they will return, prior to repatriation.
4   Internally displaced people, because they often move several times into and through mined and UXO-affected areas and may return to previously unaffected areas which have been mined in the interim, are especially vulnerable.
5   Nomadic groups whose migratory patterns traverse mined and UXO-affected areas.
6   Serious food shortages and poverty encourage risk taking where productive land is mined.

The sectors of a population requiring education may, therefore, be divided into four distinct groups: refugees, internally displaced peoples, nomadic groups and populations resident in mined and UXO-affected areas. Each group will benefit from a different educational approach designed as a response to the risks faced by that group.

How not to do Mine Awareness – Global Responses to Localised Problems

One of the most popular buzzwords in use among development organisations is 'empowerment', and yet one of the fastest growing sectors of response by those agencies is mine awareness which, it could be argued, is often implemented in a manner best described as disempowering. UNICEF have for some time been involved in a cooperation with DC Comics to produce Superman (and other superhero) comic books containing mine-awareness messages for children. This is a massive project, involving the production of some 650,000 books for Nicaragua and Costa Rica alone, of which, it seems, 90,000 will be published in English – and yet it is hard to find a symbol less empowering than Superman. As Alejandro Bendaña of the Centre for International Studies in Managua puts it, 'It is not educational to teach children or their communities that solutions are magical, that they come "from above", from the outside and from the United States, with white blue-eyed characters. Nor does it contribute to national self-esteem ... .'[3] To make matters worse the actual mine-education content of these books is questionable and too hidden within an unrealistic storyline to be readily understood. There is not even a gesture towards sustainability or community participation in this approach and, far from being empowering, the books are an imposition without even the saving grace of being good mine-awareness resources. After concerns were expressed about the Central American comic books UNICEF first indicated their intention to withdraw their endorsement but, almost immediately afterwards, announced their intention to cooperate with DC Comics and USAID to publish yet another Superman mine-awareness comic for Kosovo. So anxious were UNICEF and the US government to indulge in self-promotion they enlisted the services of the First Lady Hillary Clinton to launch the comic at the White House.[4] In reporting that 'about 150' civilians had already been killed or injured by landmines since the end of the conflict, of whom children and 'young adults' accounted for 71 per cent, UNICEF was only partly accurate. A World Health Organisation (WHO) report claimed that in a 30-day period in June and July there were 170 casualties from mines and unexploded ordnance, of which more than half were attributable to NATO-dropped UXO.[5] By far the greatest percentage of the ordnance threatening the children and young adults of Kosovo were cluster bomblets – according to the *Express* at least ten thousand of them – and the question as to whether, in those circumstances, the White House was the most appropriate venue for a press launch appears not to have occurred to UNICEF. The White House release quoted Tehnaz Dastoor, said to be a 'UNICEF landmine expert', as telling the press conference, 'We need direct and understandable ways to alert children to the dangers around them.' However, other experts did not see Superman as the solution. Handicap International had asked asked their office in Bosnia to evaluate the Superman comic used there. Their comments are enlightening:

> The drawings of superheros, super-strong and always powerful, create in children the illusion to be untouchable and invincible. These comic book heros present to them the world in its most positive version and put emphasis on a standardized society where the laws and regulations are made to protect the honest people, the poorest and the most innocent. This is an image that is far from reality. War, the expression of the worst violence and hatred, appears in these comics like a parentheses that ends once the armed conflict stops ... the conflicts seem impossible to stop without an all powerful external intervention, by preference American. This association game and its symbols contribute then to reinforce a distancing from the dangers that persist; that is that through the presence of mines, the war continues in time of peace ... The representations of the country that we see in these comics are those that someone can see during or just after the war. Today in Bosnia the countryside has changed a good deal, the houses are largely reconstructed, the countryside has been cleaned up, as if society seeks as quickly as possible to smooth over the traces of a past that brought such suffering. In spite of the paint and the paving ... the fields and forests, the paths and the rivers, and many other areas as well are still polluted by the presence of mines ... to tie the dangers of antipersonnel mines which actually do menace the children on a daily basis with the personalities of a superhero comic book, always in a situation without solution, is far from the gravity of the problem we have to resolve. To give the children the false hope that nothing can hurt them because someone (who does not exist) will always arrive, does not give them the possibility to integrate the consequences of their acts. It would be better to base the campaigns of awareness on the sentiment that the restrictions related to mines begin with themselves ... The

educational and preventative roles should depend on real people. For a small child this role should be assumed by an adult. For an adolescent, this role can be taken by an adult or by another young person of the same age. The stories and experiences of children who have been the victims of mines will better influence this population than an imaginary Superman who, in an unrealistic fashion, is successful at everything.[6]

I am unrepentant for voicing such blunt criticism of UNICEF's involvement in mine awareness partly because I share the, largely unspoken, concern of many; that it has more to do with making the world aware of UNICEF than making vulnerable communities aware of the threat from landmines – not as part of a planned policy but rather a result of an institutionalised culture of self-advertisement. However, as to the inappropriate nature of many mine-awareness initiatives, this is widespread and I have through my own involvement in such programmes been as guilty as anyone, in the belief that lives were being saved and, most paternalistically, that changes in living patterns were being influenced to reduce risk to the community. But there is little evidence to support claims that substantial numbers of lives are saved by the awareness process; in fact I have yet to see any empirical study which shows that any lives have been saved at all. Of course that itself does not mean that no one is alive who might have been killed or injured if it were not for the lessons taught by mine-awareness teachers – there certainly must be – but equally there are many people killed and maimed who have attended such classes. As for changing the way people lead their lives, it is hard not to be embarrassed by such patent hogwash. Perhaps, by way of excuse, it is more true to say that we have conspired to deceive ourselves rather than anything more sinister.

To try to put this in context let me suggest a scenario where teams of educationalists and veterinarians (and perhaps butchers) from Nicaragua, Afghanistan and Angola had arrived in England at the height of the mad-cow disease crisis and launched similar awareness initiatives. There is no need to stretch this analogy any further – but I would recommend that anyone involved in existing mine-awareness programmes or planning a future initiative should seriously examine just that kind of role reversal to understand better the nature of imposed educational projects.

No one should take this to mean that I am opposed to mine-awareness programmes *per se*. They have a role in the reduction of risk, but there is a need for a dramatic change in how mine awareness is implemented both philosophically and practically. There is, for instance, no good reason why any mine-awareness programmes are managed by expatriate staff, nor why the communities involved cannot have a major input, from inception, in project design. At present expatriate staff receive training from clearance specialists or technical literature and then integrate this material into a wider development education framework. In the best instances the resulting curriculum may be excellent and effective, but it is doubtful that anything is achieved which could not have been achieved had the curriculum been designed indigenously. The argument is not whether some expatriates should be involved at field level – that may often be a useful and cost-effective input – but rather whether the process which is imported has any advantage over a locally produced initiative, albeit perhaps with outside encourage-ment. There is nothing very complex to teach – the messages are simple and common sense and adaptable to many educational fora, from the classroom to the marketplace to the *madrassa*.[7]

There is a point made by some specialists in development education that many developing countries use a system of learning by rote or chant, and that this is insufficiently imaginative to interest children in the need to avoid mined areas and of the danger inherent in touching landmines and ordnance. The recommended approach is a child-centred, interactive learning experience. (It is perhaps worth noting that, in England, schools have recently introduced the 'numeracy hour' because children have been found to be leaving school lacking the basic arithmetical skills since the introduction of child-centred learning. The numeracy hour is, essentially, a rote learning lesson.) I can only speak from my own observation and discussions in many mined communities. Children are certainly entertained by imported learning experiences, but there is no evidence that they actually retain more information than from traditional indigenous teaching styles. There is some evidence, especially among very young children, that confusion plays a large part in their reaction to imported educational methods. I should emphasise here that I refer only to mine-awareness lessons – I have no way of knowing whether these observations have any wider development educational relevance.

It would be careless to ignore the cultural sensitivity considera-tions inherent in using landmines as a medium by which to introduce a non-traditional teaching methodology – Superman and

Wonder Woman may be the extreme case – but there are many ways to antagonise a community and the distrust that may be bred could have far greater implications for the mine-eradication effort as a whole.

A Proven Approach – Mine Action Teams

As director of the MAG I had always been aware of mutual bad feeling between expatriate technical demining specialists and mine-awareness staff. This ranged from pointed banter to mutual distrust and sometimes threatened the structure of our work in some countries. At the time I tended to take the side of the mine-awareness staff and assume that the fact that all of our specialist employees were ex-military made them unwilling to accept the worth of this non-technical intrusion into their field of expertise. I failed to find any solution although, to their credit, the technical- and education-based sides of our operations learned to coexist and share information, albeit as very demarcated responses. We gained great international kudos for our mine-awareness initiatives and they were undoubtedly imaginative and largely indigenised – it was too easy to disregard any concerns about how they measured up against our prime objectives. Happily I had mine-awareness staff who asked harder questions of themselves and were aware that many of the people who died and were maimed by landmines had attended our awareness lessons. Was it simply that limits existed as to our ability to influence behaviour, or was the whole concept wrong?

In 1995 possible answers began to emerge from within the organisation (from both educational and technical sources and, in summary, they concluded that they needed to work together) to integrate mine awareness with survey, marking and emergency clearance in what, after a period of development and experiment, became known as mine action teams. I can claim no credit for the growth of these teams, it happened at the time I was leaving the organisation and, in any case, was developed at field level in all the countries where MAG worked.

What was particularly interesting was that much of the impetus for this approach came from communities who were frustrated by continued visits from mine-awareness teams and began to say 'Yes, but when will you clear our land?' Faced with years of work and insufficient funding it was all too often an impossible question to answer, but it would be different if the team arrived and offered an improved situation by doing something practical – conducted a Level Two survey of the area, cleared some of the most dangerous areas as a very limited technical response (minefield reduction) and made the risk areas visible for all to see by marking the minefield perimeters. The mine-awareness trainers would then teach the children how to recognise the markers and explain their importance – a far greater value than, for instance, teaching students to recognise mines which are buried, or organising training exercises where children practice retracing their footsteps after a simulated mine accident.

Although the mine action team-approach began, and has continued, as an NGO strategy it has the potential to be integrated on a larger scale into a national Level Two survey process.

Refugees, Internally Displaced People and Nomadic Groups

Although, inevitably, much attention has been focused on the education of children because they are, by reason of their age and size, particularly at risk. But the fact cannot be avoided that most casualties are men in their late teens, twenties and early thirties – and few young men in these age groups would pay much attention to what a teacher of any kind had to say. This attitude cannot be totally condemned, since those who fall victim are normally well aware of the danger they face and are often taking a calculated risk for economic reasons – the economy, for example, of the subsistence farmer and his family. The same conditions apply to the woman who collects firewood with her children (one of the most dangerous tasks in a mined area), the woodcutter in the forests of northwest Cambodia, the herder on the hillsides of Afghanistan. All these people will listen politely to mine-awareness lessons in the full knowledge that the next day they will be forced, by their poverty, to break most of the rules they are learning. That is not to say that the lessons are not useful – they may teach these vulnerable people to recognise a tripwire, the profile of a fragmentation mine tied to a tree or how to keep their bleeding child or neighbour alive long enough to reach a hospital. But none of them will remotely match the impact of a fence which says, in effect, 'this side safe, that side mined' or, of course, the dream solution, the arrival of a group of deminers who destroy the mines. This is not a commentary of hopelessness but a recognition of limitations.

There are, however, three population groups who can benefit across all age groups, to a much greater degree than others, from welldesigned mine-awareness programmes.

Refugees

Refugees in camps on the borders of their home country will have some knowledge of landmines as a danger. There is a constant movement of men from such camps going and returning across the border – this is usually related to ongoing conflict but may also be in relation to trade, family business or just scouting trips to get a better understanding of the security situation, maybe in and around home villagers. The latter type of journey will increase during any period when repatriation is being considered as an option by all or part of the refugee population. Some of those journeys will result in family members falling victim to landmines, perhaps losing a limb, and all will bring back information about life at home, including the problem of mines.

However, the refugee's actual understanding of the nature of landmines and the threat they pose may be vague or inaccurate. The ideal situation is to introduce the subject of mines and UXO into the curriculum of camp schools and as special talks at mother and child clinics, religious meetings and adult-education classes. It is best that the lessons at this stage are simple and avoid specific references to areas which are thought to be mined. Even if the teacher's information is accurate it is likely to be contradicted by men who return from fighting or scouting in the home country – there are few things more annoying than returning from a trip during which you risked your life to find that someone who might never have crossed the border is claiming to have information from home, and it is almost a duty to dismiss such information as unreliable gossip. Human nature is cross-cultural in such matters. The result is a loss of credibility among the refugee population and for no good reason, nothing could be gained in using real examples, accurate or otherwise, too far in advance of repatriation. Most families will not be able to return until a repatriation is well under way.

The ideal situation will link the mine-awareness initiative with Level One assessment and Level Two survey during the months leading up to any organised repatriation. While it may not meet with the approval of everyone involved, the refugees have a right to know what the landmine situation is in their own towns and villages and to know whether they will be able to repair their irrigation systems and plant a crop. It is also during this period that training with children must focus on the dangers of exploring unchecked areas or collecting war 'souvenirs'. It was noticeable that children returning to Afghanistan, many of whom were born in the refugee camps, simply forgot the lessons taught them in the camps and ran into the fields in their excitement. Some, of course, were killed or maimed and each one, however we may choose to view it, was a failure of mine-awareness training. But, regardless of failures, refugees must receive relevant training and be given honest risk information in the weeks immediately preceding repatriation. It should be emphasised that posters, in this regard, are worthless – there is far too much happening in the lives of refugee families, perhaps returning to their homeland after years of camp life, to expect them to be influenced by posters in UNHCR and camp administration offices.

One approach which might be worth considering is to train mine-awareness monitors from among early returnees who can be tasked to keep the danger of mines in people's minds as they disembark from buses and trucks at their final destination.

Internally Displaced People

The internally displaced have none of the protection or attention afforded to refugees and more hardship than most people can even imagine. It is not unusual for IDPs to resettle and move several times in a year, driven in front of the war and often caught between advancing forces. Every time they abandon a home they leave something more behind and eventually end up, exhausted, physically and psychologically damaged, in flyblown tents or crammed into rotting freight cars in abandoned sidings. Every IDP camp has its share of orphans and parents who have lost their children, but families manage somehow to stay together as well. Their ambitions are simply to survive, to live out the war, but the odds are stacked against them.

IDPs often leave their homes expecting to stay away just for a short time, until the fighting has passed. When they leave there may be no mines and very often they escape to an area where there are mines and they perhaps see their first casualties, probably from among their own group. If they move back to their home villages they commonly find that their homes and fields are now laid with mines and scattered with unexploded mortars, hand grenades and rockets. Eventually they assume that nowhere is safe, but they often have little choice about risking their lives – the alternative is probably to go hungry.

How can these transient communities be taught to be aware of mines? Certainly the answer lies within the group – these people are survivors. Some of the most effective awareness projects with IDPs have been the result of comparatively simple 'train the trainer' projects culminating in the IDPs running their own classes with the minimum of outside input. This is essential: any process must be sustainable and survive further migrations. Wherever possible, awareness projects with IDPs should be linked to assistance in other sectors, particularly health, and any opportunity to employ staff from within displaced groups should be taken – even a few days' work can be an enormous boost to the group economy.

Nomadic Groups

In mine-awareness terms it may well be that some nomadic herders are far more aware of the mines threat than anyone else in the country. But the long-term impact on nomads of mine-laying across their traditional migration routes can be devastating. It is not uncommon, for instance, for enforced changes in migration routes to bring nomads looking for alternative pasture into conflict with farmers. Any programme targeted at nomads needs to be designed with a good understanding of the migration pattern and should be prepared to act as a conduit for mine data of value to Level Two survey teams.

THE REAL CHALLENGE – RESPONDING TO THE VICTIMS OF WAR

There is a popular concept which seems to have grown out of the international movement to ban landmines, a belief that mine victims have some greater right to medical care, prostheses and vocational training than other victims of war. I am certain that no one planned it that way – the campaign just focused massive media attention on the plight of a specific group of war victims. But the idea itself is not simply a matter of wrong thinking; it is potentially dangerous and socially divisive to see the cause of injury to be more relevant than the injury itself, especially when allocating resources for treatment and support. The answer lies in a comprehensive response to all war injured, including soldiers and fighters, who become civilians in peacetime. Because landmine and UXO injuries will rise during, at least, the immediate post-conflict period, the response must embrace the treatment and needs of those casualties until a medical and social system is in place which can adequately respond to new victims. This may not be a popular view but I believe that some organisations need to become less specialist and widen their operational horizons in order to provide a fuller service to their patients. The present system, which frankly is a generous description of the hotch-potch of response which exists to aid war victims in most countries, requires patients to negotiate an obstacle course of organisational, bureaucratic and financial hurdles where pure luck may determine the level and suitability of treatment rather than any less random factors. Take, as an example, the case of a civilian who stands on a mine in a field near an outlying village in almost any African country. Examine the factors which will normally determine his or her survival for a sufficient time in which to reach expert medical assistance.

- Alone or accompanied? If alone, survival depends on the casualty's ability to shout for help and probably drag themselves to the nearest village or at least a path where people are likely to find them.
- Accompanied or found? Can the other person reach them without becoming a victim themselves? If so, do they know how to arrest bleeding? Are they strong enough to carry or assist the victim to the village?
- Is there anyone in the village with medical training? If not, the patient may die of blood loss or other unnecessary complications.
- Do helpers fit a tourniquet? If so, does anyone among those who will accompany the casualty during evacuation recognise the need to loosen it regularly? If not, the patient may lose all or part of a limb which could otherwise have been saved, or worse.

- How far away is the nearest suitable medical facility? If more than two hours' travel the patient's chances of survival without medical assistance decrease considerably.
- What means of evacuation are available? Motor vehicle, boat, mule or donkey, cart? There may be none of those, in which case a makeshift stretcher may be the only option – distance is then a major factor in determining the casualty's chances of survival.
- Can the patient or his or her family afford the costs of evacuation? This may sound harsh, but fuel, for instance, must be bought for a vehicle or boat. In a subsistence community it is unlikely that transport of any kind will be free of cost, especially if the vehicle is taken away from its normal work for a considerable time. This is not evidence of a callous attitude, it is simply one of the realities of living on the edge of poverty.
- How cooperative are soldiers at roadblocks, border guards and any other officials along the way in allowing the casualty and those who accompany him or her to pass without delay?

The list could be longer – these are obstacles relevant to just about every mine-affected country, and each locality will have its own additional problems threatening the survival of a victim in the immediate period following the explosion. But can anything be done to improve the odds of survival for the victim? One might imagine that if such an opportunity existed it would be the highest priority for organisations committed to providing support and succour to those who fall prey to landmines and other munitions, but this, in fact, is not the case. A non-combatant casualty can rarely expect to come into contact with national or international agencies until, at least, the nearest surgical facility; usually a provincial hospital. Paradoxically the situation may often be better while conflict continues than it is after the war ends.

First, it is essential to recognise that many national military forces, and even some irregular armies, have a far greater capacity to deal with war injuries than do peacetime medical services – the military is likely to have a dedicated corps of doctors, paramedics and nurses. The medical corps will have considerable, and often virtually unlimited, access to means of evacuation, including helicopters, fixed-wing aircraft, ships and purpose-designed four-wheel-drive ambulances. The evacuation line will include frontline and intermediate surgical and medical facilities, a reliable drug supply and surgeons expert in war-related injuries. It is important to emphasise that some armies, especially when the conflict is internal or prolonged, may not have the same level of support as, say, a NATO army, but the gap between what is available to the soldier in war and the level of support likely to be available for civilians in peacetime, especially in the immediate post-conflict period, is extreme. It is often only the work of the ICRC, local Red Cross and Red Crescent societies and medical NGOs which bridges the gap between war and peace; sadly, military medical services are rarely deployed in support of the civilian sector in the post-conflict period.

So what can be done to improve this situation, to keep casualties alive long enough for them to reach expert medical aid? The philosophical, sane, answer is for humanity to invest as much in peace as in war, but the victims cannot wait for changes which, on the evidence of history, may never happen. The practical answer is to develop basic life-preserving skills within vulnerable communities, an approach which can be equated to the campaigns in Scandinavia and Europe which encouraged a greater community knowledge of first aid and exhaled air resuscitation. One organisation which has focused on this approach is the Norwegian NGO the Trauma Care Foundation, which explains the concept as follows:

> In remote rural areas with poor medical infrastructure and protracted evacuation more than 50 per cent of mine victims die before reaching hospital. The majority of deaths are due to blood loss, the first two hours after injury is critical. An efficient pre-hospital chain of survival for trauma victims must therefore include immediate simple life support by first responders. The first responders in the minefields of the South are villagers, farmers and children.

Working closely with mine-clearance NGOs, the Trauma Care Foundation has developed a first-aid training course for villagers in mine-infested areas. The following shows the curriculum used by the organisation in North Iraq, one of the most intensively mined regions in the world.

Model for a Two-day, First-aid Training Course[8]

Participants: Maximum 15 persons. Some children 12–15 years.
Equipment: Laerdal Resusci Anne,[9] adult and infant models.

Day One: Lesson 1 (30 minutes)

Subject: Basic needs of the body. How does oxygen enter and circulate? Ask about what we need to live. How long (days, hours, minutes) can we be without food, water, air? Thus: breathing air is the most important. Show how a candle flame dies when put under a glass. Describe the airway down to the lungs. Describe how the blood carries oxygen to all body parts – use the symbol of a tree carrying water to all leaves, or the channel system used for irrigation. Make all understand that the heart is nothing but a water pump, and that pumps need water input to work.

Lesson 2 (45 minutes)

Subject: If breathing is so important, how can you help someone to breathe?
Use ten minutes to demonstrate on Anne and Baby Anne how to open the airway and do mouth-to-mouth (MTM) rescue breathing. Then let everyone try with the dummies, first on the adult dummy. Then: what can we do with the weak victim who is breathing? Let all students train [practise] recovery position repeatedly on each other.

Lesson 3 (45 minutes)

Subject: How can you stop bleeding?
Two reasons why bleeding is a killer: One, blood carries the oxygen (leaking in an irrigation channel is a rural emergency). Two, blood loss is heat loss; a cold body means cold blood, and cold blood will not clot. Train the triad of limb support: Constant manual compression on the artery proximal to the bleeding wound – packing the bleeding wound with any cloth available – elevation of the bleeding limb. The points for upper and lower limb artery compression must be trained exactly. Explain why the tourniquet is a limb killer and a non-reliable method for bleeding control. Do not forget: How can you prevent a casualty getting cold during transport?

Evening: informal Discussions

Day Two: Lesson 4 (45 minutes)

Subject: If the heart stops – MTM breathing and chest compression.
Demonstrate how and where to check the pulse beat – in adults and infants. Let students train on each other. Use ten minutes to show chest compression on the dummies. Then let students train chest compression first, then chest compression with MTM alone, then compression and MTM working in pairs. (A good opportunity to asssess how much students retained from the first day's training.)

Lesson 5 (1 hour)

Subject: Make your own rescue plan for the village.
Make it clear that with the knowledge they have now gained, they are real life savers. Now it all depends upon rapid and orderly response to an accident. Use a recent accident from this (or any other) village as an example for discussion. Make all students participate in developing a local action plan to handle mine casualties, drowning and other actual emergencies. Discuss in particular the role of children – as victims and rescuers. How to call for immediate help? Can some village first responder be on call at any time? How to call for the nearest medic/nurse? How to extract casualties from within a minefield? How to transport the victim to the medic/the nearest health facility? Should some transport facilities be prepared in advance? First aid must be given all the way to the hospital – who should be responsible for that?

First-aid Training Course – Reassessment after Four Months

Why Reassessment?

Life-saving first aid is a qusetion of very simple procedures – but details are essential to make them work. Revisit the same village with a one-day refreshment course to correct mistakes, consolidate knowledge and self-confidence, and discuss problems and achievements since the first training course. Finding out how much your students retained from their first training course is the only way to assess your skills as an instructor.

How to do the Reassessment

Start with tea and talking together. Discuss at length and in detail all accidents or emergencies where first aid was provided. Be careful not to let the students feel they did badly, even if things could have been done better; better use mistakes to improve and consolidate the local action plan for emergencies. Practical experience is our greatest teacher. Also ask some test questions to find out how much they remember from the first training.

- Let the students do MTM breathing and full cardio pulmonary resuscitation (CPR) on the dummies, single and in pairs. Correct faulty techniques carefully.
- Let the students demonstrate the recovery position and manual artery compression (upper and lower limb) on each other. Correct faulty techniques.
- Again stress the importance of their skill in first aid. Identify the most competent students to be further trained as first aid instructors for her/his village area.

Training Instructors for Village Training Courses

The first-aid instructor must not only be expert in CPR and basic life support procedures. She/he must also be able to answer questions regarding the medical management of complex injury cases, and to be competent in designing village first-aid action plans. The instructor training should be done by a doctor or an experienced medic. The 30–50-hour training course should include:

- lessons in trauma physiology and the impact of the main types of mines
- lectures in basic A–B–C (airway–breathing–circulation) control
- lectures in basic life support to infants and children
- lectures in basic limb support with stress on the devastating effects of tourniquets
- practical training in CPR and basic life support procedures
- lectures and training in teaching methods
- practical and theoretical examinations with certification.

Criteria for Selecting First-aid Instructors

- They must know the culture and problems of village life; arrogant city manners are not required.
- They should have practical experience in mine/war casualty management.
- They should be literate.

Guidelines for First-aid Instructors

Musts

- Prepare each village training course carefully.
- Speak loudly and clearly.
- Answer all questions in a friendly and respectful manner.
- Report each training and each reassessment exactly.

Must Nots

- Forget that you once knew as little as the village students.
- Behave in an arrogant way.
- Forget that each of the students may save *your* life if you teach her/him well.
- Let anyone leave the training with the feeling that she/he failed.

The values of such training are obvious; it is truly empowering – offering a practical solution to a major problem. Cost is minimal and it is sustainable within the community, offering benefits far beyond the immediate problems related to landmines and UXO. The simple process of introducing a basic knowledge of first aid into rural areas, particularly those which are remote from expert medical aid, will lessen the loss of life and increase the survival chances for those who succumb to the day-to-day accidents which are common in such communities: drowning, motor accidents, choking and falls to name just a few. The concept of planning ahead, being ready to respond as a group to a mine accident, is in itself an important part of encouraging the community to take on mine-victim assistance themselves. Recognising that each person could be a future victim and investing in advance in a group response can overcome many of the problems I have already mentioned in relation to means of evacuation – payment mechanisms can be arranged to compensate the vehicle owner for instance. The key lies in one word – *respect*. There is a need for the international community to recognise and respect the capacity which exists within even the remotest post-conflict community to take remedial action themselves. The external contribution required is often minimal – the Trauma Care Foundation model, which could realistically be mounted on a national level, is a fine example of such an initiative. Of course, as with all innovative projects, this type of initiative has its detractors. Most criticism is based on the 'a little knowledge is dangerous' argument and, although few would dare to rephrase that argument in such terms, there is more than a hint of 'these people can't be trusted yet' hiding behind the careful phraseology. There might be some justification in opposing this kind of grassroots approach if there was any alternative, but that is simply not the case and – as long as post-conflict surgical response is limited, at best, to provincial capitals – it never will be the case. Which returns us to reality – somehow casualties must keep themselves alive until they can get a fingerhold on the system, such as it is, so any intervention at or near the point of injury must be actively encouraged.

One of the sights which never fails to anger and shame me is that of an amputee on crutches. There is only one question to ask – why? It is not as if a prosthesis is a high-cost item and, even when materials are imported, it is surely not beyond the means of inter-national donors to make a commitment that every amputee will receive a good-quality artificial limb. Some readers will undoubtedly call halt at this point – what do I mean by saying prostheses are not high cost? Well, everything is comparative, and here I have chosen to compare the cost of a prosthesis, including manufacture, import of materials, staff training – everything that goes to make up a future with dignity for an amputee – with the cost of a cruise missile, a cluster bomb or a shipment of landmines. In my book that makes even the lightest, highest-technology limb a bargain item.

One development which would dramatically improve prosthetic services in countries where the incidence of amputation is high is a determined policy of decentralisation of prosthetic facilities. The aim should be to site the facilities where demand for their services are greatest rather than require the amputee to reach the prosthetic centre. It is common for the main facility to be sited in the capital city, and this may be justified using arguments based on logistic considerations which may, subject to close scrutiny, amount to reasons of little more than organisational and staff convenience rather than operational necessity. The defining factor for many victims who survive an explosion and live to reach the surgical ward is whether they can subsequently travel to a prosthetic facility. In some countries this may be a comparatively simple process, but in others it is little more than a lottery where, for instance, distances involved may be huge and travel costs beyond the resources of most patients. It is not unusual to interview amputees in remote areas who are unaware that prosthetic facilities exist to which they might have access. It is essential that prosthetic organisations locate workshops in locations dictated by geographical concentration of amputees rather than less relevant considerations. Local manufacture of wheelchairs designed to meet the needs of individuals should be encouraged and subsidised as part of victim-assistance programmes.

A FUTURE FOR WAR VICTIMS

The term 'vocational training' is commonly employed when discussing those maimed and blinded as a result of conflict. The terminology is perfect, but too often the scope of such training is limited by the predominance of external perceptions and concepts of what might constitute a viable horizon for an amputee or a blind person in what is commonly a subsistence community. There are some obvious and accepted fields in which war victims can be trained – one which has become common is for amputees to work in prosthetic centres. But just having a job is only a first step: how many amputees have an opportunity to advance to management roles or to become fully qualified physiotherapists, for instance? The question is, should a woman or man whose life is shattered by war be grateful for whatever opportunity presents itself and limit their ambitions at that level, or should they seek to advance themselves with the same enthusiasm and expectations as an able-bodied person? Of course, the right answer is obvious and political correctness would demand that any organisation accepted no other standard, but the fact is that most war injured survive on the very edges of community life and the few who manage to train in a new career have little chance, if any, of achieving management status. There are exceptions and they nearly all arise when the organisation involved takes an imaginative approach driven by a commitment to offer open-ended opportunity. This is an area riven with rhetoric, where everyone involved feels the need to say the correct thing and where an organisation with radical plans to offer openings to those damaged by conflict might well be discouraged by unexpected criticism. I have experienced this type of response myself and admit to having been caught off-balance by the strength of opposing opinion with which our efforts were met. The experience is relevant and interesting and may offer some lessons of value for those who work with the war disabled.

A Case Study – Widows and Amputees in Minefields

In 1994 Chris Horwood, the MAG country director in Cambodia, suggested that MAG should examine the possibility of employing amputee and female deminers. He had for some time been reviewing our local employment policies and, while employing former fighters from all factions meant that they were involved in a positive contribution to their country's recovery from conflict, as Chris put it during our discussions: 'some of our staff have laid more mines as soldiers than they will ever clear if they spend their whole life as deminers'. I fully supported the initiative, with the one proviso: that the full practical and cultural implications must be researched in detail before we made a final policy decision. The reasoning behind considering the recruitment of women to the MAG teams was less an equality issue than a recognition that an opportunity existed to respond to the needs of mine victims. That was transparent in our decision to employ amputees, but less so in the case of women. But mine victims – those who suffer the consequences of each explosion – are not confined to the victims who actually stand on a mine. A widow in Cambodian society, for instance, has few options for her own and her children's survival – when the woman has been widowed as a result of a landmine incident, these women and children are mine victims. So when MAG began recruiting women the policy was to give preference to widows and similarly socially disadvantaged applicants. In a country where the recruitment of women was, at least in theory, unrestricted, we could find no reason not to press ahead with interviews and, from the beginning, agreed that female recruits would have complete parity of salary and contractual terms with male demining staff. The key considerations with regard to amputee deminers were practical rather than cultural. It was decided after considerable research that we would hire only below-knee amputees who had full mobility in all positions and were otherwise in good health. The only special consideration related to the prosthesis itself; the standard artificial limb has a comparatively high metal content which would influence the mine detector – in effect the deminer would be at risk of continually detecting his or her own leg, a serious safety factor. In cooperation with the ICRC in Cambodia a special non-metal limb was designed and fitted for each deminer.

On 29 May 1995 6 women and 22 amputee deminers completed their training. Five of the women had been widowed when their husbands were killed by landmines. The new deminers were integrated into existing teams in Battambang Province and began work on 5 June. The pilot project received wide and positive coverage in the Cambodian and international media and I was confident that from Chris Horwood's original idea we had moved quickly and responsibly to putting into practice a very practical, logical and ground-breaking concept, so I was more than a little bemused when we found ourselves inundated with criticism from within the NGO community. Many comments were merely rather silly, but none the less annoying, gripes – we had, said some, 'only done it as a fund-raising gimmick'. But other criticisms were more serious. We were accused of discriminating against non-widows and of encouraging lone parents to undertake high-risk work, and alarmingly we were also charged with 'using the misery of disabled people to raise MAG's profile'. In retrospect I should have recognised these attacks for what they were – the rantings of disciples of political correctness, gender theory and developmental 'soundness' – and ignored them. For some days I tried to respond seriously until I suddenly recognised the ultimate irony which underpinned every one of these criticisms: each one assumed that the women and amputees involved had no minds or opinions of their own and needed these, non-Khmer, critics to defend them from MAG.

The lesson is clear and important because too many people are discouraged from speaking or writing honestly and openly for fear of incurring the wrath of these self-appointed judges of correctness. I have no argument with the need to consider the rights of women and children and, for that matter, since it is a concern of special relevance in post-conflict situations, the family group. The need to have sound developmental principles at the heart of any programme or intervention is a key factor at every stage from the very first planning phase through to the completion of the project. But the linkage of these important issues to the ephemera of political correctness serves no one's interests, least of all the refugees, displaced people, disenfranchised farming families and war victims who stand to lose most when initiative is stifled for fear of mindless criticism.

There are lessons here for donors too. I have on several occasions been asked whether there is a 'gender element' within a new mine-action initiative. What could I say to such a patently ridiculous question? What was I expected to say? Of course, because the target community depended on my ability to fund the clearance of mines and UXO from their land, I lied or, more precisely, I responded with a distortion of the truth. I said something along the lines of 'we ensure that women in the community are consulted regarding the prioritising of land for clearance' or, in a more general vein, 'we recognise the need for a gender-specific approach and use our community-awareness projects to identify areas where women are most vulnerable and focus on those areas within our wider programme'. We got the funding, but why? Because the donor was asking a question required by fashion and any positive answer was good enough – a tick in a box indicating 'yes, this programme has a gender element': any answer was sufficient because no answer was really required. We were playing a game. But while this kind of charade is being played out, the real gender issues are being afforded less attention than they deserve. Men and women who fear for the lives of their little boys and girls, men whose wives are disfigured, women whose husbands get torn apart – there should be no time for gender games when real men and women are at risk and can be helped.

So what specific assistance can be offered to war victims? The first step is to make them aware that opportunity exists and need not be limited by traditional horizons. Very often improved mobility can be a first step in offering a wider choice to the disabled. This need not be a high-technology or expensive input, there is an Afghan double above-knee amputee in the Solaymankhel Valley of Paktya Province who adapted his Massey Ferguson 240 tractor to allow him to carry out all the tasks needed for him to continue farming his land. There is no reason why this sort of simple mechanical adaptation cannot be carried out on an *ad hoc* basis and organisations should be encouraged to keep records and sketches or photographs of such projects and circulate them for use by others. Perhaps an NGO could research this kind of project and publish a simple handbook which could be regularly updated and reprinted. A common mobility problem in many countries is seasonal – trying to negotiate muddy tracks in the rainy season can prove impossible in a standard wheelchair. There are solutions available but they may not be obvious. Tun Channareth, *Rhet,* with whom I shared the platform at the Nobel Peace Prize ceremony[10] is a double amputee who knows the solutions to wheelchair mobility in adverse conditions – he designs and manufactures wheelchairs for use in Cambodia. If Rhet could be funded to internationalise his workshop, to form an NGO for instance, he could provide the same service in many other countries and train local staff to design and build personalised wheelchairs.

Another great challenge is finding ways to offer renewed opportunity to the huge number of blinded war victims. Being blind in a a war-ravaged country is probably one of the most appalling disabilities and few casualties get more than the most basic post-hospital support, yet many can benefit dramatically from simply undergoing a full ophthalmic examination. This is particularly true of landmine casualties and similar blast-related incidents where dust and minute fragments may be blasted into the face of the casualty. Sometimes damage to the eye is irreversible, but often while the cornea is destroyed the eye may be otherwise unharmed and partial or even full sight may be recovered by a corneal transplant.

Although these instances are probably fairly common there is no existing or planned initiative actively to identify such war victims – their future depends on chance. The really obscene truth, in a world which justifies the expenditure of billions of dollars on weaponry and mounts military actions using humanitarian and human rights concerns as justification is that even when the potential for a corneal transplant exists most victims in developing countries will not benefit because they cannot afford the cost involved. One such victim was a 20-year-old Eritrean, Abraham Gebrayesus, who lost an arm and was blinded, losing one eye totally, when, as a small boy he fell victim to an anti-personnel mine. Despite his disability he learned braille and went on to study law – a remarkable enough achievement for an able-bodied village boy, but quite extraordinary for a blind amputee. And yet Abraham had been diagnosed for some considerable time as being a patient who would regain sight in his one eye if a transplant could be carried out. Happily a group of friends were able to raise funds for him to fly to South Africa where, through contacts in the ICBL, he was operated on successfully at a South African military hospital. For the first time since he was a little boy Abraham could see and his future as a lawyer, committed to disabled rights, in Asmara is assured by, if nothing else, his own extraordinary determination. But why was pure chance an element in this instance, as with virtually every other similar case? Let me offer what some may perceive as a controversial view.

There are so many organisations compiling databases related to the use and impact of landmines and yet very few which appear to have clearly identified how these databases will be used to good purpose. International donors should only fund such projects where they are linked directly to practical programmes implemented by expert organisations which are committed to providing actual treatment for war victims held on the database. The justification for such action by donors is obvious: record keeping without response is a purely academic pastime and the need is for action to alleviate suffering and distress and to provide a widening of opportunity, rather than casual observation which, in the circumstances, seems a perverse form of voyeurism.

It seems right to finish this book with a challenging observation. The past eight years have culminated in a wide recognition that anti-personnel mines and randomly targeted weapons such as cluster bombs are unacceptable by reason of their disproportionate impact on non-combatants and their persistent nature. There is a real hope that the first decade of the new millennium will see an extension of the ban to include *de facto* anti-personnel mines such as cluster bombs and anti-handling devices and perhaps even anti-tank mines. We could even hope that major powers and manufacturers such as the United States and China become party to the treaty and are joined by others like Pakistan, India, Russia and Egypt. But while this may prevent the recurrence of disasters such as Afghanistan, Cambodia and Angola, legislation has done nothing to relieve the plight of mine victims and their communities. If the same energy is harnessed by NGOs to concentrate on remedial action as was focused on achieving international legislation it would be possible to make mine-affected communities safe and revolutionise the evacuation and treatment of war victims within the same time period. But NGOs, particularly the major agencies, must take a step back from their increasingly cosy relationships with government and be prepared to take their arguments to street level in order to make post-conflict response a voting issue.

Appendix
Resource Information

There are many sources of information regarding landmines and unexploded ordnance covering every aspect from eradication to campaigning. As with all resources they vary greatly in quality, reliability, relevance and ease of usage. The list which follows is not comprehensive, nor should inclusion of a particular organisation be taken as a recommendation of any kind; it seeks to provide a wide range of sources for donors, researchers, media and any reader whose interest has been whetted by the preceding pages. Any reader who wishes to access a wider range of information will find no difficulty by using links from the websites included below.

ORGANISATIONS INVOLVED DIRECTLY IN LANDMINE AND
UXO ERADICATION

Afghan Technical Consultants (ATC), 45–D-4 Old Jamrud Road, University Town, Peshawar, PO Box 1149, Pakistan. Tel: +92 91 40412/840122, Fax: INT+92 91 44780, Email: atc@pes.comsats.net.pk

Austcare, 69–71 Parramatta Road, Camperdown, NSW 2050, Australia. Tel: +61 2 9565 9111, Fax: +61 2 9550 4509

Halo Trust, 804 Drake House, Dolphin Square, London SW1V 3NW, UK. Tel: +44 20 7821 9244, Fax: +44 20 7834 0198

Demining Agency for Afghanistan (DAFA), House 32A, Samangali Road, Jinnah Town, PO Box 548, Quetta, Pakistan. Tel: +92 81 825237, Fax: +92 81 825247

Gerbera, Bahnhofstrasse 4, 15711 Koenigs Wusterhausen, Germany. Tel: +49 3375 290721, Fax: +49 3375 201580

Handicap International, Rue de Spa 67-B, 1000 Brussels, Belgium. Tel: +32 2 280 1601, Fax: +32 2 230 6030, Email: anne.cappelle@handicap.be

Mechem, PO Box 912454, 0127 Silverton, South Africa. Tel: +27 12 803 7290, Fax: +27 12 803 7189

Mine Evaluation and Training Agency (META), Hadda Farm, Jalalabad, Afghanistan. Tel: +92 91 824520, Fax: c/o MCPA, Email: meta@paknet2.ptc.pk

Mines Advisory Group, 45/47 Newton Street, Manchester M1 1FT, UK. Tel: +44 161 236 4311, Fax: +44 161 236 6244, Email: maguk@cybase.co.uk

Mine Clearance Planning Agency, House No 291, Street 56, F-10/4 Islamabad, Pakistan. Tel: +92 51 21151, Fax: +92 91 211471, Email: mcpa@mcpa-afg.sdnpk.undp.org or abdul@undp.org.pk

Mine Dog Centre (MDC), GT Road, Pabbi, GPO Box 1324, Peshawar, Pakistan. Tel: +92 91 229236, Fax: +92 91 229179, Email: mdc@psh.brain.net.pk

Norwegian Peoples Aid (NPA), Postbox 8844 Youngstorget, N-0028 Oslo 1, Norway. Tel: +47 2203 7700, Fax: +47 2220 0870

Organisation for Mine Clearance and Afghan Rehabilitation (OMAR), House 15, Street 1, D-1, Phase 1, Hayatabad, Peshawar, Pakistan. Tel: +92 91 812084, Fax: +92 91 812085, Email: omarintl@pes.comsats.net.pk

RONCO Consulting Corporation, 2301 M Street NW, Suite 400, Washington DC 20037, USA. Tel: +1 202 785 2791, Fax: +1 202 785 2078

Stiftung Menschen Gegen Minen (MGM), Diessemer Bruch 150, 47805 Krefeld, Germany. Tel: +49 2151 555755, Fax: +49 2151 511448, Email: info@mgm.org

UXO Lao, PO Box 345, Vientiane, Lao PDR. Tel: +856 21 414 896, Fax: +856 21 415 766

ORGANISATIONS WORKING DIRECTLY WITH LANDMINE- AND
UXO-AFFECTED COMMUNITIES

Brot für die Welt, Stafflenbergstr. 76, 70184 Stuttgart, Germany. Tel:
+49 711 2159 108, Fax: +49 711 2159 100, Email: w.mai@BROT-
FUER-DIE-WELT.ORG
Relief organisation with major interest in mine-affected
communities

Gesellschaft für technische Zusammenarbeit (GTZ), Postfach 5180,
65762 Eschborn, Germany. Tel: +49 6196 791 1334, Fax: +49 6196
797130
German government overseas technical assistance

Handicap International, 14 Avenue Berthelot, F-69361 Lyon Cedex
07, France. Tel: +33 7869 7979, Fax: +33 7869 7994
Prosthetic workshops

Medico International, Obermainanlage 7, D-60314 Frankfurt am
Main, Germany. Tel: +49 69 944380, Fax: +49 69 436002, Email:
medico_international@t-online.de
Wide range of projects with mine-affected communities

Medical Emergency Relief International (MERLIN) 14 David Mews,
Porter Street, London W1M 1HW, UK. Tel: +44 20 7487 2505, Fax:
+44 20 7487 4042, Email: schembri@merlin.org.uk
Emergency programmes in post-conflict situations

Mennonite Central Committee 21 South 12th Street, PO Box
500, Akron, PA 17501–0500. Tel: +1 717 859 1151, Email:
mailbox@mcc.org
MCC have worked in Laos since 1975 and ran their own small-scale
UXO-clearance project until they were instrumental in facilitating
and funding the MAG programme in 1993. Persistent and fearless
campaigners and very knowledgeable on the US use of cluster bombs
in Southeast Asia.

Motivation, Brockley Academy, Brockley Lane, Backwell, Bristol BS19
3AQ, UK. Tel: +44 1275 464 012, Fax: +44 1275 464 019
Provision of wheelchair production facilities and training

Trauma Care Foundation, (Tromsoe Mine Victim Resource Centre), Norway Fax: +47 776 90099, Email: tmc@rito.no
Mine victim assistance and medical training for first providers

Vietnam Veterans of America Foundation (VVAF), 2001 S Street NW, Suite 740, Washington DC, USA. Tel: +1 202 483 9222, Fax: +1 202 483 9312, Email: bob@vi.org
Primarily prostheses and rehabilitation projects in post-conflict communities

UNITED NATIONS LANDMINE AND UXO ACTION –
KEY CONTACT POINTS

United Nations Mine Action Service (UNMAS), DC-1500, New York, NY 10017, USA. Fax: +1 212 963 2498, Email:MineClearance@un.org

UNMAS chief, Mr Tore Skedsmo Tel: +1 212 963 2627

UNMAS public information officer, Tel: +1 212 963 1161

UNMAS database coordinator, Tel: +1 212 963 0062

United Nations Development Programme (UNDP), 1 United Nations Plaza, 4th Floor, New York, NY 10017, USA. Fax: +1 212 906 5379

Emergency Response Division (ERD)
Ian Mansfield, team leader Mine Action Tel: +1 212 906 5193
Judy Grayson, mine advocacy specialist, Tel: +1 212 906 6579

United Nations Office for Project Services (UNOPS) 220 East 42nd Street, 14th Floor, New York, NY10017, USA. Fax: +1 212 906 6963

Division chief, Mine Action Unit, Ms Marylene Spezzati, Tel: +1 212 906 6135

Officer in charge, Mine Action Unit, Dimitri Samaras, Tel: +1 212 906 6872

United Nations Children's Fund (UNICEF), UNICEF House, United Nations, New York, NY 10017, USA. Fax: +1 212 326 7037

Ms Tehnaz Dastoor, Project officer, Landmine Focal Point, Office of Emergency Programmes, Tel: +1 212 326 7068

Office of the United Nations High Commissioner for Refugees (UNHCR), 15 Chemin Louis Dunand, 'VNG', CH1211, Genève, Switzerland. Fax: +41 22 739 7371

Chief, Programme and Technical Support Section, Mr Kolude Doherty, Tel: +41 22 739 8178

The World Bank, 1818 H Street NW, Washington DC 20433, USA. Fax: +1 202 522 3247

Expert, Post Conflict Unit, Steven Holtzman, Tel: +1 202 473 3455

United Nations Mine Action Coordination Mechanism
Chair, Mr Bernard Miyet, Under-Secretary-General for Peacekeeping Operations, Fax: +1 212 963 9222

United Nations Mine-Action Programmes – Field Representatives

Afghanistan

Ian Bullpitt, Programme manager
Mohammad Iqbal, Programme officer
Mine Action Centre for Afghanistan, House 292, Street 55, F-10/4 (PO Box 1809), Islamabad, Pakistan. Tel: +92 51 211 451, Fax: +92 51 211 450

Angola

Pieter de Villiers, Programme manager
Instituçâo Nacional Angolána de Removaçâo dos Obstaculos Explosivos (INAROE), Avenida Comandante Valodia 206, 5 Andar, Luanda, Angola. Tel: +244 2 334 321 or via UN tie-line +1 212 963 1950 Ext 4525, Fax: +244 2 342 710 or via UN tie-line +1 212 963 1950 Ext 4548

Bosnia and Herzegovina

Peter Isaacs, Programme manager
Mine Action Centre, Marshal Tito Barracks, BFPO 543 England, Sarajevo, Bosnia & Herzegovina. Tel: +387 71 667 310, Fax: +387 71 667 311

Cambodia

Lt-Gen Khem Saphoan, Director General CMAC
Richard Warren, Programme Coodinator
Cambodian Mine Action Centre, PO Box 116, Phnom Penh,
Cambodia. Tel: +855 23 981 083, Fax: +855 23 360 096

Croatia

Richard Todd, Programme Manager
Mine Action Centre, Ilica 207, Bldg A, Zagreb, Croatia. Tel: +385 1
378 0005, Fax: +385 1 378 0101

Iraq

Phil Lewis, Project coordinator
Mine Action Programme, Fax c/o: +1 212 963 4793

Laos

Phil Bean, Technical advisor
c/o UXO Lao, PO Box 345, Vientiane, Lao PDR. Tel: +856 21 414 896,
Fax: +856 21 415 766

Mozambique

Michel Cipiere, Advisor
National Demining Commission, rua da Resistência, 1946 7th Floor,
Maputo, Mozambique, Tel: +258 1 418 577, Fax: +258 1 418 578

Mr Jacky d'Almeida, Programme director
J. Armstrong, Technical advisor
Accelerated Demining Programme, 2770 avenida de Angola,
Maputo, Mozambique. Tel: +258 1 466 011, Fax: + 258 1 46 013

ORGANISATIONS AND COMPANIES WORKING IN MINE-
RELATED FIELDS

The following is a selection, there are many more depending on your
area of interest or enquiry. The internet websites below will provide
all the links you require if you need more information.

European Commission DG1A, Wetstraat 200, 1040 Brussels,
Belgium. Tel: +32 2 296 2100, Fax: +32 2 299 2198
European donors with an interest in the landmine and UXO
problem

Geneva International Centre for Humanitarian Demining, 7bis,
avenue de la Paix, Case postale 1300, 1211 Geneva, 3003 Berne,
Switzerland. Tel: +41 22 730 8571, Fax: +41 22 730 8925
New kids on the block with funds from the Swiss government and a
core of ex-UN staff. Ambitions to be a centre of excellence and seem
keen to start at the top. May turn out to be some use when they
loosen their ties and roll their sleeves up ... may be worth watching

International Campaign to Ban Landmines (ICBL)
Use their website at <www.icbl.org> for campaign information,
updates and links, or contact Liz Bernstein, the ICBL coodinator at
PO Box 401, Fergus, ON N1M 3EZ, Canada. Tel: +1 519 787 8043,
Fax: +1 519 787 8058, Email: banemnow@icbl.org

Mine Action Unit – Canadian International Development Agency
(CIDA), 200 Promenade du Portage, Hull (Québec), Canada. Tel: +1
819   953   0420,   Fax: +1   819   997   2637,   Email:
NICOLAS_DROUIN@acdi-cida.gc.ca
Canadian government funding agency

Mine Information and Training Centre (MITC)
Battlefield Engineer Wing, Combat Engineer School, Gibraltar
Barracks, Blackwater, Camberley, Surrey GU17 9LP, UK. Tel: +44
1252 863623, Fax: +44 1252 863255
Touted by the British minister of defence as 'A one-stop shop for
guidance and information on counter-mine measures ... .'

Physicians for Human Rights, 100 Boylston Street, Suite 702, Boston MA 02116, USA. Tel: +1 617 695 0041, Fax: +1 617 695 0307, Email: cobey@worldnet.att.net
Advocacy and reports on landmine/UXO issues

UK Working Group on Landmines, The 1st Floor, 89 Albert Embankment, London SE1 7TP, UK. Tel: +44 20 78200 222, Fax: +44 20 78200 057, Email: ukwglm@msn.com
Good national campaign with excellent resources on landmine production and use.

LANDMINE- AND UXO-RELATED WEBSITES

This is just a selection of the best and most interesting from the many websites which have been spawned by the global landmine crisis.

<http://diwww.epfl.ch/lami/detec/minelinks.html>
Detech Demining Technology website contains long list of links to demining-related sites

<www.angola.org>
Site gives overview of the situation in Angola; usually more about goldmines than landmines, which accurately indicates the government's priorities

<www.army.mod.uk/ukmitc>
Website of the British Army Mine Information and Training Centre (MITC) based at the Combat Engineer School; not very informative but may improve with time

<www.camnet.com.kh/cambodia.daily/Land_Mines/land_mines.htm>
A good informative site which includes the bad with the good. Also try the NGO Forum at
<www.camnet.com.kh/ngoforum>

<www.handicap-international.org/presentation/icbl/>
Handicap International French-language landmine campaign site

<www.icbl.org>
The main site of the International Campaign to Ban Landmines

<www.un.org/Depts/Landmine>
United Nations landmine resource centre and what they call the database

<www.icrc.org/eng/mines>
The International Committee of the Red Cross landmine page in English, French and Spanish

German Initiative to Ban Landmines

<www.mag.org.uk>
Mines Advisory Group. Excellent information about MAG programmes, philosophy, etc., plus photographs

<www.manitese.it/mine>
Italian Campaign to Ban Landmines, Italian-language site

<www.mennonitecc.ca/mcc/programs/peace/land-mines.html>
The Mennonite Central Committee site – good updates on landmines/UXO problems related especially to cluster bombs and Laos

One of the best landmine campaign websites with good links to other landmine-related sites

COMMERCIAL SERVICE SUPPLIERS OF LANDMINE- AND UXO-ERADICATION OPERATIONS

Once again this is a personal and by no means comprehensive selection of companies with experience of providing services and equipment for use in humanitarian operations.

Aardvaak Clearmine Ltd, Shevock Farm, Insch, Aberdeenshire AB52 6XQ, Scotland. Tel: +44 1464 820122, Fax: +44 1464 820985
Manufacturers of a flail unit and bolt-on flails which, alone among purpose-built mechanical clearing systems, have proved to be operationally viable as components within a large-scale eradication programme

Aeromega Helicopters, Stapleford Aerodrome, Stapleford, Tawney, Essex RM4 1RL, UK. Tel: +44 208 500 3030, Fax: +44 1708 688566
Helicopter support is not always a consideration for budgetary reasons but it may be a consideration in some circumstances and Aeromega have experience of working with NGOs and in remote areas of the world; a worthwhile contact

Ebinger Prüf- und Ortungstechnik GmbH, Hansestrasse 13, 51149 Köln, Germany. Tel: +49 2203 36063/64, Fax: +49 2203 36062
Mine and bomb detection equipment. Ebinger have an excellent reputation within the humanitarian clearance fraternity; their equipment is used in many humanitarian clearance operations

Guartel Ltd, 16 Alliance Court, Alliance Road, London W3 0RB, UK. Tel: +44 20 8896 0222, Fax: +44 20 8896 0333
Bomb and mine detector manufacturers

Hans Schiebel Elektronische GesmbH, Margaretenstrasse 112, A-1050 Vienna, Austria. Tel: +43 1 546260, Fax: +43 1 545 2339
Bomb and mine detector manufacturer producing equipment used in many humanitarian clearance programmes

HMT Insurance Brokers Ltd, Old Bank House, 26 Station Approach, Hinchley Wood, Esher, Surrey KT10 0SR, UK. Tel: +44 20 8398 2362, Fax: +44 20 8398 4568
Insurance brokers specialising in the insurance of organisations and staff, including local employees, involved in landmine- and UXO-clearance operations and those agencies working in mine-affected areas

Laerdal Medical, PO Box 377, N 4001 Stavanger, Norway. Tel: +47 515 170, Fax: +47 515 23557, Email: <tore.laerdal@laerdal.no>
Manufacturers of the Mine Anne dummy and other training dummies

Lightweight Body Armour Ltd, 2 Macadam Close, Drayton Fields, Daventry NN11 5BT, UK.
Suppliers of protective clothing and headgear for landmine- and UXO-clearance operatives

RBR International, 88/94 Old Kent Road, London SE1 4NU, UK. Tel: +44 20 7703 1005, Fax: +44 20 7703 5505
Suppliers of protective clothing and headgear for landmine- and UXO-clearance operatives.

John Rodsted, 6 Tallaroon Court, Greensborough, 3088 Melbourne, Victoria, Australia. Tel: +61 3 9432 6688, Fax: +61 9432 6699, Email: rodsted@hotmail.com
Professional photographer who has specialised for some years in photographing minefields, the people who clear them and the communities affected by them. Has a comprehensive and constantly updated library of images from the worst-mined countries of the world available in London

Tri-Med Ltd, 7 Hanson Street, London W1P 7LJ, UK. Tel: +44 20 7637 1601, Fax: +44 20 7255 1000
Shipping agents and suppliers. The world is full of them – average, bad, terrible and indifferent. Tri-Med are none of those, and I've used them since the mid-1980s. They do the business, anywhere, anytime and they've never let me down – you need that when you have demining teams waiting for equipment

RECOMMENDED READING AND VIEWING

Arkin, W.M., Durrant, D. and Cherni, M., *On Impact. Modern Warfare and the Environment, A Case Study of the Gulf War* (London: Greenpeace, 1991).
A detailed study of the use of weaponry and its impact in Kuwait and Iraq against the requirements of the international laws of armed conflict and protection of the environment

Best, Geoffrey, *War and Law Since 1945* (Oxford: Oxford University Press, 1994).
This book should be required reading for every soldier, arms manufacturer and politician. The chapters on 'Humanitarian Practice' and 'Methods and Means' are especially relevant to the landmines and UXO problem

Croll, Mike, *The History of Landmines* (London: Leo Cooper, 1998).
A businesslike history of the landmine by this ex-sapper officer and Halo Trust deminer.

Davies, Paul, *War of the Mines. Cambodia, Landmines and the Impoverishment of a Nation* (London: Pluto Press, 1994).
Davies tells the story of Rattanak Mondul, a remote district in Cambodia devastated by landmines, through the experiences of its people. With excellent photography by Nic Dunlop the book makes sad but essential reading

Eaton, R., Horwood, C. and Niland, N. *Study Report. The Development of Indigenous Mine Action Capacities* (New York: United Nations Lessons Learned Unit, Dept of Humanitarian Affairs, 1998).
This remarkable report comes in five volumes and covers UN demining programmes in Afghanistan, Cambodia, Mozambique and Angola. It is perhaps the most honest, outspoken and credible internal assessment ever conducted by the UN; only time will tell if lessons have been learned. The report is also available on the internet at: <www.reliefweb.int> under 'Resources' then 'Library', or at <www.reliefweb.int/dha_ol> under 'Publications'

Gray, Bruce, *Landmines: The Most Toxic and Widespread Pollution Facing Mankind* (Sydney: ICBL Australia, 1997).
An interesting paper, one of the the very few documents which examines the environmental impact of landmines. Available at: <http://fn2.freenet.edmonton.ab.ca/~puppydog/bgray.htm>

Hidden Killers. The Global Landmine Crisis (Washington: US Dept of State, Bureau of Political-Military Affairs, 1994)
An interesting, if somewhat Washington-centric, overview of the global landmine situation

Horwood, Chris, *The Use of Dogs for Operations Related to Humanitarian Mine Clearance* (Lyon: Handicap International, 1998).
A comprehensive and timely study with an excellent section on the use of dogs in the minefield reduction role

Hurley, Graham, *The Perfect Soldier* (London: Macmillan, 1996).
A novel very loosely (thank God) based around the work of MAG and their teams in Angola

Husum, Hans *Save Lives, Save Limbs* (Penang: Third World Network, 1999).
Training the first providers at village level in mine-affected countries; essential reading for aid and development workers

King, Colin (ed.) *Jane's Mines and Mine Clearance* (London: Jane's Information Group, 1996).
Just about every mine in the world described with photographs and technical drawings. This is an excellent technical resource if you can afford Jane's prices: unless you are involved in demining or a serious researcher, I wouldn't bother – borrow someone else's

Living with UXO. National Survey on the Socio-Economic Impact of UXO in Lao PDR (Vientiane: UXO Lao and Handicap International, 1997).
Level One survey of Lao PDR. Should be read in conjunction with Warner's *Backfire* and, perhaps, the self-promoting ramblings of Henry Kissinger

McGrath, R. and Stover, E., 'Injuries from land mines', *British Medical Journal*, Vol. 303, 1991, p. 1492.

McGrath, R. and Stover, E. *Landmines in Cambodia: The Coward's War* (New York: Human Rights Watch and Physicians for Human Rights, 1991).
We set out to alert the world to the madness of landmines with this report; King Sihanouk waved it dramatically at the UN General Assembly, HRW and PHR called for a ban. In a way this was the first shot fired by the landmines campaign, although it didn't formally start until some time later

McGrath, R. and Whitton, M., *Report of the Mines Survey of Afghanistan* (Peshawar: Mines Advisory Group, 1991).
The first widescale Level One survey undertaken and MAG's very first project. The methodology was good and the results accurate. Worth reading in conjunction with the later survey conducted by MCPA using similar methodology

McGrath, R. *Hidden Death: Landmines and Civilian Casualties in Iraqi Kurdistan* (New York: Human Rights Watch, 1992).
The follow-up to *The Coward's War* with detailed reports of minefields

McGrath, R. and Rone, J., *Land Mines in Angola: An Africa Watch Report* (New York: Human Rights Watch, 1993).
It is hard to believe in retrospect that, when I researched this report, very few organisations or donors had even considered the potential

problems of 30 years of mine-laying on a post-conflict Angola. But then the conflict only paused and now the war and the mine-laying goes on

Prokosch, Eric, *The Technology of Killing. A Military and Political History of Antipersonnel Weapons* (London: Zed Books, 1995).
A bible and standard reference for anyone interested in landmines and other anti-personnel weapons. Well written and superbly researched

SIPRI, *Anti-personnel Weapons* (London: Taylor and Francis, 1978).
Still a prime source of information on early US cluster bombs and submunitions

Warner, Roger, *Backfire: The CIA's Secret War in Laos and Its Link to the War in Vietnam* (New York: Simon and Schuster, 1995).
A fascinating, horrifying and invaluable insight into the bombing of Laos which left the country devastated and scattered with millions of unexploded ordnance, mines and submunitions which may well take decades to clear

Winslow, Philip C., *Sowing the Dragon's Teeth. Landmines and the Global Legacy of War* (Boston: Beacon Press, 1997).
A very personal and journalistic view of the landmines crisis in Angola. An interesting outsider's perspective on the MAG–Medico–VVAF integrated programme in Moxico Province

Videos

A Footstep Away. Award-winning film by Yorskshire TV for the Discovery Channel showing MAG work in Iraqi Kurdistan; unarguably the best film ever made on the landmine issue

Land Mines, a 60 Minutes Report, 29 October 1995 (CBS News).
Mildly surreal US TV look at mine clearance in Cambodia

Liberating the Land – Mines Advisory Group Projects in Cambodia (Mines Advisory Group).
A look at humanitarian mine clearance in Cambodia

Secret War, Secret Slaughter. Unexploded Ordnance in Laos (Mines Advisory Group).
Highly political and hard-hitting look at the US bombing of Laos and its aftermath

Towards an International Ban on Landmines (ICBL and Bicycle Trail Films 1995).
Nic Dunlop slides with music and voiceover; good opening or end to seminars, fundraisers, etc.

Endnotes

PREFACE

1. Rae McGrath, *Mines in Afghanistan. A Handbook for Development Workers* (Peshawar: Norwegian Afghanistan Committee, 1990).
2. Rae McGrath, *Landmines – Legacy of Conflict* (Oxford: Oxfam/Mines Advisory Group, 1994).
3. MCPA was originally called the Mines Clearance Planning Cell (MCPC).
4. The term 'demining' comes from the French *deminage* which was adopted in the early days of the Afghan programme.

1   AN INTRODUCTION TO LANDMINES AND UNEXPLODED ORDNANCE

1. British war ministry, *Military Engineering (Vol IV) 'Demolitions and Mining'*, Chapter XII, Section 86, Paragraph 2 (London: British War Ministry, 1934).
2. *Military Engineering (Vol IV)*, Chapter XII, Section 88, Paragraph 1.
3. *Military Engineering (Vol IV)*, Chapter VII, Section 61, p. 131.
4. *Military Engineering (Vol IV)*, Chapter VIII, Section 61, p. 134.
5. C. Smith, *The Military Utility of Landmines ...?* (London: Centre for Defence Studies, King's College, University of London).
6. *Hidden Killers, The Global Landmine Crisis*, Report to US Congress Bureau of Political-Military Affairs (Washington, US Department of State, 1994).
7. M. Lumsden, *Anti-personnel Weapons* (Stockholm: SIPRI, 1978).
8. Lumsden, *Anti-personnel Weapons*.
9. US Defense Intelligence Agency, *Landmine Warfare – Trends and Projections*, declassified 'secret' document (Washington: US Department of Defense Intelligence, 1992).
10. The late Samuel Cummins in conversation with the author.
11. *Landmine Warfare – Trends and Projections*.
12. *Landmine Warfare – Trends and Projections*.
13. Non-governmental organisations such as the Norwegian and Swedish Afghanistan Committees for Afghanistan began operations in Afghanistan soon after the Soviet invasion in 1979.
14. W.M. Arkin, D. Durrant, M. Cherni, *On Impact – Modern War and the Environment, A Case Study of the Gulf War* (London: Greenpeace, 1991).
15. Robert S. McNamara, *In Retrospect – The Tragedy and Lessons of Vietnam* (New York and Toronto: Times Books, 1995), pp. 244–5.
16. Eric Prokosch, *Cluster Weapons* (Essex: Human Rights Centre, University of Essex, 1995), p. 15.
17. McNamara, *In Retrospect*, p. 14, quoting USAF Tactical Air Command Report TAC-TR-65-114 Annex C, Attachment 1.

18. Roger Warner, *Backfire – The CIA's Secret War in Laos and its Link to the War in Vietnam* (New York: Simon and Schuster, 1995), p. 157.
19. Mines Advisory Group, *Xieng Khouang Project Report*, July 1996 to June 1997 (Manchester: MAG).
20. Arkin *et al.*, *On Impact*. Each rocket contained 644 submunitions.
21. Smith, *The Military Utility of Landmines ...?*, p. 86.
22. General Alfred Gray, Jr (former US marine corps commandant), addressing ADPA Symposium, 9 September 1993.

2   LANDMINES AND UNEXPLODED ORDNANCE – POST-CONFLICT IMPACT

1. ICRC, *Mine Injury Statistics – An Update from the ICRC Surgical Office* (Geneva: International Committee of the Red Cross, March 1995), and F. Kakar, F. Bassani, C.J. Romer and S.W.A. Gunn, 'The consequences of landmines on public health', *Prehospital and Disaster Medicine Journal*, Vol. II, No. 1. January–March 1996.
2. The component parts of the explosive chain differ in many landmines as does the composition of the mine casing. The example used is typical.
3. The scenario is a composite description drawn from the testimony of survivors of several such incidents.
4. ICRC, *Outline of Mine Victim Statistics in Bosnia and Herzegovina January 1992 to July 1997*, (Geneva: ICRC, 1998).
5. FAO/WFP, Special Report, *Crop and Food Supply Assessment Mission to Afghanistan* (Rome: FAO/WFP, August 1997). Quotes are taken from section 1, p. 1; section 2, p. 3; section 3, p. 4.
6. 'Internally displaced people' is a generic term used to define all persons displaced within the borders of their native country. IDPs, as a general rule, do not fall within the mandate of the United Nations High Commissioner for Refugees and are not afforded international protection as such.
7. *Field Report. Cambodia* (Manchester: MAG, January 1998).
8. Sir J.H. Simpson, 1939. Quoted in Gaim Kibreab, *Refugees and Development in Africa* (Trenton, NJ: Red Sea Press, 1997), p. 5.
9. Zhia Rizvi, UNHCR 19 March 1980. Quoted in W. Shawcross, *Quality of Mercy* (London: Fontana, 1985), p. 312.
10. Shawcross, *Quality of Mercy*, p. 91.
11. R. McGrath and E. Storer, *Landmines in Cambodia – The Coward's War* (New York: Human Rights Watch and Physicians for Human Rights, 1991).
12. McGrath and Storer, *The Coward's War*, p. 90.
13. B. Boutros-Ghali, *The 50th Anniversary Annual Report on the Work of the Organisation* (New York: United Nations, 1996), p. 182.
14. UNHCR, *Repatriation and Reintegration of Angolan Refugees, June 1995 – December 1997. Plan of Action* (Geneva: UNHCR, 1997).
15. UNITA (Uniao Nacional para a Independencia Total de Angola) is the opposition guerilla army led by the former foreign minister of Angola,

Jonas Savimbi. Although it has representatives in the the government following elections, at the time of writing UNITA is again involved in armed conflict with government forces. MPLA (Movimento Popular de Libertacao de Angola) is the governing Angolan party led by President Santos.

3   THE SURVEY PROCESS

1. Bjorn Johansson, UNHCR mission chief in Phnom Penh. Reported in McGrath and Storer, *Landmines in Cambodia – The Coward's War.*
2. *Detection and Clearance of Mines: Field Engineering and Mine Warfare,* Pamphlet No. 6, Part II (London: The War Office, 1947).
3. Handicap International for Lao PDR Ministry of Labour and Social Welfare, *Living with UXO – Report of the National Survey on the Socio-Economic Impact of UXO in Lao PDR* (Vientianne: Lao National UXO Programme, 1997).
4. Ausaid is the overseas aid and development department of the Australian government.
5. UNDHA, *Angola – The Development of Indigenous Mine Action Capacities* (New York: Lessons Learned Unit, Policy and Analysis Division, UNDHA, 1997), p. 1, para 4.
6. UNDHA, *Angola – The Development of Indigenous Mine Action Capacities,* p. 39, para 133.
7. UNMAS became the United Nations department responsible for mine action worldwide in 1998. The full UN agency responsibilities in relation to mine action as defined in the UN Policy Document *Mine Action and Effective Coordination* are as follows:

UNMAS

- Focal point for resource mobilisation in support of mine action.
- Coordination of the preparation of mine action project portfolios.
- Preparation of annual pledging conference for mine action.
- Management of the Voluntary Trust Fund for Mine Clearance.
- Coordination of headquarters donor meetings.
- Consolidated reporting to donors on mine action.
- Coordination with the UN Fund for International Partnerships.
- Initiation of interagency and steering committee meetings to discuss resource mobilisation priorities.

OCHA (Office for the Coordination of Humanitarian Affairs)

- Coordination of country-specific consolidated appeals.
- Management of the Central Emergency Revolving Fund.

UNICEF

- In cooperation with UNMAS is the UN focal point on mine-awareness education.

UNDP

- Responsibility for addressing the socioeconomic consequences of landmine contamination.
- Supporting local/national demining capacity building. Where the problem of landmines is 'not only a humanitarian emergency', will have primary responsibility for the development of integrated, sustainable national/local mine-action programmes.

UNOPS (UN Office for Project Services)

- The principal 'service provider' within the UN system for integrated mine-action and capacity-building programmes.
- To implement mine-action programmes in cooperation with UNMAS, UNDP and others.

   The document also defines less direct roles for the WFP, the FAO, the World Bank, the Department for Disarmament Affairs (DDA) and the WHO.

8. The fact that some countries can afford the cost of eradicating landmines and UXO does not, of course, exclude the possibility that external donors may contribute to the cost of operations, especially where a moral imperative for such a contribution exists.
9. R. McGrath, M. Whitton, *Report of the Afghanistan Mines Survey* (Peshawar: MAG, 1991).
10. One essential item which should be carried by all surveyors is a plastic-covered identity card with the holder's photograph and, normally on the reverse, a short explanation of the project emphasising its humanitarian nature. When staff are to conduct survey work in areas known to be high risk it is useful for them also to carry a letter of introduction signed by a political or religious leader who is trusted and respected in the target area.
11. It can be useful for surveyors to carry a small flip-chart notebook with pictures of mines and common UXOs to avoid confusion – soldiers often have nicknames for individual devices which may have no similarity to the official designation. An area-specific book can be printed for each surveyor using the US Department of Defense *MineFacts* CD-ROM as a printing source for device photographs. For security reasons the notebook cover should be imprinted with a similar project summary as the reverse of the surveyor's identity card (see note 10).

12. Whenever OHP slides are used, especially to emphasise lists of priority points, photocopies should be distributed to trainees at the conclusion of the lesson.

13. If a question is consistently misunderstood by trainees it is likely that the question itself is badly expressed and consideration should be given to revising the wording used.

14. Reproduced with the kind permission of the Mines Advisory Group. (Some changes in presentation style have been made for the purposes of clarity.)

15. Extracts from the *Report of the Afghanistan Mines Survey*, section 2.4, reproduced with the kind permission of the Mines Advisory Group.

16. It should be emphasised that, for NGO projects to contribute in this way to the overall programme, there is need for a substantially increased level of support and recognition from the UN agencies involved.

17. *International Standards for Humanitarian Mine Clearance Operations*, section 3, para 37.

18. MCPA, *Minefield and Battlefield Survey* (Afghanistan: MCPA, 1997).

19. The term 'fighter' is used here as a generic term to refer to soldiers fighting with non-government forces, guerilla armies, freedom fighters and, in general, the military arms of non-state actors.

20. Attempting to obtain information of this kind while fighting continues is extremely dangerous and should not normally be attempted. Risks may still be high for some time after combat ceases and any attempt to obtain military information *at any time* should be done with extreme caution and, if possible, with official permission.

21. McGrath and Storer, *Landmines in Cambodia – The Coward's War*.

22. It is worth noting that the Afghan mapping pack project had one extra-ordinary success. At that time, in 1990, it was generally believed that the far western province of Farah, bordering Iran, did not have a substantial landmine problem. A three-dimensional map drawn in colour on a large square of parchment was delivered to the MCPA office in Peshawar in northwest Pakistan having been passed from messenger to messenger *en route*. The map gave an accurate portrayal of heavy mine use in the area of the respondent's village and influenced the decision to include Farah in the subsequent Afghanistan mines survey. The survey showed that, far from being unaffected, the province was among the most heavily mined in the country – a discovery which would not have been made for a considerable time had it not been for the villager's mine map. The original map, now framed, has pride of place in my home study.

23. The Chamkani Programme was a multidisciplinary agricultural and reconstruction initiative funded by World Vision International and managed by myself. The programme incorporated the first humanitarian-based widescale mine-clearance project, although the UK NGO Halo Trust had been conducting a limited-scale landmine and UXO project based in Kabul for some time prior to the Chamkani initiative.

24. *Karez* = a traditional lined underground irrigation system common in parts of Afghanistan.

25. MCPA, *Standing Operational Procedures* (Afghanistan: MCPA, 1997).

26. *Shura* = an Afghan community committee.
27. I founded the MAG in 1990 and was director until 1996.
28. Michael Ferguson, *GPS Land Navigation* (Boise, Idaho: Glassford Publishing, 1997).
29. Extract from MCPA, *Standing Operational Procedures* (Afghanistan: MCPA, 1997).
30. MDG = Mine Dog Group. The term used in Afghanistan for a clearance unit based around the use of dogs.
31. The MCPA works within the United Nations coordinated response known as UNOCHA (United Nations Office for the Coordinator of Humanitarian Assistance to Afghanistan).
32. Two Gurkhas serving with the British army were killed along with two KLA fighters soon after NATO/Kfor forces moved into Kosovo.
33. For details of area reduction and minefield marking see Chapter 4.
34. Information from Sayed Aqa, former director of the MCPA.

4.1 ERADICATING LANDMINES AND UNEXPLODED ORDNANCE

1. John Ryall, 'The invisible enemy', *New Yorker*, Issue 69, No. 40, 29 November 1993, pp. 120–35.
2. The protective properties of a helmet do not require that it is especially heavy – good protection is afforded by many modern materials. The shape of the helmet or, more precisely, the profile it presents to blast is an equally important factor; the helmet with visor down should be uniformly curved serving to divert the blast wave around and over the head with as little resistance as possible. There should be no flat surfaces facing the front.
3. One of the first dogs to be killed in Afghanistan was being carried in a converted ambulance used by the Ronco dog teams when the vehicle hit a mine while manoeuvring on a narrow track.
4. Chris Horwood, *The Use of Dogs for Operations Related to Humanitarian Mine Clearance* (Lyon: Handicap International, 1997), Paper 1, Section 27.
5. Extract from MCPA, *Standing Operational Procedure, Survey of Battle Area Clearance (BAC) Residential Areas* (Afghanistan: MCPA, 1997). Reproduced with permission.

4.2 SUSTAINABLE MANAGEMENT STRUCTURES FOR NATIONAL DEMINING PROGRAMMES

1. R. Eaton, C. Horwood and N. Niland, *Study Report: The Development of Indigenous Mine Action Capacities* (New York: UNDP/DHA Lessons Learned Unit, 1998).
2. *Jirgha* = a meeting of tribal, community or military traders or key people in Afghanistan to resolve important issues, disagreements or conflicts or to make administrative decisions.

5   RESPONDING TO THE NEEDS OF MINE-AFFECTED COMMUNITIES

1. The term 'landmine survivor' gained popularity after the US-based NGO, Landmine Survivors Network (LSN) was set up by Ken Rutherford and Jerry White, both amputees as a result of landmine explosions in Somalia and Israel respectively.
2. The programme, based in Pakistan, was run by the US-based organisation, International Rescue Committee (IRC) and was probably the first attempt to run such a programme on this scale with refugees. IRC also ran a similar programme in the Cambodian refugee camps in Thailand.
3. Alejandro Bendaña, *Anti-personnel Mines and Demining in Nicaragua: Achievements and Limitations*, first independent report by the Center for International Studies, Managua, Nicaragua, March 1999 (summarised English version).
4. UNICEF press release, *New Superman Comic Book on Landmines Launched, Comic Will Help Educate Kosovo's Children*, Washington, 2 August 1999.
5. 'Nato Bomb ... That Killed Five Boys', *Daily Express*, 6 August 1999.
6. Sylvian Lecoin and Silva Spanjic, *Superman and the Mines*, internal report, Handicap International Sarajevo. Lecoin is a clinical psychologist and Spanjic a psychologist-educator.
7. *Madrassa* = an Islamic school.
8. Reproduced with permission of the Trauma Care Foundation.
9. Laerdal Resusci Anne is a lifesize human dummy used for resuscitation and other realistic medical emergency training.
10. Tun Chanareth accepted the 1997 Nobel Peace Prize on behalf of the ICBL; I delivered the Nobel lecture on behalf of the campaign.

Glossary

Note: The definitions used here are of a simple explanatory nature for non-specialists, they are not necessarily those used by landmine and UXO specialists

anti-lift device A device designed to detonate a landmine when an attempt is made to move, neutralise or disarm it. May be an integral component or can be added at the time of emplacement. In the latter case it may be a purpose-designed device or of an improvised nature.

anti-personnel mine A landmine designed to be initiated by a person or persons and thereby cause death or injury.

anti-tank mine A landmine designed to be initiated by a heavy vehicle and thereby destroy or immobilise it.

area-denial philosophy A military concept based on the belief that weapons such as air-delivered landmines and cluster weapons can be used to make large areas of territory too dangerous for an enemy force to occupy. Has also been used to deny areas for use by civilian population. Has obvious post-conflict resettlement implications.

bench mark A fixed and permanent visible reference point at a safe location close to a minefield. May be either natural or manufactured.

blast mine A landmine which relies on its explosive blast properties for effect.

bomblet A submunition normally transported to a point near the intended target in a large carrier bomb, often referred to as a cluster bomb, which may carry hundreds of bomblets. On arrival at a predetermined point close to the target the bomblets are released and disperse over an area determined by the weapon type and other factors.

bounding mine An anti-personnel landmine which operates in two phases. When the victim initiates the firing mechanism, normally by applying direct pressure, by tripping a wire or through physical proximity, an initial detonation drives the inner case of the mine to a height normally determined by a tether wire, commonly between 1 and 3 metres. When the mine reaches the predetermined height the main explosive content is detonated, driving fragmentation outwards at ballistic speed.

breach The engineering process of clearing a lane into or through a minefield.

canalise A military strategy based on the belief that enemy forces can be channelled into strategically favourable areas by denying alternative land through use of a wide range of weaponry, especially remotely delivered landmines.

contact mine A landmine which is detonated by direct contact, normally pressure.

cover A military term meaning protection from incoming fire.

dead ground Military terminology for an area of land occupied by, or at risk of occupation from, an enemy force which is out of line-of-sight when viewed from a defensive position and will, therefore, provide cover for the enemy.

displaced people A term used to describe people who have been displaced from their homes usually by war or natural disaster, but who have not left their own country and cannot be classified as refugees. Also know as IDPs (internally displaced people).

dud rate Refers to the percentage of failures from a batch of munitions. Commonly used in the case of cluster bomblets which fail to explode on impact or when referring to the failure of self-destruct devices.

force multiplier The concept that use of a certain weapon can even the odds in favour of an outnumbered military force or increase the strength of a superior force.

fragmentation mine A landmine which relies on fragments, usually of metal, driven outwards at ballistic speed for its major effect.

pull switch A switch incorporated into the explosive chain of a mine which is initiated when an attached tripwire is pulled.

sapper A British soldier of the Royal Engineers. Originally referred exclusively to private soldiers but now often used as a generic term for the Royal Engineers – the Sappers.

start point A fixed point adjacent to a minefield from where all survey, marking and clearance operations begin.

turning point Any point at which the perimeter of a minefield changes direction. Part of the means by which safe areas are demarcated from mined areas in a minefield.

Index

For a list of Mine Types see end of index

Mine Types